101 Extra Python Challenges

- With Solutions / Code Listings -

Philippe Kerampran

101Computing.net

About the Author

Philippe Kerampran has worked as an ICT & Computer Science teacher in a comprehensive UK High School/Academy & 6th Form Centre since 2006. As a Head of Department he has introduced a computing curriculum and computer science courses at GCSE and A Level. He is passionate about finding ways to share his enjoyment of computing with students while developing their abilities to become independent and resourceful learners.

From the Same Author:

- 101 Computing Challenges (2014)
- 101 Python Challenges with Solutions / Code Listings (2017)
- 101 Extra Python Challenges with Solutions / Code Listings (2019)

First Printing: 2019

ISBN: 978-0-244-79056-1

Published by:

101 Computing
Email: info@101Computing.net
Website: www.101Computing.net

"Whether you want to uncover the secrets of the universe, or you just want to pursue a career in the 21st century, basic computer programming is an essential skill to learn."

_____

Stephen Hawking
Theoretical Physicist, Cosmologist & Author

Contents at a Glance

3

101 Programming Challenges

A Brief Introduction

Welcome to this second selection of 101 Python challenges from the 101computing.net website. As its predecessor - *101 Python Challenges with solutions / code listing, published in 2017* - the aim of this follow up book is to help you develop and apply your programing skills by solving carefully selected challenges. The book is organised into ten chapters to progressively introduce a range of key procedural programming concepts.

Coding skills are acquired through practice and are dependent on problem solving abilities. This is the reason why a challenge-based approach is strongly encouraged to help you boost your programming skills. At first you may find that the 101 challenges of this book are aimed at different levels of abilities. By completing these challenges and reverse-engineering the given code listings, you will progressively acquire new skills and be exposed to new procedural programming concepts. This should quickly raise your confidence in your ability to tackle more advanced challenges. This should also develop your ability to decompose a problem into sub-problems, recognise coding patterns, and identify computational approaches to solve these challenges.

Please bear in mind that there is rarely a unique solution to a given problem. So, as you progress through these challenges, you may start to question and evaluate the effectiveness of the proposed solutions. You may also investigate alternative approaches that could be used sometimes even more effectively! Solving a challenge is a key step forward; finding the most efficient or elegant approach to do so should also be considered as being a rewarding part of the process!

Recommended Resources

You are nearly ready to get started with your first challenge. The good news is that, provided you have internet access, you will not need to install anything on your computer to get started. All of the challenges can be completed online using the web address given for each challenge (also accessible using the QR codes provided). Each web address points towards the blog post of the challenge and each bog post includes a widget from trinket.io, an online Python environment that lets you type and run Python code within your web browser.

If you are serious about coding, you will most likely want to install Python on your own computer. We would also strongly recommend that you investigate installing a Python IDE (integrated Development Environment). There are several free Python IDEs available, but if you are not sure which one to choose from, we shall recommend PyScripter which is a free, open-source IDE. It will make it a lot easier to type your code (Syntax highlighting and checking as you type, indentation options) and to troubleshoot and debug your code using the built-in debugging tools (breakpoints, stepping options and variables windows). Should you be planning to build 2D arcade games, you may also want to install the Pygame library. (See challenge 101: Pong Game).

Python *Version 3.6.0 or above*	https://www.python.org/downloads/
PyScripter IDE	https://en.wikipedia.org/wiki/PyScripter
Pygame – Python Library	http://www.pygame.org

Beyond this Book

The 101 challenges from this book are just a selection from a wider range of programming and computing challenges from the 101computing.net blog. I am regularly posting and amending existing challenges on this blog so do not hesitate to visit the blog on a regular basis.

You can also register on the blog or follow me on different social networks to be kept informed when new blog posts are being published:

101Computing.net Blog	https://www.101computing.net/
Twitter	https://twitter.com/101computing
Facebook	https://www.facebook.com/101Computing/
Youtube	https://www.youtube.com/c/101Computing

I would like to hear from you:

You may be willing to give feedback on this book or on the blog and you may have suggestions on how I could improve these resources further. I would love to hear what you have to say. You can contact me through the social networks listed above or via e-mail: info@101computing.net.

And now?

Well that's it, let's get coding. You are ready to move on to challenge #1.

Happy coding!

Chapter #1: Getting Started

Let's get started with our first few challenges. Though these challenges will be based on fairly basic algorithms (mainly based on sequencing), these will enable you to get used to the Python syntax as well as cover a range of key programming concepts that are essential and heavily used in most, if not all programs.

When working on these first challenges, bear in mind that the computer will run your code one line at a time from the top (line 1) to the end of your program. This is what we call **sequencing**.

Our first few challenges will cover the following programming techniques:

- Sequencing,
- Input / Output,
- Variables,
- Data Types,
- Casting Variables,
- Assignment Operator,
- Arithmetic Operators.

1. A Puzzling Algorithm

For this challenge, we will use a flowchart to implement and test an algorithm.

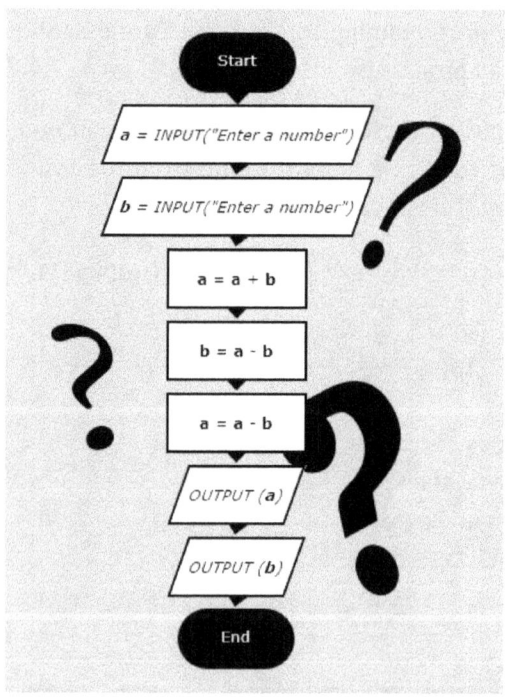

We will use the test plan provided at the web address provided below to predict and verify the output of this algorithm for different input values.

This will enable us to find out what this puzzling algorithm actually does! It will also help us find out more about how variables work and how they can be used to retrieve user inputs and how their values can be changed and displayed on screen (output).

Web Address

https://www.101computing.net/a-puzzling-algorithm/

```
1.  #A Puzzling Algortihm
2.  #Input
3.  a = int(input("Enter a number:"))
4.  b = int(input("Enter a number:"))
5.
6.  #Process
7.  a = a + b
8.  b = a - b
9.  a = a - b
10.
11. #Output
12. print("a = " + str(a))
13. print("b = " + str(b))
```

Test this algorithm with a range of different values for variables *a* and *b*. The program should swap the content of both variables. This is a very unusual and puzzling approach to swap the content of two variables. Now that you have completed this challenge we strongly recommend you complete the next challenge called "The Box Swap Puzzle" which will show you a more widely used approach used to swap the content of two variables.

2.   The Box Swap Puzzle

For this challenge we will write a program that asks the user to enter two values between 1 and 10 and assign these values to two variables called *number1* and *number2*.

We will then compare these two numbers to find out which number is the highest number. If *number1* is lower than *number2*, our program will swap the content of the variables *number1* and *number2* using "the box swap approach" as described in the following picture.

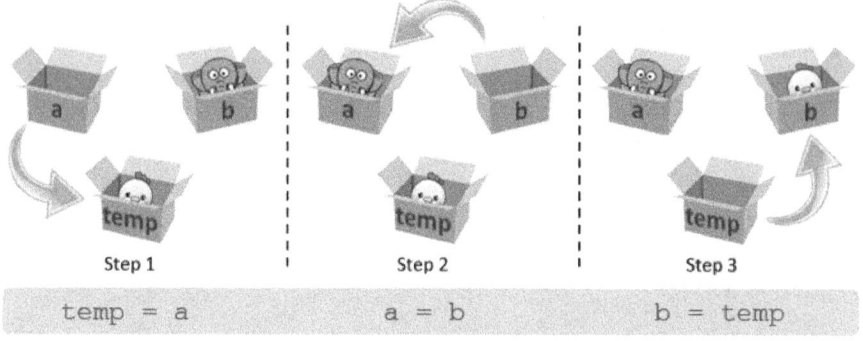

Step 1	Step 2	Step 3
temp = a	a = b	b = temp

Finally, our program will output both numbers. *Number1* should have the highest value and *number2* the lowest value.

Web Address

https://www.101computing.net/the-box-swap-puzzle

Python Code

```python
1.  #Swapping the content of two variables
2.
3.  #Retrieve user inputs
4.  number1 = int(input("Enter a number between 1 and 10:"))
5.  number2 = int(input("Enter a number between 1 and 10:"))
6.
7.  #Perform a permutation only if number1 is lower than number
    2
8.  if number1<number2:
9.      temp = number1
10.     number1 = number2
11.     number2 = temp
12.
13. #Output the 2 numbers
14. print("In descending order...")
15. print(number1)
16. print(number2)
```

3. Three Numbers Sort

This challenge uses the "box swap" approach used in the previous challenge but this time to sort three numbers in ascending order. Our program will ask the user to enter three values between 1 and 10 and assign these values to three variables called *number1*, *number2* and *number3*. It will then perform some permutations (swapping the content of variables) to sort and output these three numbers in ascending order.

Web Address

https://www.101computing.net/the-box-swap-puzzle

Python Code

```
1.  #Ordering 3 numbers in ascending order
2.
3.  #Retrieve user inputs
4.  number1 = int(input("Enter a number between 1 and 10:"))
5.  number2 = int(input("Enter a number between 1 and 10:"))
6.  number3 = int(input("Enter a number between 1 and 10:"))
7.
8.  #Perform permutations to order all three numbers
9.  if number1>number2:
10.    temp = number1
11.    number1 = number2
12.    number2 = temp
13.
14. if number2>number3:
15.    temp = number2
16.    number2 = number3
17.    number3 = temp
18.
19. if number1>number2:
20.    temp = number1
21.    number1 = number2
22.    number2 = temp
23.
24. #Output 3 numbers in ascending order
25. print("In ascending order...")
26. print(number1)
27. print(number2)
28. print(number3)
```

4. Original Price Calculator

Shopping during the sales can sometimes be very confusing. With discounted prices at 10%, 20%, 50% or even 70%!

For this challenge we are going to write a Python script that prompts the user to enter a discounted price in pounds (or in your own currency) (e.g. £90) and the discount rate that this price benefits from (e.g. 25%).

Our program will then calculate and display the original price (price before discount) of the item (e.g. £120).

How much did this item cost in the first place?

Web Address

https://www.101computing.net/original-price-calculator/

Python Code

```
1.  # Original Price Calculator
2.
3.  #Retrieve User Inputs
4.  discountedPrice = float(input("Discounted Price?"))
5.  discount = float(input("Percentage Discount?\n(e.g. Type 20
    for 20%):"))
6.
7.  #Process
8.  originalPrice = discountedPrice / (1 -discount/100)
9.
10. #Output
11. print("The original price was £" + str(originalPrice))
```

5. Weight on the Moon Calculator

Your weight is a measure of the amount of gravity exerted on your body by the planet Earth. On planet Earth, gravity has a value of 9.81 N/Kg (Newtons per kilogram). Because the Moon has about one-sixth of the gravity that Earth does, you would weigh less standing on it. On the Moon, gravity has a value of 1.622 N/Kg.

We can hence use the following formula to calculate your weight on the Moon:

$$weight\ on\ the\ Moon = \frac{weight\ on\ Earth}{9.81} \times 1.622$$

For this challenge, we are writing a short Python program, based on the Input / Process / Output model. Our program will:

INPUT:

Ask the user to input their weight in kg and store this value in a variable called *weightOnEarth*.

PROCESS:

Apply the formula to calculate the equivalent lunar weight and store it in a variable called *weightOnMoon*.

OUTPUT:

Display the weight on the Moon on screen.

We can also apply the same approach to calculate and output the weight of the end-user on all the different planets of the Solar system.

Web Address

https://www.101computing.net/weight-on-the-moon-calculator/

18

```
1.  #Weight on the Moon Calculator
2.
3.  #Input
4.  weightOnEarth = float(input("Enter a weight/mass in kg:"))
5.
6.  #Process -
    Calculate weight on the Moon, rounded to 2 decimal places.

7.  weightOnMoon = round( weightOnEarth * 1.622 / 9.81 , 2)
8.  weightOnMercury = round( weightOnEarth * 3.7 / 9.81 , 2)
9.  weightOnVenus = round( weightOnEarth * 8.87 / 9.81 , 2)
10. weightOnMars = round( weightOnEarth * 3.711 / 9.81 , 2)
11. weightOnJupiter = round( weightOnEarth * 24.79 / 9.81 , 2)
12. weightOnSaturn = round( weightOnEarth * 10.44 / 9.81 , 2)
13. weightOnUranus = round( weightOnEarth * 8.69 / 9.81 , 2)
14. weightOnNeptune = round( weightOnEarth * 11.15 / 9.81 , 2)
15.
16. #Output
17. print("Your weight on the Moon is: " + str(weightOnMoon) + "
    kg.")
18. print("Your weight on Mercury is: " + str(weightOnMercury) +
    "kg.")
19. print("Your weight on Venus is: " + str(weightOnVenus) + "kg
    .")
20. print("Your weight on Mars is: " + str(weightOnMars) + "kg."
    )
21. print("Your weight on Jupiter is: " + str(weightOnJupiter) +
    "kg.")
22. print("Your weight on Saturn is: " + str(weightOnSaturn) + "
    kg.")
23. print("Your weight on Uranus is: " + str(weightOnUranus) + "
    kg.")
24. print("Your weight on Neptune is: " + str(weightOnNeptune) +
    "kg.")
```

6. Complementary Colours Algorithm

Complementary colours are pairs of colours which, when combined or mixed, cancel each other out by producing a grayscale colour like white or black. When placed next to each other, they create the strongest contrast for those two colours. Complementary colours may also be called "opposite colours".

When representing colours using the RGB colour code, we can use the following formula to work out the complementary RGB colour code:

$$colour = (red, green, blue)$$

$$complementaryColour = (255 - red, 255 - green, 255 - blue)$$

Our aim is to write a Python program, based on the INPUT, PROCESS and OUTPUT model in order to:

INPUT:

Ask the user to enter an RGB colour code.

PROCESS:

Apply the complementary colour code formula to work out the RGB code of the complementary colour.

OUTPUT:

Display the complementary colour code on screen.

Web Address

https://www.101computing.net/complementary-colours-algorithm/

20

```
1.  #Complementary Colours Algorithm
2.
3.  #INPUT
4.  red = int(input("Red value:"))
5.  green = int(input("Green value:"))
6.  blue = int(input("Blue value:"))
7.
8.  #PROCESS
9.  complementaryRed = 255 - red
10. complementaryGreen = 255 - green
11. complementaryBlue = 255 - blue
12.
13. #OUTPUT
14. print("Colour: (" + str(red) + "," + str(green) + "," + str(
    blue) + ")")
15. print("Complementary Colour: (" + str(complementaryRed) + ",
    " + str(complementaryGreen) + "," + str(complementaryBlue) +
    ")")
```

7. Entry Fees Calculator

For this challenge we will create a program to calculate the entry fees to an aqua park for a small group of visitors or a family. Our program will have to implement the following pricing policy:

Our program will:

- Ask the user how many adult tickets are needed,
- Ask the user how many child tickets are needed,
- Calculate the total cost of this order,
- Decide if this order qualifies for a 5% discount and if so, calculate the new total cost of the order,
- Output the total cost of the order.

Web Address

https://www.101computing.net/entry-fees-calculator-using-a-flowchart/

```
1.  #Aqua Park - Entry Fees Calculator
2.
3.  #Retrieving User Inputs
4.  adults = int(input("Number of adults: "))
5.  children = int(input("Number of children: "))
6.
7.  #Calculate Cost
8.  cost = adults * 15 + children * 11
9.
10. #Decide if this order qualifies for a 5% discount
11. if cost>=50:
12.   print("Your order qualifies for a 5% discount.")
13.   cost = cost * 95 /100
14.
15. #Output
16. print("Total Cost: £" + str(cost))
```

Chapter #2: What if...

In the previous challenges we used sequencing, which is based on the idea that a computer program starts at line 1, reads and executes the line and progresses to the next line, and so on until it reaches the last line of the program.

We are now going to investigate **selection** using IF statements. Selection allows the computer to choose alternative pathways bypassing a few lines of code if a condition is not met.

In the next challenges we will use:

- Selection using IF Statements,
- Nested IF Statements,
- Comparison Operators,
- Boolean Operators.

8. Stopping Distance Calculator

In this challenge, we will write a Python program to estimate the total stopping distance of a vehicle based on its speed. The stopping distance consists of two components. The first component is the reaction distance covered by the vehicle due to the reaction time/delay of the driver between the moment an obstacle is spotted on the road and the moment the brakes are applied. The second component is the braking distance which is the distance a vehicle will travel from the point when its brakes are fully applied to when it comes to a complete stop. The braking distance is primarily affected by the original speed of the vehicle and the coefficient of friction between the tires and the road surface.

Based on the law of physics, we can write the stopping distance formula as follows:

Stopping Distance (SD)

Reaction Distance (RD)   Braking Distance (BD)

$$Stopping\ Distance = RD + BD$$

$$RD = v.tr$$

$$BD = \frac{v^2}{2\mu g}$$

v	Velocity (speed) of the vehicle in m/s
t_r	Reaction time in seconds (s)
μ	Friction coefficient
g	Gravity (9.81 m/s^2)

For this challenge we will use a response time (tr) of 1.5 seconds, the average response time of a driver. In reality this response time varies depending on the age of the driver, their experience and their condition: e.g. a tired driver will have a slower response time than an alert driver.

The value of the friction coefficient μ depends on the condition of the road (e.g. dry/wet/icy) as well as the types, condition and pressure of the tyres. We will use the following values for the friction coefficient:

Road Condition	Dry	Wet	Icy
Friction Coefficient	$\mu = 0.7$	$\mu = 0.5$	$\mu = 0.3$

Our aim is to write a Python program based on the INPUT / PROCESS / OUTPUT model that will:

- INPUT: Ask the user to enter the speed of a car in mph (Miles per hour)
- PROCESS: Convert this speed in mps (meters per second)
- PROCESS: Apply the stopping distance formula (using $\mu = 0.7$ and tr = 1.5s)
- OUTPUT: Display the estimated stopping distance of the car in meters.

To convert the speed of the vehicle from mph (miles per hour) to mps (meter per second) you will need to apply the following formula:

$$Speed\ in\ mps = \frac{Speed\ in\ mph}{2.237}$$

Web Address

https://www.101computing.net/stopping-distance-calculator/

Python Code

```
1.  #Stopping Distance Calculator
2.
3.  mu = 0.7 # Friction Coefficient
4.  tr = 1.5 # Response Time
5.  g = 9.81 # Gravity
6.
7.  #INPUT
8.  #Ask the user to enter the speed of the vehicle in mph
9.  speed_mph = float(input("Enter the speed of the vehicle in m
    iles per hour:"))
10. road_condition = input("Enter the road condition: Dry, Wet o
    r Icy").lower()
11.
12. #PROCESS
```

```
13. #Convert the speed from miles per hour to meters per second
14. v = speed_mph / 2.237
15.
16. #Workout the friction coefficient based on the road conditio
    n
17. mu = 0.7
18. if road_condition=="dry":
19.     mu = 0.7
20. elif road_condition=="wet":
21.     mu = 0.5
22. elif road_condition=="icy":
23.     mu = 0.3
24. else:
25.     print("Road condition not recognised. Assumption: Dry road
    .")
26.     mu = 0.7
27.
28. #Calculate the reaction distance, braking distance and overa
    ll total stopping distance
29. rd = v * tr
30. bd = v**2 / (2 * mu * g)
31. stopping_distance = rd + bd
32.
33. #OUTPUT
34. #Display the stopping distance in meters
35. print("Stopping distance: " + str(int(stopping_distance)) +
    " meters.")
```

9. Mixed Numbers Challenge

In Maths a fraction consists of two numbers: a numerator and a denominator.

$$\frac{numerator}{denominator}$$

An improper fraction is a fraction where the numerator is greater than or equal to the denominator. For instance: $\frac{7}{4}$, $\frac{12}{10}$, $\frac{21}{3}$ are all improper fractions.

A proper fraction is a fraction where the numerator is lower than to the denominator. For instance: $^7/_9$, $^{12}/_{21}$, $^3/_4$ are all proper fractions.

A mixed number is a number consisting of a whole number and a proper fraction. For instance: $3\,^1/_2$, $1\,^3/_{10}$, $21\,^3/_4$ are all mixed numbers.

We can easily convert an improper fraction into a mixed number by calculating the quotient and the remainder from the improper fraction.

$$\text{Mixed number} = \text{Quotient}\,^{\text{Remainder}}/_{\text{Denominator}}$$

In this challenge, we are using a Python script to ask the user to enter a fraction (by inputting both its numerator and denominator). Our script will then decide if the fraction is an improper fraction and if it is, it will calculate and output the fraction as a mixed number.

Web Address

https://www.101computing.net/mixed-numbers-challenge/

Python Code

```
1.  #Mixed Numbers Challenge
2.
3.  print("- Improper Fraction to Mixed Number Conversion -")
4.  numerator = int(input("Enter the numerator:"))
5.  denominator = int(input("Enter the denominator:"))
6.
7.  #An improper fraction is a fraction where the numerator is g
    reater than or equal to the denominator.
8.  if numerator>=denominator:
9.    print("This is an improper fraction.")
10.   #Calculate the quotient and the remainder of this improper
      fraction and output the resulting mixed number on screen
11.   quotient = numerator // denominator
12.   remainder = numerator % denominator
13.   print("It can be written as a mixed number:")
14.   if remainder>0:
15.     print(str(quotient) + " " + str(remainder) + "/" + str(d
      enominator))
16.   else:
17.     print(str(quotient))
18. else:
19.   print("This is a proper fraction.")
```

10. Area Calculator

In this challenge we will implement an algorithm to calculate the area of various shapes as listed below:

Shape	Name	Area
Square diagram with width	Square	$width^2$
Rectangle diagram with width and length	Rectangle	width x length
Circle diagram with radius	Circle	$pi \times radius^2$
Triangle diagram with height and base	Triangle	base x height / 2

Our program will:

- Ask the user which of the above four shapes they would like to calculate the area of.
- Based on the chosen shape, our program will ask the end user to enter the required dimensions (e.g. width, or width and length or radius or base and height).
- Calculate and display the area of the chosen shape.

Web Address

https://www.101computing.net/area-calculator-python-challenge/

Python Code

```
1.  #Area Calculator Python Challenge -
    www.101computing.net/area-calculator-python-challenge/
2.
3.  shape=input("What shape would you like to calculate the area
    of?").lower()
4.
5.  if shape=="square":
6.    width = float(input("Width?"))
7.    area = width**2
8.    print("Area = " + str(area))
9.
10. elif shape=="rectangle":
11.   width = float(input("Width?"))
12.   length = float(input("Length?"))
13.   area = width * length
14.   print("Area = " + str(area))
15.
16. elif shape=="circle":
17.   radius = float(input("Radius?"))
18.   area = 3.14 * (radius**2)
19.   print("Area = " + str(area))
20.
21. elif shape=="triangle":
22.   base = float(input("Base?"))
23.   height = float(input("Height?"))
24.   area = base * height / 2
25.   print("Area = " + str(area))
26.
27. else:
28.   print("Invalid shape!")
```

11. Acute, Obtuse and Reflex Angles

Angles are often used in computer science especially when creating 2D or 3D user interfaces. Angle measurements are given in either radians or degrees. In this blog post we will use degrees. As the angle increases, the name of the angle changes as explained below:

Type of Angle	Description
Acute Angle	an angle that is less than 90°
Right Angle	an angle that is 90° exactly
Obtuse Angle	an angle that is greater than 90° but less than 180°
Straight Angle	an angle that is 180° exactly
Reflex Angle	an angle that is greater than 180°

For this challenge we will write a Python script that will ask the user to enter an angle between 0° and 360°.

The program will then find out and output the type of angle (Acute, Right, Obtuse, Straight or Reflex) using the table of values provided above.

Web Address

https://www.101computing.net/acute-obtuse-and-reflex-angles/

Python Code

```
1.  #Acute, Obtuse or Reflex Angle? -
    www.101computing.net/acute-obtuse-and-reflex-angles/
2.
3.  angle = int(input("Please enter an angle between 0 and 360 d
    egrees:"))
4.  #Complete the code here...
5.  if angle>=0 and angle<90:
6.    print("This is an acute angle.")
7.  elif angle==90:
8.    print("This is a right angle.")
9.  elif angle>90 and angle<180:
10.   print("This is an obtuse angle.")
11. elif angle==180:
12.   print("This is a straight angle.")
```

```
13. elif angle>180 and angle<=360:
14.    print("This is a reflex angle.")
15. else:
16.    print("Try again with a value between 0 and 360 degrees.")
```

12. ATM Algorithm

An ATM, a.k.a. Cash Withdrawal Machine, uses a computer program to interact with the customer and count the number of banknotes to dispense based on the customer's requested amount.

In the UK, ATM's tend to only stock £20 banknotes and £10 banknotes and apply the following rules:

- The minimal amount that can be withdrawn is £10,
- The maximal amount that can be withdrawn is £200,
- The amount to be withdrawn must be a multiple of 10 e.g. £10, £20, £30, £40, ... £180, £190, £200.

The aim of this challenge is to implement a basic algorithm that asks the end-user to enter an amount to withdraw, checks that it is a multiple of 10, and counts the number of £20 and £10 banknotes to dispense.

Web Address

https://www.101computing.net/atm-algorithm/

Python Code

```
1.  #ATM Algorithm - www.101computing.net/atm-algorithm/
2.
3.  while True:
4.      print("Welcome to Python Bank ATM - Cash Withdrawal")
5.      amount = int(input("How much would you like to withdraw to
        day?"))
6.      if (amount % 10) != 0:
7.          print("You can only withdraw a multiple of ten!")
8.      else:
```

```
9.      if amount<10 or amount>200:
10.        print("You can only withdraw between £10 and £200")
11.      else:
12.        notes20 = amount // 20
13.        notes10 = (amount % 20) / 10
14.        print("Collect your money: ")
15.        print("    >> £20 Banknotes: " + str(notes20))
16.        print("    >> £10 Banknotes: " + str(notes10))
17.        print("Thank you for using this Python Bank ATM.")
18.        print("Good Bye.")
```

13. Automatic Petrol Pump Algorithm

In this challenge we will implement an algorithm to be used in an automatic petrol pump to interact with the customer and calculate the total cost of filling up their vehicle.

The fuel options and tariffs at this petrol station are as follows:

- Unleaded: £1.17 per litre,
- Super Unleaded: £1.27 per litre,
- Diesel: £1.21 per litre,
- Diesel Premium: £1.34 per litre.

The petrol pump will interact with the customer by asking the following questions:

- What fuel do you require?
- Do you want to fill up (full tank capacity) and if not how many litres of fuel do you require?

The petrol pump will use this information provided by the customer as well as the tariffs provided above to calculate the total cost of this order.

To simulate a real life situation, we will assume that the customer's vehicle has a tank capacity of 55 litres.

We will also assume that when the customer reaches the petrol station, the vehicle still has some fuel left. To simulate this we will generate a random number between 0 and 55. This number will represent the number of litres left in the tank before filling up.

If the customer requires a full tank, the algorithm will calculate the quantity needed as follows:

Quantity Needed = Full Tank Capacity – Current Fuel Level

If the customer specifies a desired quantity (in litres), the algorithm will fill up the tank with the required quantity. However, if the required quantity combined with the current level of fuel in the tank exceeds the full tank capacity, the required quantity will be replaced to just the quantity that is needed using the same formula as mentioned above.

Web Address

https://www.101computing.net/automatic-petrol-pump-algorithm/

Python Code

```
1.  #Automatic Petrol Pump Algorithm -
    www.101computing.net/automatic-petrol-pump-algorithm/
2.  import random
3.
4.  currentFuelLevel = random.randint(0,55)
5.  print("You have " + str(currentFuelLevel) + " litres left in
    your tank.")
6.
7.  tankCapacity = 55 #litres
8.  unleadedPrice = 1.17
9.  superUnleadedPrice = 1.27
10. dieselPrice = 1.21
11. dieselPremiumPrice = 1.34
12.
13. print(" ---- Our Tariffs ----")
14. print("A -
    Unleaded: £" + str(unleadedPrice) + " per litre")
15. print("B -
    Super Unleaded: £" + str(superUnleadedPrice) + " per litre"
    )
16. print("C - Diesel: £" + str(dieselPrice) + " per litre")
```

```
17. print("D -
      Diesel Premium: £" + str(dieselPremiumPrice) + " per litre"
      )
18.
19. fuelChoice = input("What fuel do you need?")
20. pricePerLitre = 0
21. if fuelChoice == "A":
22.    pricePerLitre = unleadedPrice
23. elif fuelChoice == "B":
24.    pricePerLitre = superUnleadedPrice
25. elif fuelChoice == "C":
26.    pricePerLitre = dieselPrice
27. elif fuelChoice == "D":
28.    pricePerLitre = dieselPremiumPrice
29. else:
30.    print("Invalid Option")
31.
32. fullTank = input("Would you like to fill up to a full tank?"
      )
33. if fullTank=="Yes":
34.    quantityNeeded = tankCapacity - currentFuelLevel
35. else:
36.    quantityNeeded = int(input("How many litres do you need?")
      )
37.    if (currentFuelLevel + quantityNeeded) > tankCapacity:
38.       quantityNeeded = tankCapacity - currentFuelLevel
39.
40. cost =  quantityNeeded * pricePerLitre
41.
42. print("Fuel Choice: " + fuelChoice)
43. print("Quantity: " + str(quantityNeeded) + " litres.")
44. print("Total Cost: £" + str(cost))
```

Chapter #3: Loop the loop

Sequencing and Selection are two extremely useful programming constructs that help us build very complex programs.

While completing some of the previous challenges you may have been tempted to repeat some lines of code to allow the user to play the program several times without having to restart it.

This can be done using **iteration**. This programming construct allows a section of code to be repeated several times using a loop. A loop acts similarly to an IF statement but, instead of allowing the computer to jump downwards within the code (to bypass code when a condition is not met), a loop allows the computer to jump upwards to a line of code that has already been executed previously. This allows a section of code to be repeated, either a fixed number of times (**Count-controlled *For* loop**) or until a condition is met (**Condition-controlled *While* loop**).

In the next few challenges we will be using:

- Iteration using Count-Controlled Loops (*For* loops),
- Iteration using Condition-Controlled Loops (*While* loops),
- Nested Loops (a loop within a loop),
- Nested Loops and IF Statements.

14. Padlock Code Challenges 1 to 3

The next few challenges are from a series of nine padlock code breaking puzzles.

For each of these puzzles, we need to write a computer program to work out a 3-digit padlock code. Our program will output the solution for a given hint. We will then be able to input this combination onto the padlock available at the web addresses provided below. This should let us check if our combination works!

Web Addresses

https://www.101computing.net/padlock-code-challenge-1/
https://www.101computing.net/padlock-code-challenge-2/
https://www.101computing.net/padlock-code-challenge-3/

Padlock 1: Hint:

code = 1 + 2 + 3 + 4 + ... + 38 + 39 + 40

Python Code – Padlock 1

```
1.  code = 0
2.  for i in range(1,41):
3.      code += i
4.
5.  print("Code:")
6.  print(code)
```

Padlock 2: Hint:

code = Total number of 3-digit combinations
where digit1 < digit2 < digit3

```
1.  code = 0
2.  for digit1 in range(0,10):
3.    for digit2 in range(0,10):
4.      for digit3 in range(0,10):
5.        if digit1<digit2 and digit2<digit3:
6.          code+=1
7.
8.  print("Code:")
9.  print(code)
```

Padlock 3: Hint:

 code = Total number of 3-digit combinations
where digit1, digit2 and digit3 are all even numbers

Python Code – Padlock 3

```
1.  code = 0
2.  for digit1 in range(0,10):
3.    for digit2 in range(0,10):
4.      for digit3 in range(0,10):
5.        if (digit1%2==0) and (digit2%2==0) and (digit3%2==0):
6.          code+=1
7.
8.  print("Code:")
9.  print(code)
```

15. Padlock Code Challenges 4 to 6

Let's carry on with our series of padlock code challenges to work out the combinations of padlocks 4, 5 and 6.

https://www.101computing.net/padlock-code-challenge-4/
https://www.101computing.net/padlock-code-challenge-5/
https://www.101computing.net/padlock-code-challenge-6/

Padlock 4: Hint:

 code = Total number of 3-digit combinations
where the sum of all three digits is an odd number

Python Code – Padlock 4

```
1.  code = 0
2.  for digit1 in range(0,10):
3.    for digit2 in range(0,10):
4.      for digit3 in range(0,10):
5.        if (digit1+digit2+digit3)%2==1:
6.          code +=1
7.
8.  print("Code:")
9.  print(code)
```

Padlock 5: Hint:

 code = Total number of 3-digit combinations
where at least two digits are equal.

Python Code – Padlock 5

```
1.  code = 0
2.  for digit1 in range(0,10):
3.    for digit2 in range(0,10):
4.      for digit3 in range(0,10):
5.        if digit1==digit2 or digit2==digit3 or digit1==digit3:
6.          code +=1
7.
8.  print("Code:")
9.  print(code)
```

code = Total number of 3-digit combinations where
one digit is equal to the sum of the other two digits

Python Code – Padlock 6

```
1.  code = 0
2.  for digit1 in range(0,10):
3.    for digit2 in range(0,10):
4.      for digit3 in range(0,10):
5.        if digit1==(digit2+digit3) or digit2==(digit1+digit3)
   or digit3==(digit2+digit1):
6.          code +=1
7.
8.  print("Code:")
9.  print(code)
```

16. Padlock Code Challenges 7 to 9

To complete this series of nine padlock challenges,
let's work out the combinations of padlocks 7, 8 and 9.

Web Addresses

https://www.101computing.net/padlock-code-challenge-7/
https://www.101computing.net/padlock-code-challenge-8/
https://www.101computing.net/padlock-code-challenge-9/

Padlock 7: Hint:

code = The largest 3-digit square number.

```
1.  code = 0
2.  number = 0
3.  while code<1000:
4.      number += 1
5.      code = number**2
6.
7.  number -= 1
8.  code = number**2
9.
10. print("Code:")
11. print(code)
```

 code = The largest 3-digit prime number.

Python Code – Padlock 8

```
1.  #A function to find out if a number is prime or not
2.  def isPrime(number):
3.      prime=True
4.      for i in range(2,number):
5.          if number % i ==0:
6.              prime=False
7.      return prime
8.
9.  code = 0
10. count = 0
11. #Update the code below to solve this challenge
12. for i in range (2,1000):
13.     if isPrime(i):
14.         code = i
15.
16. print("Code:")
17. print(code)
```

code = The average of all prime numbers between 0 and 999 (rounded to the nearest value).

Python Code – Padlock 9

```
1.  #A function to find out if a number is prime or not
2.  def isPrime(number):
3.      prime=True
4.      for i in range(2,number):
5.          if number % i ==0:
6.              prime=False
7.      return prime
8.
9.  code = 0
10. count = 0
11. for i in range (2,1000):
12.     if isPrime(i):
13.         code += i
14.         count += 1
15.
16. code = round(code / count)
17.
18. print("Code:")
19. print(code)
```

17. Finding the Factors of...

For this challenge we will use an algorithm to find all the factors of a given number.

Factors are numbers we can multiply together to get another number. For instance, factors of 15 are 1, 3, 5 and 15, because 1×15=15 and 3×5 = 15.

Web Address

https://www.101computing.net/finding-the-factors-of/

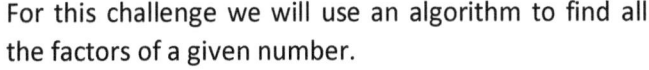

Python Code

```
1. #Finding the factors of...
2.
3. number = int(input("Enter a number:"))
4. print("The factors of " + str(number) + " are:")
5. for i in range(1, number+1):
6.   if number % i == 0:
7.     print(i)
```

18. Star Rating Validation

The aim of this Python challenge is to validate a user input using both a type check and a range check.

In this program, the user will be asked to enter a star rating by entering a number value between 0 and 5. This could for instance be used to rate a movie (5 Stars = Excellent ,0 Star = Disappointing).

The program will check that the end-user has entered a number (type check) between 0 and 5 (range check) and if not, it will display an error message and repeat the question until a valid rating between 0 and 5 is entered.

Web Address

https://www.101computing.net/flowchart-to-python-code-star-rating-validation/

Python Code

```
1. #Star Rating Validation
2.
3. #A function to check that a user input is an integer
4. def inputNumber(message):
5.   while True:
6.     try:
7.       userInput = int(input(message))
8.     except ValueError:
9.       print("Not an integer! Try again.")
10.       continue
11.     else:
12.       return userInput
```

```
13.         break
14.
15. #MAIN PROGRAM STARTS HERE:
16. starRating = inputNumber("Enter a star rating bettwen 0 and
    5?")
17. while starRating<0 or starRating>5:
18.    print("Invalid star rating. Please try again!")
19.    starRating = inputNumber("Enter a star rating bettwen 0 an
    d 5?")
20.
21. print("Thank you!")
```

19. Pomodoro Timer

The Pomodoro Technique is a time management method that can be used for a wide range of tasks. Many students use this technique to organise their revision time before an exam.

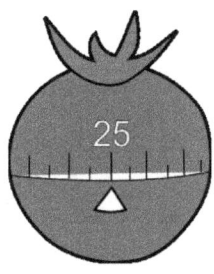

This Pomodoro Technique was developed by Francesco Cirillo in the late 1980s. It uses a timer to break down work into short intervals, typically 25 minutes in length, separated by short breaks (3 to 5 minutes). Each interval is known as a pomodoro, from the Italian word for "tomato" because Francesco Cirillo used a tomato-shaped kitchen timer when he was a university student.

The technique is an iterative process based on the following steps:

1. Decide on a task to complete,
2. Work on this task for 25 minutes (using a timer),
3. When the timer stops/rings, put a check mark on a post-it note,
4. If you have fewer than 4 check marks:
    a. Take a short break (3 to 5 minutes),
    b. Repeat this process from step 2,
5. After 4 check marks (pomodoros):

a. Take a long break (15 to 30 minutes),
b. Reset your check mark counter to zero,
c. Repeat this process from step 2.

https://www.101computing.net/pomodoro-timer/

Python Code

```
1.  #Pomodoro Timer
2.  from time import sleep
3.
4.  interval = 25 * 60 #25 minutes
5.  shortBreak = 5 * 60 #5 minutes
6.  longBreak = 30 * 60 #5 minutes
7.
8.  print("..ooOO The Pomodoro Technique OOoo..")
9.  sleep(2) #wait 2 seconds
10.
11. task=input("Define the task you would like to work on:")
12. print("Your Task: " + str(task))
13. checkmarks=0
14. carryOn=("Yes")
15.
16. while carryOn=="Yes":
17.     print("Starting pomodoro timer (25 Minutes)")
18.     sleep(interval)
19.     print("End of pomodoro interval")
20.     checkmarks=checkmarks + 1
21.     print("Check Marks: " + str(checkmarks))
22.
23.     if checkmarks==4:
24.         print("Take a long break - 30 minutes")
25.         sleep(longBreak)
26.         checkmarks=0
27.     else:
28.         print("Take a short break - 5 minutes")
29.         sleep(shortBreak)
30.     carryOn = input("Would you like to carry on? Yes or No")
31.
32. print("Goodbye!")
```

20. Bidding Process

For this challenge we will consider the bidding process used within online auction websites such as eBay.

Our aim is to create a system that will accept bids from the end-user, check if the bid being placed is greater than the current bid and if so, update the value of the current bid.

You will find at the web address provided below the flowchart for our Bidding System.

Web Address

https://www.101computing.net/bidding-process-flowchart/

Python Code

```
1.  #Bidding Algorithm
2.
3.  def startAuction():
4.    currentBid = 0
5.    bidding=True
6.    #Keep bidding till the user asks to stop
7.    while bidding==True:
8.      userInput = input("Would you like to place a bid?\nEnter
      'Yes' or 'No':").strip().title()
9.      if userInput =="Yes":
10.        newBid = int(input("How much would you like to bid for
      ?"))
11.        #Only accept higher bids.
12.        if newBid > currentBid:
13.          currentBid = newBid
14.          print("Current bid:" +str(currentBid))
15.        else:
16.          print("Invalid bid! You must place a higher bid!")
17.          print("Current bid remains at: " +str(currentBid))
18.      else:
19.        bidding = False
20.
21.    print("End of bidding - Final Value: " +str(currentBid))
22.
23. startAuction()
```

21. Euler's Number

The number *e* is a famous irrational number called Euler's number after Leonhard Euler a Swiss Mathematician (1707 – 1783). Number *e* is considered to be one of the most important numbers in mathematics.

The first few digits are: 2.71828182845904523536028747135527... It has an infinite number of digits with no recurring pattern. It cannot be written as a simple fraction.

Number *e* is the limit of $(1 + 1/n)^n$ as n approaches infinity:

$$e = \lim_{n \to \infty} \left(1 + \frac{1}{n}\right)^n$$

Euler's number, *e*, can also be calculated as the sum of the infinite series:

$$e = \sum_{n=0}^{\infty} \frac{1}{n!} = \frac{1}{1} + \frac{1}{1} + \frac{1}{1\times2} + \frac{1}{1\times2\times3} + \cdots$$

A less common approach to calculate number *e* is to use a continued fraction based on the following sequence:

$$e = [2; 1, 2, 1, 1, 4, 1, 1, 6, 1, \ldots, 1, 2n, 1, \ldots]$$

Continued Fraction:

$$e = 2 + \cfrac{1}{1 + \cfrac{1}{2 + \cfrac{1}{1 + \cfrac{1}{1 + \cfrac{1}{4 + \cfrac{1}{1 + \cfrac{1}{1 + \cdots}}}}}}}$$

In this challenge, we are using a python script to estimate the value of *e* using these three approaches.

Web Address

https://www.101computing.net/eulers-number/

Python Code

```
1.  #Calculating an approximation of Euler's Number
2.
3.  #Method 1: e = limit of (1 + 1/n)^n as n approaches infinity
4.  print("Method 1: e = limit of (1 + 1/n)^n as n approaches in
    finity")
5.  n=10000000
6.  e = (1+1/n)**n
7.  print(e)
8.
9.  #Method 2: Using an infinite series (Iterative approach)
10. print("\nMethod 2: Using an infinite series (Iterative appro
    ach)")
11. e = 1
12. quotient = 1
13. for i in range(1,100):
14.     quotient = quotient * i
15.     e = e + 1/quotient
16. print(e)
17.
18. #Method 3: Using a continued fraction (Iterative approach)
19. print("\nMethod 3: Using a continued fraction (Iterative app
    roach)")
20.
21. n = 100 # number of iterations
22. e = 0
23. for i in range(n, 0, -1):
24.     if i % 3 == 1:
25.         j = 2 * int(i / 3)
26.     else:
27.         j = 1
28.     e = 1.0 / (e + j)
29. e = e+1
30. print(e)
```

We have all heard of the famous English pirate called
Blackbeard who sailed the seven seas during the XVIII
century. Through his numerous acts of piracy,
Blackbeard accumulated a huge collection of riches including golden coins,
jewels, golden plates and precious stones. Blackbeard was wise enough
not to carry his treasure on his vessel. Instead he buried his treasure in a
secret location, somewhere in the middle of the Pacific Ocean.

Recently, a team of SCUBA divers found a message in a bottle while
SCUBA diving near Coral Bay, Western Australia. Inside this old bottle of
rum, they found two pieces of parchment believed to have belonged to
Blackbeard.

The first piece of parchment
is a map. Looking at the
shapes of the three islands on
the map, the SCUBA divers
have been able to locate the
location of these islands
somewhere a few miles off
the coast of Australia. They
strongly believe that this map
will help them find the exact
location of Blackbeard's
treasure.

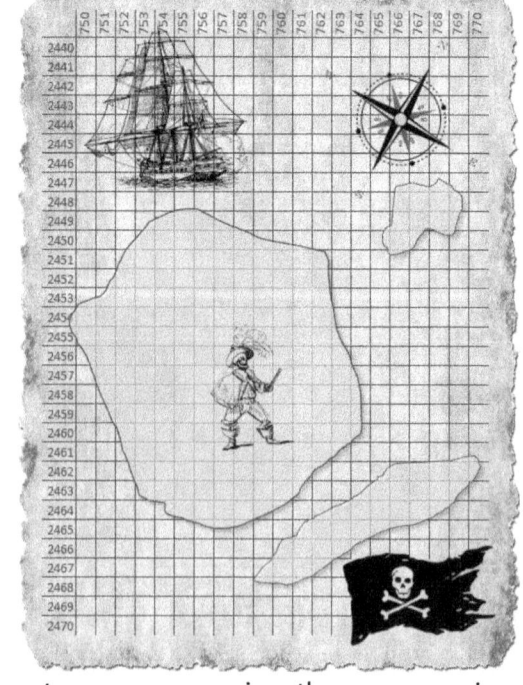

The second parchment is
believed to be the key to help
locate the position of the
treasure on the map.

Your task is to write a computer program, using the programming
language of your choice, in order to find the row number and the column
number to solve the following equation:

Row x Column = 1889121

Looking at the map, we can deduce that the row number could be any number between 2440 and 2470 and that the column number could be any number between 750 and 770.

Your computer program will enable you to pinpoint the exact location of Blackbeard's treasure on this map! Once you have found your row and column numbers enter them on the form provided at the web address below to check if you have located the treasure!

Web Address

https://www.101computing.net/blackbeards-treasure-map/

Python Code

```
1.  #Blackbeard's Treasure Map
2.
3.  for row in range(2440,2770):
4.    for col in range(750,770):
5.      if (row*col) == 1889121:
6.        print("The treasure's location is:")
7.        print("Row:" + str(row))
8.        print("Col:" + str(col))
9.        break
```

23. Min, Max, Range, Mean, Median & Mode

In this challenge we will write a Python script to calculate the Min, Max, Range, Mean, Median and Mode from a list of numbers.

Web Address

https://www.101computing.net/min-max-mean-median-and-mod-flowcharts

```
1.  #Min, Max, Mean, Median and Mode Challenge
2.
3.  list=[7,14,81,56,9,17,14,9,14,43]
4.
5.  #Calculating the Min value...
6.  min = list[0]
7.  for i in range(0,len(list)):
8.    if list[i]<min:
9.      min = list[i]
10.
11. print("Min = " + str(min))
12.
13. #Calculating the Max value...
14. max = list[0]
15. for i in range(0,len(list)):
16.   if list[i]>max:
17.     max = list[i]
18.
19. print("Max = " + str(max))
20.
21. #Calulating the Range value:
22. rangevalue = max - min
23. print("range = " + str(rangevalue))
24.
25. #Calculating the Mean value...
26. total = 0
27. for i in range(0,len(list)):
28.   total += list[i]
29.
30. mean = total / len(list)
31. print("Mean = " + str(mean))
32.
33. #Calculating the Median value...
34. midPosition = len(list)//2
35. median = list[midPosition]
36.
37. print("Median = " + str(median))
38.
39. #Calculating the Mode value...
40. #Start by creating a dictionary of all occurences appearing
    in the list
41. numCount={}
42. for i in range(0,len(list)):
43.     value=list[i]
44.     if value in numCount.keys():
45.       numCount[value] += 1
```

```
46.      else:
47.         numCount[value] = 1
48.
49. #Then find the key with highest count in this dictionary
50. maxCount=0
51. for key in numCount.keys():
52.   if numCount[key] > maxCount:
53.     maxCount=numCount[key]
54.     mode = key
55.
56. print("Mode = " + str(mode))
```

24. Protractor Challenge

A protractor is an instrument used in Maths when measuring or drawing angles.

Our challenge is to use Python to draw a protractor on screen, using all the graduations for a scale going from 0° to 180°.

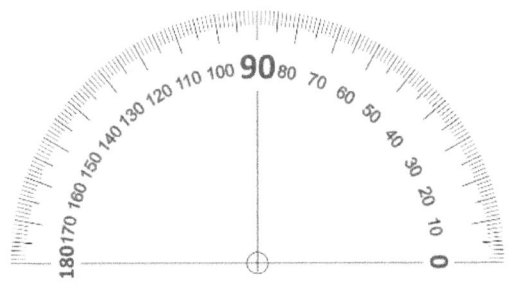

Web Address

https://www.101computing.net/python-turtle-protractor-challenge/

Python Code

```
1.  #Python Turtle Protractor
2.  import turtle
3.
4.  myPen = turtle.Turtle()
5.  myPen.shape("turtle")
6.  myPen.speed(100000)
```

```
 7.  myPen.color("#333333")
 8.
 9.  myPen.penup()
10.  myPen.goto(-10,0)
11.  myPen.pendown()
12.  myPen.setheading(0)
13.  myPen.forward(20)
14.  myPen.penup()
15.  myPen.goto(0,-10)
16.  myPen.pendown()
17.  myPen.setheading(90)
18.  myPen.forward(20)
19.
20.  #Add graduations every 10deg.
21.  for angle in range (0,180,10 ):
22.     myPen.penup()
23.     myPen.goto(0,0)
24.     myPen.setheading(angle)
25.     myPen.forward(130)
26.     myPen.pendown()
27.     myPen.forward(40)
28.
29.  #Add graduations every 5deg.
30.  for angle in range (0,180,5):
31.     myPen.penup()
32.     myPen.goto(0,0)
33.     myPen.setheading(angle)
34.     myPen.forward(140)
35.     myPen.pendown()
36.     myPen.forward(30)
37.
38.  #Add graduations every 1deg.
39.  for angle in range (0,180,1):
40.     myPen.penup()
41.     myPen.goto(0,0)
42.     myPen.setheading(angle)
43.     myPen.forward(150)
44.     myPen.pendown()
45.     myPen.forward(20)
46.
47.  myPen.penup()
48.  myPen.goto(-80,-50)
49.  myPen.write("My Protractor", None, None, "22pt bold")
50.
51.  myPen.hideturtle()
```

25. Moroccan Mosaic

Moroccan mosaic, aka Zellige (الزليج بح), is a form of Islamic art and one of the main characteristics of Moroccan architecture. It consists of geometrically patterned mosaics, used to ornament walls, ceilings, fountains, floors, pools and tables. Each mosaic is a tilework made from individually chiselled geometric tiles set into a plaster base.

In this challenge, we will investigate how to create our own mosaic using various geometric patterns. We will use Python Turtle to draw a regular polygon (e.g. pentagon, hexagon, etc.) and repeat and rotate this shape several times to create a circular pattern/mosaic. We will then be able to use our program to recreate these patterns:

 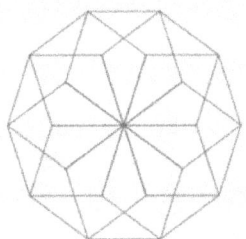 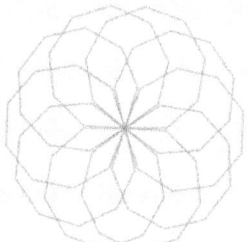

Web Address

https://www.101computing.net/moroccan-mosaic/

Python Code

```
1.  #Moroccan Mosaic using Python Turtle
2.  import turtle
3.  myPen = turtle.Turtle()
4.  myPen.shape("arrow")
5.
6.  myPen.speed(1000) #Set the speed of the turtle
7.
8.  #A Procedure to draw a mosaic by repeating and rotating a
    polygon shape.
9.  def drawMosaic(color,numberOfSides,size,numberOfIterations):
```

```
10.  myPen.color(color)
11.  for i in range(0,numberOfIterations):
12.    for j in range (0,numberOfSides):
13.      myPen.forward(size)
14.      myPen.left(360 / numberOfSides)
15.    myPen.left(360 / numberOfIterations)
16.
17. #Main Program Starts Here
18. hexColourCode = input("Colour Code (e.g.#0B5CCB):")
19. numberOfSides = int(input("Number of sides (e.g. 5):"))
20. size = int(input("Side width in pixels (e.g. 100):"))
21. numberOfIterations = int(input("Number of iterations  (e.g.
     20):"))
22.
23. drawMosaic(hexColourCode,numberOfSides,size,numberOfIteratio
     ns)
24.
25. myPen.hideturtle()
```

26. Infinite Quarter Series

The infinite quarter series is a series where each term is a quarter of the previous one:

$$1/4 + 1/16 + 1/64 + 1/256 + \cdots$$

We can visually represent this series by dividing a canvas (or price of paper) into 4 quadrants and colouring in one quadrant (bottom left). Then we repeat this process by dividing the top right quadrant into 4 and so on. By doing so infinitely we will colour in a third of the initial canvas. This is because this infinite series converges to the value of 1/3.

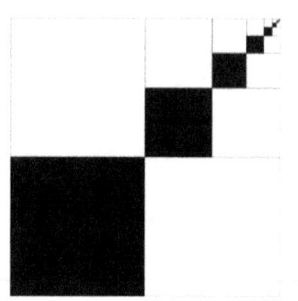

It is possible to visually represent this series using a triangle instead of a square.

The two python programs are used to visually represent the infinite quarter series using both visual representations.

Web Address

https://www.101computing.net/infinite-quarter-series/

Python Code: Visualisation #1

```
1.  #Infinite Quarter Series
2.  import turtle
3.  import random
4.
5.  boardWidth = 40
6.  needleLength = 30
7.  numberOfNeedles = 50
8.
9.  myPen = turtle.Turtle()
10. myPen.hideturtle()
11. myPen.speed(0)
12. myPen.color("purple")
13.
14. def drawSquare(x,y,width,color):
15.     myPen.penup()
16.     myPen.goto(x,y)
17.     myPen.pendown()
18.     myPen.fillcolor(color)
19.     myPen.begin_fill()
20.     for side in range(0,4):
21.       myPen.forward(width)
22.       myPen.left(90)
23.     myPen.end_fill()
24.
25. myPen.penup()
26. x=-200
27. y=-200
28. width=400
29. sum=0
30.
31. for n in range(1,11):
32.     sum += (1/4)**n
33.     drawSquare(x,y,width,"white")
34.     width=width/2
35.     #Fill in 1/4
```

```
36.    drawSquare(x,y,width,"purple")
37.    x+=width
38.    y+=width
39.
40. print("After " + str(n) + " iterations:")
41. print("Sum = " + str(sum))
```

Python Code: Visualisation #2

```
1.  #Infinite Quarter Series
2.  import turtle
3.  import random
4.  import math
5.
6.  boardWidth = 40
7.  needleLength = 30
8.  numberOfNeedles = 50
9.
10. myPen = turtle.Turtle()
11. myPen.hideturtle()
12. myPen.speed(0)
13. myPen.color("purple")
14.
15. def drawTriangle(x,y,width,color):
16.    myPen.penup()
17.    myPen.goto(x,y)
18.    myPen.pendown()
19.    myPen.fillcolor(color)
20.    myPen.begin_fill()
21.    for side in range(0,3):
22.      myPen.forward(width)
23.      myPen.left(120)
24.    myPen.end_fill()
25.
26. myPen.penup()
27. x=-200
28. y=-200
29. width=400
30. sum=0
31.
32. drawTriangle(x,y,width,"purple")
33. width=width/2
34. for n in range(1,11):
35.    sum += (1/4)**n
36.    drawTriangle(x,y,width,"white")
37.    drawTriangle(0,y,width,"white")
38.
```

```
39.    x+=width/2
40.    y+=width*math.sin(math.radians(60))
41.    width=width/2
42.
43.
44. print("After " + str(n) + " iterations:")
45. print("Sum = " + str(sum))
```

27. Text Based Animations

In this challenge we will use Python code to create text-based (ASCII) animations. Each of these animations is using a main loop that repeats the given code every 0.2 seconds and clears the screen between two iterations (frames).

You will find some examples of text-based animations at the web address provided below.

Web Address

https://www.101computing.net/text-based-animations/

The code given below will focus on the following animations:

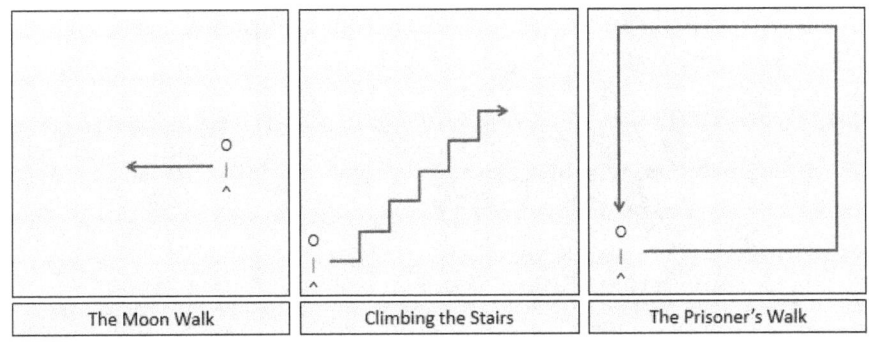

| The Moon Walk | Climbing the Stairs | The Prisoner's Walk |

```
1.  #Rocket Animation
2.  import os
3.  import time
4.
5.  def animate_MoonWalk():
6.      distanceFromLeft = 30
7.      while True:
8.          print("\n" * 10)
9.          print((" " * distanceFromLeft) + "O")
10.         print((" " * distanceFromLeft) + "|")
11.         print((" " * distanceFromLeft) + "^")
12.         time.sleep(0.2)
13.         os.system('clear')
14.         distanceFromLeft -= 1
15.         if distanceFromLeft <0:
16.             distanceFromLeft = 30
17.
18. #Main Program Starts Here....
19. animate_MoonWalk()
```

Python Code: Climbing the Stairs

```
1.  #Climbing the Stairs Animation
2.  import os
3.  import time
4.
5.  def animate_stairs():
6.      steps = 0
7.      while True:
8.          print("\n" * (20-steps))
9.          print((" " * steps) + "O")
10.         print((" " * steps) + "|")
11.         print((" " * steps) + "^")
12.         time.sleep(0.2)
13.         os.system('clear')
14.         steps += 1
15.         if steps > 20:
16.             steps = 0
17.
18. #Main Program Starts Here....
19. animate_stairs()
```

```
1.   #The Prisoner's Walk Animation
2.   import os
3.   import time
4.
5.   def animate_stairs():
6.     steps = 0
7.     while True:
8.       for steps in range(0,10):
9.         print("\n" * 10)
10.        print((" " * steps) + "O")
11.        print((" " * steps) + "|")
12.        print((" " * steps) + "^")
13.        time.sleep(0.2)
14.        os.system('clear')
15.      for steps in range(10,-1,-1):
16.        print("\n" * steps)
17.        print((" " * 10) + "O")
18.        print((" " * 10) + "|")
19.        print((" " * 10) + "^")
20.        time.sleep(0.2)
21.        os.system('clear')
22.      for steps in range(10,-1,-1):
23.        print((" " * steps) + "O")
24.        print((" " * steps) + "|")
25.        print((" " * steps) + "^")
26.        time.sleep(0.2)
27.        os.system('clear')
28.      for steps in range(0,10):
29.        print("\n" * steps)
30.        print("O")
31.        print("|")
32.        print("^")
33.        time.sleep(0.2)
34.        os.system('clear')
35.
36. #Main Program Starts Here....
37. animate_stairs()
```

Chapter #4: Subroutines

As we are now working on more complex programs, our code listings become fairly long. One approach to organise our code more effectively is to use **subroutines** so that functional sections of code can be grouped into subroutines. This makes it easy to read, understand and troubleshoot the code. Subroutines, such as **functions** and **procedures**, are also very useful as they allow you to call them whenever you need them. This reduces the need to duplicate lines of code within your program when the same functionality is required at different stages of your program.

Finally, you may write some subroutines that could be reused within other programs. This is a lot easier to do when the code is organised into subroutines. To facilitate code reusability of your subroutines you may also want to create your own **library**. A library is a collection of subroutines with a common theme. For instance in challenge 44 you will create your own library of conversions functions.

Another aspect of functions is that they enable us to implement a forth programming construct called **recursion**. (Remember so far we have only used three programming constructs: sequencing, selection and iteration). To investigate how a recursive algorithm works, you can jump to challenge 96.

In this chapter we will investigate:

- Functions and Procedures,
- Passing Parameters,
- Creating a Python Library,
- Recursive Algorithms.

28. Splash Screen & Progress Bar

The aim of this challenge is to create two procedures that could be used in any of our Python project to add a splash screen or/and a progress bar.

A splash screen usually appears for a few seconds while a game or program is launching. It can contain basic information such as the name of the game and its version number.

A progress bar is a graphical control element used to visualise the progression of an extended computer operation, such as a download, file transfer or installation. Sometimes, the graphic is accompanied by a textual representation of the progress in a percent format.

Web Address

https://www.101computing.net/splash-screen-and-progress-bar/

Python Code

```
1.  #Splash Screen & Progress
2.  import os
3.  import time
4.
5.  def progress_bar(seconds):
6.    for progress in range(0,seconds+1):
7.      percent = (progress * 100) // seconds
8.      print("\n")
9.      print("Loading...")
10.     print("<" + ("=" * progress) + (" " * (seconds-
    progress)) + "> " + str(percent) + "%")
11.     print("\n")
12.     time.sleep(1)
13.     os.system('clear')
14.
15. def splash_screen(seconds):
16.   print("\n")
17.   print(" **********************")
18.   print(" *                    *")
19.   print(" *    SPLASH SCREEN    *")
20.   print(" *        v1.0         *")
21.   print(" *                    *")
```

```
22.    print(" *********************")
23.    time.sleep(seconds)
24.    os.system('clear')
25.
26. #Main Program Starts Here....
27. splash_screen(3)
28. progress_bar(10)
29. username=input("Type your username:")
```

29. How many Bytes in...

In this challenge we will write a set of functions to calculate how many Bytes there are in a given number of kilobytes, megabytes, gigabytes, terabytes or petabytes.

By completing this challenge we will investigate how subroutines (functions/procedures) are used in Python to create sections of code that can be called/reused many times within a program. Subroutines mean that a section of code can be identified using a name (identifier). This enables us to add more instructions to the already existing functions used in Python such as print or input.

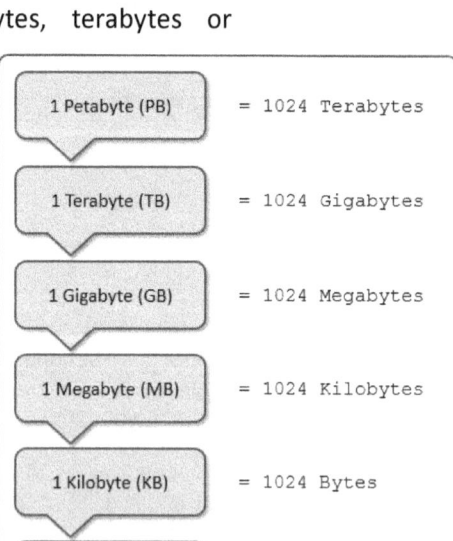

1 Petabyte (PB)	= 1024 Terabytes
1 Terabyte (TB)	= 1024 Gigabytes
1 Gigabyte (GB)	= 1024 Megabytes
1 Megabyte (MB)	= 1024 Kilobytes
1 Kilobyte (KB)	= 1024 Bytes
1 Byte (B)	= 8 bits

Web Address

https://www.101computing.net/how-many-bytes-in/

```
1.  #How many bytes in a kilobyte, megabyte, gigabyte, terabyte,
    petabyte
2.
3.  def kilobytes_to_bytes(numberOfKilobytes):
4.      bytes = 1024 * numberOfKilobytes
5.      return bytes
6.
7.  def megabytes_to_bytes(numberOfMegabytes):
8.      bytes = 1024 * 1024 * numberOfMegabytes
9.      return bytes
10.
11. def gigabytes_to_bytes(numberOfGigabytes):
12.     bytes = 1024 * 1024 * 1024 * numberOfGigabytes
13.     return bytes
14.
15. def terabytes_to_bytes(numberOfTerabytes):
16.     bytes = 1024 * 1024 * 1024 * 1024 * numberOfTerabytes

17.     return bytes
18.
19. def petabytes_to_bytes(numberOfPetabytes):
20.     bytes = 1024 * 1024 * 1024 * 1024 * 1024 * numberOfPet
    abytes
21.     return bytes
22.
23. #Main Program Starts Here
24. option = input("What unit would you like to convert from: KB
    , MB, GB, TB, PB?").upper()
25.
26. if option=="KB":
27.     numberOfKilobytes = int(input("Enter a number of kilobytes
    :"))
28.     numberOfBytes = kilobytes_to_bytes(numberOfKilobytes)
29.     print("There are " + str(numberOfBytes) + " Bytes in " + s
    tr(numberOfKilobytes) + " KB.")
30. elif option == "MB":
31.     numberOfMegabytes = int(input("Enter a number of megabytes
    :"))
32.     numberOfBytes = megabytes_to_bytes(numberOfMegabytes)
33.     print("There are " + str(numberOfBytes) + " Bytes in " + s
    tr(numberOfMegabytes) + " MB.")
34. elif option == "GB":
35.     numberOfGigabytes = int(input("Enter a number of gigabytes
    :"))
36.     numberOfBytes = gigabytes_to_bytes(numberOfGigabytes)
```

64

```
37.    print("There are " + str(numberOfBytes) + " Bytes in " + s
       tr(numberOfGigabytes) + " GB.")
38. elif option == "TB":
39.    numberOfTerabytes = int(input("Enter a number of terabytes
       :"))
40.    numberOfBytes = gigabytes_to_bytes(numberOfTerabytes)
41.    print("There are " + str(numberOfBytes) + " Bytes in " + s
       tr(numberOfTerabytes) + " TB.")
42. elif option == "PB":
43.    numberOfPetabytes = int(input("Enter a number of petabytes
       :"))
44.    numberOfBytes = petabytes_to_bytes(numberOfPetabytes)
45.    print("There are " + str(numberOfBytes) + " Bytes in " + s
       tr(numberOfPetabytes) + " PB.")
```

30. Binary Shifts

Everything that is stored on a computer is stored as binary code. Binary code is made of bits (0 or 1). We often use Bytes to store data. A Byte is made of eight bits and can be used to store any whole number between 0 and 255.

A binary left shift is used to multiply a binary number by two. It consists of shifting all the binary digits to the left by 1 digit and adding an extra digit at the end with a value of 0.

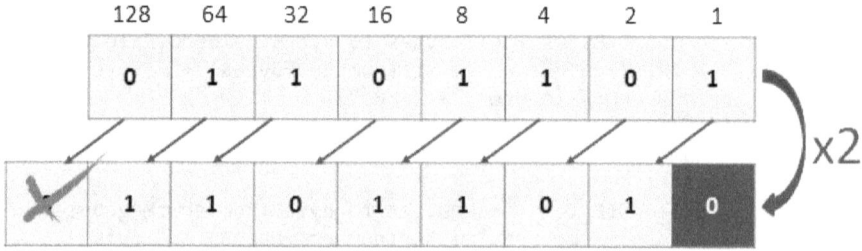

A binary right shift is used to divide a binary number by two. It consists of shifting all the binary digits to the right by 1 digit and adding an extra digit at the beginning (to the left) with a value of 0.

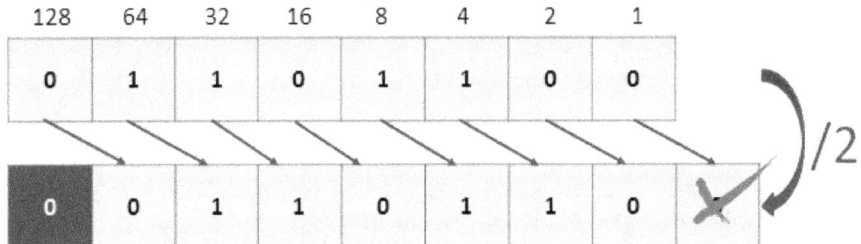

A two-digit left shift consists of two consecutive left shifts on a binary number and is the equivalent of timing this number by 2^2=4.

A three-digit left shift consists of three consecutive left shifts on a binary number and is the equivalent of timing this number by 2^3=8. (And so on...)

A two-digit right shift consists of two consecutive right shifts on a binary number and is the equivalent of dividing this number by 2^2=4.

A three-digit right shift consists of three consecutive right shifts on a binary number and is the equivalent of dividing this number by 2^3=8. (And so on...)

The purpose of this challenge is to write a Python script to perform a binary shift. Our Python program will:

- Ask the user to enter an 8-bit binary number,
- Ask the user whether they would like to perform a left shift or a right shift,
- Ask the user whether the number of digits they want to shift,
- Output the resulting 8-bit binary number.

Web Address

https://www.101computing.net/binary-shift-using-python/

```
1.  #Binary Left and Right Shift
2.
3.  #A function to perform a left shift
4.  def leftShift(binary,numberOfBits):
5.    for i in range(0,numberOfBits):
6.      binary = binary[1:8]
7.      binary = binary + "0"
8.
9.    return binary
10.
11. #A function to perform a right shift
12. def rightShift(binary,numberOfBits):
13.   for i in range(0,numberOfBits):
14.     binary = binary[0:7]
15.     binary = "0" + binary
16.
17.   return binary
18.
19. #Main Program Starts Here
20. #Retrieving and validating user inputs:
21. binary = input("Input a number in binary:")
22. while len(binary)!=8:
23.   binary = input("Input a number in binary, using 8 bits:")

24.
25. leftright = input("Would you like to perform a left or right
      binary shift?").lower()
26. while leftright not in ["left","right"]:
27.   binary = input("Try again - answer left or right:")
28.
29. numberOfBits = int(input("How many digits would you like to
      shift?"))
30. while numberOfBits<1 or numberOfBits>8:
31.   numberOfBits = int(input("Try again -
      enter a number between between 1 and 8:"))
32.
33. if leftright=="right":
34.   binary = rightShift(binary,numberOfBits)
35.   print("Right Shift by " + str(numberOfBits))
36.   print(binary)
37.
38. elif leftright=="left":
39.   binary = leftShift(binary,numberOfBits)
40.   print("Left Shift by " + str(numberOfBits))
41.   print(binary)
```

31. Binary Permutations

Everything that is stored on a computer is stored as binary code. Binary code is made of bits (0 or 1). We often use Bytes to store data. A Byte is made of eight bits and can be used to store any whole number between 0 and 255. This is because, with 8 bits, you can generate 256 different permutations.

The aim of this challenge is to write a procedure called *binaryPermutations()* that will take one parameter called *numberOfBits* and outputs all possible binary permutations depending on the number of bits.

For instance *binaryPermutations(4)* would output the following 16 binary permutations

• 0000	• 0100	• 1000	• 1100
• 0001	• 0101	• 1001	• 1101
• 0010	• 0110	• 1010	• 1110
• 0011	• 0111	• 1011	• 1111

To complete this challenge we will use a recursive function. A recursive function is a function that:

- Includes a call to itself,
- Has a stopping condition to stop the recursion.

A recursive algorithm is an alternative approach to using a loop (iteration).

Web Address

https://www.101computing.net/binary-permutations-challenge/

Python Code

```
1.  #Binary Permutations Challenge
2.
3.  #A recursive function to list all possible permutations of a
    binary number
4.  def listAllBinaryPermutations(numberOfBits,binary = ""):
```

```
5.    if numberOfBits>0:
6.        listAllBinaryPermutations(numberOfBits-1,binary+"0")
7.        listAllBinaryPermutations(numberOfBits-1,binary+"1")
8.    else:
9.        print(binary)
10.
11. #This call will generate 256 binary permutations
12. listAllBinaryPermutations(8)
```

32. Factorial Challenge

In Mathematics, the factorial of n is denoted by n! and calculated by the product of integer numbers from 1 to n.

For instance:

$$5! = 5 \times 4 \times 3 \times 2 \times 1$$
$$5! = 120$$

In this challenge we will write a Python program that asks the user to enter a positive number. In return the program will output the factorial of this number. We will use two different approaches to solve this challenge:

- Method 1: Using an iterative approach
- Method 2: Using a recursive approach

Our iterative approach will be based on the following formula:

n! = n x (n-1) x (n-2) x (n-3) x ... x 4 x 3 x 2 x 1

Our recursive approach will be based on the following formula:

n! = n x (n-1)!

Note: The factorial calculations given above work for any positive integer greater than 0. There is however an exception for the value 0 as 0! = 1.

Python Code

```
1.  #Factorial Challenge
2.
3.  # iterative Function (Returns the result of: 1x2x3x4x5x...xn
    )
4.  def iterativeFactorial(n):
5.      if n==0: return 1
6.      total=1
7.      for i in range(1,n+1):
8.          total *= i
9.      return total
10.
11. # Recursive Function (Returns the result of: 1x2x3x4x5x...xn
    )
12. def recursiveFactorial(n):
13.     if n==0: return 1
14.     if (n > 1):
15.         return n * recursiveFactorial(n - 1)
16.     else:
17.         return n
18.
19. #User input & validation (positive number)
20. number=int(input("Input a positive number:"))
21. while number<0:
22.     number=int(input("Try again -
    Input a positive number:"))
23.
24. print ("Using an interative approach")
25. print ("1x2x3x...x" + str(number-
    1) + "x" + str(number)+ "=")
26. print(iterativeFactorial(number))
27.
28. print ("\nUsing a recursive approach")
29. print ("1x2x3x...x" + str(number-
    1) + "x" + str(number)+ "=")
30. print(recursiveFactorial(number))
```

Chapter #5: Data Structures

In most, if not all our challenges so far, we have used variables to store values within our code. Each variable was used to store a single value: an integer, a float, a Boolean or a string.

In Python, it is also possible to store a collection of values within a variable. Such a variable is called a **list**.

An alternative data structure that can also be used in Python is a **dictionary**. By completing the next few challenges you will gain a good understanding of the similarities and differences between lists and dictionaries.

The next few challenges focus on the use of lists and dictionaries within a Python program and will cover:

- Using Lists in Python,
- Using a List of Lists,
- Using Dictionaries,
- Using Graphs.

For this challenge we will create a program to be used by a teacher at a start of a lesson to take the register. The program will go through a class list and for each pupil in the list, will ask the teacher if the pupils is present (y) or absent (n).

The program will then output the total number of students in the class, the number of students present and the number of students who are absent.

Our program will use a list called pupils to store the names of all the students in the class.

Web Address

https://www.101computing.net/my-class-register/

Python Code

```
1.  #My Class Register
2.
3.  pupils = ["Joe","Sonny","Yassine","Emma","Ines","Satveer","L
    ily","Reuben","Lucy","Tom"]
4.  counter = 0
5.  presentCounter = 0
6.
7.  for name in pupils:
8.    print(name)
9.    counter = counter + 1
10.   present = input("Is this pupil in today? (y or n)").lower(
    )
11.   if present=="y":
12.     presentCounter = presentCounter + 1
13.
14. print("There are " + str(counter) + " pupils in the class!")

15. print(str(presentCounter) + " pupils are in.")
16. absentCounter = counter - presentCounter
17. print(str(absentCounter) + " pupils are absent.")
```

For this challenge we will use a two-dimensional array (in Python a list of lists) to store the average temperature (in Celsius degrees) and the rainfall (in mm) for each of the twelve months of the year for Quebec City, Canada.

We will populate our array called *quebec* with the following data:

	January	February	March	April	May	June	July	August	September	October	November	December
Avg. Temperature (°C)	-11.1	-9.7	-3.8	4.1	11.2	16.6	19.9	18	13.3	7.3	0.5	-8.1
Precipitation / Rainfall (mm)	83	71	71	71	80	114	117	107	105	82	93	107

Source: https://en.climate-data.org/location/663/

The aim of this challenge is to use a Python script to scan through all this data to calculate and display:

- The average temperature throughout the year,
- The hottest month of the year,
- The total amount of rainfall throughout the year,
- The average rainfall throughout the year,
- The coldest month of the year,
- The difference in rainfall between the wettest and the driest month of the year,
- The average temperature during the wettest month of the year,
- The average temperature during the driest month of the year,
- The average Temperature during the three winter months, December, January, February.

The data provided above can also be represented using an "Average Temperature and Rainfall Chart". You can use this chart to compare and check the outcomes of your Python script with the information provided on this chart.

Average Monthly Temperature and Rainfall in Quebec City, Canada

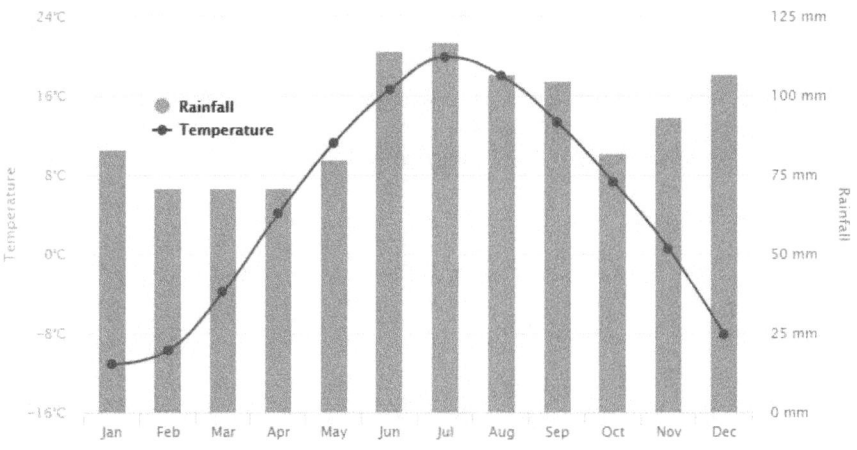

Web Address
https://www.101computing.net/weather-statistics-challenge/

Python Code

```
1.   #Weather Statistics Challenge
2.
3.   #---------------------------#
4.   #List of List - [[Month,Average Temperature,Rainfall]]
5.   #Temperatures are in Celsius Degrees
6.   #Precipitation/rainfall in mm
7.   #---------------------------#
8.
9.   quebec = []
10.  quebec.append(["January",-11.1,83])
11.  quebec.append(["February",-9.7,71])
12.  quebec.append(["March",-3.8,71])
13.  quebec.append(["April",4.1,71])
14.  quebec.append(["May",11.2,80])
15.  quebec.append(["June",16.6,114])
16.  quebec.append(["July",19.9,117])
17.  quebec.append(["August",8,107])
18.  quebec.append(["September",13.3,105])
19.  quebec.append(["October",7.3,82])
20.  quebec.append(["November",0.5,93])
21.  quebec.append(["December",-8.1,107])
22.
23.
```

```
24.  #---------------------------#
25.  #Average Temperature throughout the year:
26.  #---------------------------#
27.  averageTemp = 0
28.  for i in range(0,12):
29.      averageTemp = averageTemp + quebec[i][1]
30.
31.  averageTemp = averageTemp/12
32.  averageTemp = round(averageTemp,1)
33.  print("---------------------------")
34.  print("In Quebec City, the average temperature through the
     year is " + str(averageTemp) + " Celsius degrees.")
35.  print("---------------------------")
36.
37.
38.  #---------------------------#
39.  #Hottest Month of the year:
40.  #---------------------------#
41.  maxTemp = quebec[0][1] #Initialise maxTemp to the temperat
     ure in January
42.  maxMonth = "January"
43.  for i in range(0,12):
44.      if quebec[i][1]>maxTemp:
45.        maxTemp = quebec[i][1]
46.        maxMonth = quebec[i][0]
47.  print("---------------------------")
48.  print("In Quebec City, the hottest month of the year is "
     + maxMonth + ".")
49.  print("The average temperature on this month is " + str(ma
     xTemp) + " Celsius degrees.")
50.  print("---------------------------")
51.
52.
53.  #---------------------------#
54.  #Total Rainfall throughout the year
55.  #---------------------------#
56.  totalRainfall = 0
57.  for i in range(0,12):
58.      totalRainfall = totalRainfall + quebec[i][2]
59.
60.  print("---------------------------")
61.  print("In Quebec City, the total rainfall for the year is
     " + str(totalRainfall) + " mm.")
62.  print("---------------------------")
63.
64.
65.  #---------------------------#
66.  #Average Rainfall throughout the year
67.  #---------------------------#
```

```
68.   averageRainfall = 0
69.   for i in range(0,12):
70.     averageRainfall = averageRainfall + quebec[i][2]
71.
72.   averageRainfall = averageRainfall / 12
73.   averageRainall = round(averageRainfall,1)
74.
75.   print("---------------------------")
76.   print("In Quebec City, the average rainfall through the ye
      ar is " + str(averageRainfall) + " mm.")
77.   print("---------------------------")
78.
79.
80.   #---------------------------#
81.   #Coldest Month of the year
82.   #---------------------------#
83.   minTemp = quebec[0][1] #Initialise minTemp to the temperat
      ure in January
84.   minMonth = "January"
85.   for i in range(0,12):
86.     if quebec[i][1]<minTemp:
87.       minTemp = quebec[i][1]
88.       minMonth = quebec[i][0]
89.   print("---------------------------")
90.   print("In Quebec City, the coldest month of the year is "
      + minMonth + ".")
91.   print("The average temperature on this month is " + str(mi
      nTemp) + " Celsius degrees.")
92.   print("---------------------------")
93.
94.
95.   #---------------------------#
96.   #Difference in rainfall between the wettest and the driest
      month of the year
97.   #---------------------------#
98.   minRainfall = quebec[0][2] #Initialise maxRainfall to the
      temperature in January
99.   minRainfallMonth = "January"
100.  for i in range(0,12):
101.    if quebec[i][2]<minRainfall:
102.      minRainfall = quebec[i][2]
103.      minRainfallMonth = quebec[i][0]
104.
105.  maxRainfall = quebec[0][2] #Initialise maxRainfall to the
      temperature in January
106.  maxRainfallMonth = "January"
107.  for i in range(0,12):
108.    if quebec[i][2]>maxRainfall:
109.      maxRainfall = quebec[i][2]
```

```
110.        maxRainfallMonth = quebec[i][0]
111.
112. diffRainfall = maxRainfall - minRainfall
113. print("----------------------------")
114. print("In Quebec City, the wettest month of the year is "
     + maxRainfallMonth + ".")
115. print("In Quebec City, the driest month of the year is " +
      minRainfallMonth + ".")
116. print("The difference in rainfall in these months is " + s
     tr(diffRainfall) + " mm.")
117. print("----------------------------")
118.
119.
120. #--------------------------#
121. #Average Temperature during the wettest month of the year
122. #--------------------------#
123. maxRainfall = quebec[0][2] #Initialise maxRainfall to the
     temperature in January
124. maxRainfallMonth = "January"
125. WettestAvgTemp = quebec[0][1]
126. for i in range(0,12):
127.    if quebec[i][2]>maxRainfall:
128.       maxRainfall = quebec[i][2]
129.       maxRainfallMonth = quebec[i][0]
130.       WettestAvgTemp = quebec[i][1]
131.
132. print("----------------------------")
133. print("In Quebec City, the wettest month of the year is "
     + maxRainfallMonth + ".")
134. print("The average tempureature during this month is " + s
     tr(WettestAvgTemp) + " Celcius Degrees.")
135. print("----------------------------")
136.
137.
138. #--------------------------#
139. #Average Temperature during the driest month of the year
140. #--------------------------#
141. minRainfall = quebec[0][2] #Initialise maxRainfall to the
     temperature in January
142. minRainfallMonth = "January"
143. DriestAvgTemp = quebec[0][1]
144. for i in range(0,12):
145.    if quebec[i][2]<minRainfall:
146.       minRainfall = quebec[i][2]
147.       minRainfallMonth = quebec[i][0]
148.       DriestAvgTemp = quebec[i][1]
149.
150. print("----------------------------")
```

```
151. print("In Quebec City, the driest month of the year is " +
     minRainfallMonth + ".")
152. print("The average tempureature during this month is " + s
     tr(DriestAvgTemp) + " Celcius Degrees.")
153. print("----------------------------")
154.
155.
156. #--------------------------#
157. #Average Temperature during the three winter months, Decem
     ber, January, February
158. #--------------------------#
159. averageWinterTemperature = (quebec[11][1] + quebec[0][1] +
     quebec[1][1])/3
160. print("----------------------------")
161. print("In Quebec City, the average temperature during the
     three winter months is " + str(round(averageWinterTemperat
     ure,2)) + " Celcius Degrees.")
162. print("----------------------------")
```

35. Colour Difference Formula

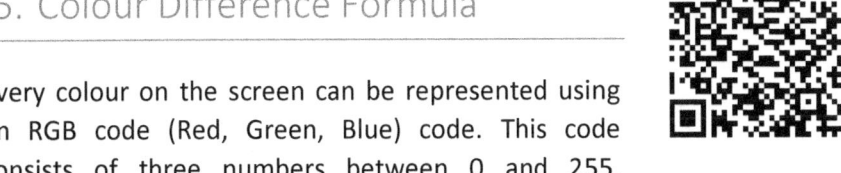

Every colour on the screen can be represented using an RGB code (Red, Green, Blue) code. This code consists of three numbers between 0 and 255, indicating how much red, green and blue are used to recreate the colour. Using the RGB colour code we can represent 256^3 = 16,777,216 colours. Let's consider the following 12 colours:

- RED (Hex: #FF0000 – RGB: 255, 0, 0)
- ORANGE (Hex: #FF7F00 – RGB: 255, 127, 0)
- YELLOW (Hex: #FFFF00 – RGB: 255, 255, 0)
- CHARTREUSE GREEN (Hex: #7FFF00 – RGB: 127, 255, 0)
- GREEN (Hex: #00FF00 – RGB: 0, 255, 0)
- SPRING GREEN (Hex: #00FF7F – RGB: 0, 255, 127)
- CYAN (Hex: #00FFFF – RGB: 0, 255, 255)
- AZURE (Hex: #007FFF – RGB: 0, 127, 255)
- BLUE (Hex: #0000FF – RGB: 0, 0, 255)
- VIOLET (Hex: #7F00FF – RGB: 127, 0, 255)

- MAGENTA (Hex: #FF00FF – RGB: 255, 0, 255)
- ROSE (Hex: #FF007F – RGB: 255, 0, 127)

The colour difference formula is used to find out the "distance" between two colours:

$$colour_1 = (R_1, G_1, B_1)$$

$$colour_2 = (R_2, G_2, B_2)$$

$$difference = \sqrt{(R_2 - R_1)^2 + (G_2 - G_1)^2 + (B_2 - B_1)^2}$$

For this challenge, our aim was to write a program that:

- asks the user to input an RGB colour code,
- calculates the differences between this colour and each of the 12 colours of the above colour wheel,
- outputs the name of the closest colour from the colour wheel. (The colour with the smallest difference)

Web Address

https://www.101computing.net/colour-difference-formula/

Python Code

```
1.  #Colour Difference Formula
2.
3.  colourWheel = []
4.
5.  colourWheel.append(["Red",255,0,0])
6.  colourWheel.append(["Orange",255,127,0])
7.  colourWheel.append(["Yellow",255,255,0])
8.  colourWheel.append(["Chartreuse Green",127,255,0])
9.  colourWheel.append(["Green",0,255,0])
10. colourWheel.append(["Spring Green",0,255,127])
11. colourWheel.append(["Cyan",0,255,25])
12. colourWheel.append(["Azure",0,127,255])
13. colourWheel.append(["Blue",0,0,255])
14. colourWheel.append(["Violet",127,0,255])
15. colourWheel.append(["Magenta",255,0,255])
16. colourWheel.append(["Rose",255,0,127])
```

```
17.
18. #Input RGB colour code
19. r=int(input("Red Value (0 to 255):"))
20. g=int(input("Green Value (0 to 255):"))
21. b=int(input("Blue Value (0 to 255):"))
22.
23. shortestDistance = 3*255^2 + 1 #1 over the maximum distance
    between two colours!
24. closestColour = ""
25. #For each colour in the wheel calculate the distance
26. for colour in colourWheel:
27.    #Apply Colour Difference Formula
28.    distance = ((colour[1]-r)**2+(colour[2]-g)**2+(colour[3]-
       b)**2)**0.5
29.
30.    if distance < shortestDistance:
31.       shortestDistance = distance
32.       closestColour = colour[0]
33.
34. #Output name of the colour with the smallest distance
35. print("The closest colour is " + closestColour + ".")
```

36. Top 10 Countries

Our aim is to create a quiz where the user has to identify the top 10 largest countries per area. The user can have as many guesses as needed and should not need to list the ten countries in the right order.

The program should stop when the user has guessed all 10 countries or when the user presses "x" to quit the game.

Web Address

https://www.101computing.net/top-10-challenge/

Python Code

```
1.  #Top 10 Challenge
2.  import time
3.
4.  print("~~~~~~~~~~~~~~~~~~~~~~~~~~~~~~~~~~~~~~")
```

```
5.  print("~                             ~")
6.  print("~         TOP 10 CHALLENGE        ~")
7.  print("~                             ~")
8.  print("~~~~~~~~~~~~~~~~~~~~~~~~~~~~~~~~~~~~~~")
9.  print("")
10.
11. #Top 10 largest countries in the world per area
12. largestCountries = ["Russia","Canada","USA","China","Brazil"
    ,"Australia","India","Argentina","Kazakhstan","Algeria"]
13. guessedCountries = []
14.
15. start = int(time.time())
16.
17. carryOn=True
18. while carryOn:
19.   #Retrieve user input
20.   country = input("Can you name one of the top 10 largest co
    untry (per area)?")
21.
22.   if country=="x":
23.     print("Game Over!")
24.     carryOn=False
25.   #Check if the given country is in the top 10
26.   elif country in largestCountries:
27.     if country not in guessedCountries:
28.       #Find the index (position) of the country in the list

29.       #Add 1 as the position in the list starts at 0
30.       position = largestCountries.index(country) + 1
31.       print("You are correct. " + country + " is in position
    : " + str(position) + ".")
32.
33.       #Add this country to the list of guessed countries
34.       guessedCountries.append(country)
35.       numberOfCountries = len(guessedCountries)
36.       if numberOfCountries==1:
37.         print("You have guessed 1 country out of 10.")
38.       elif numberOfCountries<10:
39.         print("You have guessed " +str(numberOfCountries) +
    " countries out of 10.")
40.       else:
41.         #The user guessed all 10 countries
42.         end = int(time.time())
43.         minutes = (end-start) // 60
44.         seconds = (end-start) % 60
45.         print("You have guessed all 10 countries in " + str(
    minutes) + " minute(s) and " + str(seconds) + " second(s).")

46.         carryOn=False
```

81

```
47.      else:
48.         print("You have already listed this country.")
49.     else:
50.        print(country + " is not in the top 10 largest countries
       .")
```

37. How Many Sweets in the Jar?

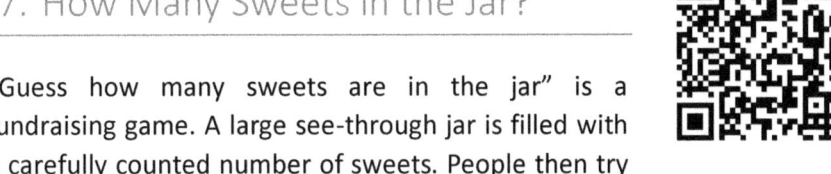

"Guess how many sweets are in the jar" is a fundraising game. A large see-through jar is filled with a carefully counted number of sweets. People then try to guess how many sweets are in the jar. Each contestant has to donate a small amount of money to have a go. Guesses are recorded (name + guess). At the end of the game, the nearest guesser wins the content of the jar.

In this challenge we are using Python Turtle to draw a jar with a random number of sweets. We then record the names and guesses (number of sweets) of each contestant. We record this information in a list of lists called *guesses*. Finally, we find the name of the contestant who has the nearest guess. Note that, on occasions, there might be several contestants placed equal first.

Web Address

https://www.101computing.net/how-many-sweets-in-the-jar/

Python Code

```
1.  #How Many Sweets in the Jar
2.  import turtle
3.  import random
4.
5.  numberOfSweets = random.randint(30,100)
6.
7.  myPen = turtle.Turtle()
8.  myPen.hideturtle()
9.  myPen.speed(0)
10. window = turtle.Screen()
```

```
11. window.bgcolor("#69C5FF")
12.
13. #Draw Jar
14. myPen.penup()
15. myPen.goto(-120,100)
16. myPen.pensize(4)
17. myPen.color("#000000")
18. myPen.pendown()
19. myPen.goto(-100,100)
20. myPen.goto(-100,-100)
21. myPen.goto(100,-100)
22. myPen.goto(100,100)
23. myPen.goto(120,100)
24.
25. #Add Sweets
26. for sweet in range(0,numberOfSweets):
27.     x = random.randint(-85,85)
28.     y = random.randint(-95,80)
29.     color = (random.randint(0,255),random.randint(0,255),rando
    m.randint(0,255))
30.     myPen.penup()
31.     myPen.goto(x,y)
32.     myPen.pendown()
33.     myPen.fillcolor(color)
34.     myPen.color(color)
35.     myPen.begin_fill()
36.     myPen.circle(10)
37.     myPen.end_fill()
38.
39. #Collect guesses from different users
40. guesses=[]
41. while True:
42.     name=input("Enter your name (or 'x' to exit):")
43.     if name=="x":
44.         break
45.     else:
46.         number = int(input("How many sweets in the jar?"))
47.         guesses.append([name,number])
48.
49. #Print all guesses:
50. print ("----- List of guesses -----")
51. for guess in guesses:
52.     print(guess[0] + ": " + str(guess[1]))
53.
54. #Print actual numbe rof sweets in the jar
55. print ("----- Actual number of sweets in the jar -----")
56. print(str(numberOfSweets) + " sweets")
57.
58. #Find out who has the closest guess and display their name
```

83

```
59. print ("----- And the nearest guess is -----")
60. nearestGuess = guesses[0][1]
61. for guess in guesses:
62.   if abs(guess[1]-numberOfSweets) < abs(nearestGuess-
      numberOfSweets):
63.     nearestGuess = guess[1]
64.
65. print("And the winner(s) is/are:")
66. for guess in guesses:
67.   if abs(guess[1]-numberOfSweets) == abs(nearestGuess-
      numberOfSweets):
68.     print(guess[0] + ":" + str(guess[1]))
```

38. The Shoelace Algorithm

The shoelace formula or shoelace algorithm is a mathematical algorithm to determine the area of a simple polygon whose vertices are described by their Cartesian coordinates in the plane.

The method consists of cross-multiplying corresponding coordinates of the different vertices of a polygon to find its area. It is called the shoelace formula because of the constant cross-multiplying for the coordinates making up the polygon, like tying shoelaces. (See table below). This algorithm has applications in 2D and 3D computer graphics, in surveying or in forestry, among other areas.

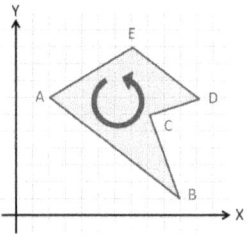

Vertices	x	y
A	2	7
B	10	1
C	8	6
D	11	7
E	7	10

$$\text{Area} = \frac{1}{2}\left|\sum_{i=1}^{n} x_i y_{i+1} - x_{i+1} y_i\right|^{*}$$

$$\text{Area} = \frac{1}{2}\left|x_1 y_2 - x_2 y_1 + x_2 y_3 - x_3 y_2 + \cdots - \cdots + x_{n-1} y_n - x_n y_{n-1} + x_n y_1 - x_1 y_n\right|$$

* where $x_{n+1} = x_1$ and $y_{n+1} = y_1$

The Shoelace Formula

To implement the shoelace algorithm we will define a polygon as a **list of vertices**, listed in anticlockwise order. Each vertex will be a list of 2 values: its x and y coordinates.

Web Address

https://www.101computing.net/the-shoelace-algorithm/

Python Code

```
1.  #The Shoelace Algorithm
2.
3.  def polygonArea(vertices):
4.      #A function to apply the Shoelace algorithm
5.      numberOfVertices = len(vertices)
6.      area = 0
7.
8.      for i in range(0,numberOfVertices):
9.          j = (i+1) % numberOfVertices #Index of the "row below" (
    using a modulo to wrap around back to the first line when yo
    u reach the bottom of the table)
10.         area = area + vertices[i][0] *  vertices[j][1] -
    vertices[i][1] *  vertices[j][0]
11.
12.     area = area /2
13.     return area
14.
15. #Vertices (x,y) Coordinates
16. A = [2,7]
17. B = [10,1]
18. C = [8,6]
19. D = [11,7]
20. E = [7,10]
21. #Define a polygon as being a list of vertices, (on anticlock
    wise order)
22. polygon = [A,B,C,D,E]
23.
24. area = polygonArea(polygon)
25. print("Polygon Vertices:")
```

```
26. print(polygon)
27. print("")
28. print("Area = " + str(area) + "cm2")
```

39. Hardware Quiz

Computer hardware consists of all the components that you will find inside the computer (Motherboard, CPU, RAM, graphic card, sound card, network card, etc.) as well as all the peripherals/devices than you can plug to a computer.

Peripherals are often categorised into three types:

- Input Devices (e.g. mouse, keyboard, microphone, etc.)
- Output Devices (e.g. monitor, speakers, printer, etc.)
- Storage Devices (e.g. hard drive, USB key, CD drive, etc.)

Our challenge consists of creating a quiz that will randomly pick and display a peripheral device and ask the end-user to decide whether the device is an input device, storage device or output device.

The user should score 10 points per correct answer. The game should carry on as long as the user is giving a correct answer.

Web Address

https://www.101computing.net/hardware-quiz/

Python Code

```
1.  #Hardware Quiz - www.101computing.net/hardware-quiz/
2.  import random
3.
4.  print("--> Harware Quiz <--")
5.  print("")
6.
7.  score=0
```

```
 8.  inputDevices = ["mouse","keyboard","webcam","microphone","sc
     anner"]
 9.  outputDevices = ["screen","printer","projector","speaker"]
10.  storageDevices = ["SSD Hard Drive","USB Key", "CD Drive", "S
     D Card Reader"]
11.
12.  #Join the three lists together
13.  allDevices = inputDevices + outputDevices + storageDevices
14.
15.  gameOver = False
16.  while not gameOver:
17.      #Select a device randomly from the list of devices
18.      randomDevice = random.choice(allDevices)
19.      print("Hardware device: " + randomDevice)
20.
21.      #Retrieve answer from the player
22.      answer = input("Is it an input, output or storage device?"
         ).lower()
23.
24.      #Check if the player is right
25.      if answer=="input" and randomDevice in inputDevices:
26.          score += 10
27.          print("Correct! Score: " + str(score) + "pts")
28.      elif answer=="output" and randomDevice in outputDevices:
29.          score += 10
30.          print("Correct! Score: " + str(score) + "pts")
31.      elif answer=="storage" and randomDevice in storageDevices:

32.          score += 10
33.          print("Correct! Score: " + str(score) + "pts")
34.      else:
35.          print("Wrong answer! Game Over!")
36.          gameOver=True
```

40. Hardware Quiz – The Odd One Out

For this challenge we will adapt the code from the previous challenge to create a quiz that displays 4 devices on screen: 3 devices from the same category (e.g. 3 input devices) and 1 device from another category (e.g. storage device). All 4 devices should be displayed in a random order.

The user should then be asked to identify the "odd one out". The user should score 10 points per correct answer. The game should carry on as long as the user is giving a correct answer.

e.g. Which device is the odd one out?

mouse, webcam, printer, keyboard

Web Address

https://www.101computing.net/hardware-quiz/

Python Code

```
1.  #Hardware Quiz: The Odd One Out
2.  import random
3.
4.  print("--> Harware Quiz: The Odd One Out? <--")
5.  print("")
6.
7.  score=0
8.  inputDevices = ["mouse","keyboard","webcam","microphone","sc
    anner"]
9.  outputDevices = ["screen","printer","projector","speaker"]
10. storageDevices = ["SSD Hard Drive","USB Key", "CD Drive", "S
    D Card Reader"]
11.
12. #Join the three lists together
13. allDevices = inputDevices + outputDevices + storageDevices
14.
15. gameOver = False
16. while not gameOver:
17.   selectedDevices = []
18.   devices = []
19.   otherDevices = []
20.   category = random.randint(1,3)
21.   if category==1:
22.     devices = inputDevices
23.     otherDevices = outputDevices + storageDevices
24.   elif category==2:
25.     devices = outputDevices
26.     otherDevices = inputDevices + storageDevices
27.   else:
28.     devices = storageDevices
29.     otherDevices = inputDevices + outputDevices
30.
31.   #Select 3 devices from the same category
```

```
32.    for i in range(3):
33.       device = random.choice(devices)
34.       #Check that we have not already picked this device, if n
   ot pick another one
35.       while device in selectedDevices:
36.          device = random.choice(devices)
37.       selectedDevices.append(device)
38.
39.    #Select the odd one out
40.    device = random.choice(otherDevices)
41.    selectedDevices.append(device)
42.
43.    #Shuffle list
44.    random.shuffle(selectedDevices)
45.
46.    #Display list of 4 devices
47.    print(selectedDevices)
48.
49.    #Retrieve answer from the player
50.    oddOne = input("Which device is the odd one out?").lower()

51.
52.    #Check if the player is right
53.    if oddOne==device.lower():
54.       score += 10
55.       print("Correct! Score: " + str(score) + "pts")
56.    else:
57.       print("Wrong answer! Game Over!")
58.       gameOver=True
```

41. Four In a Row Challenge

This challenge is based on the game of Connect 4. Using Python Turtle we have created an animation that randomly position red and yellow tokens on a Connect4 grid. The aim of this challenge is to stop the animation when the computer detects if four consecutive tokens of the same colour are aligned.

The code provided uses a variable called *connect4*, used to store a two-dimensional array (6×7) of integer values. In Python, a 2D-array is a list of lists. Within this array, a 0 represents an empty place, a 1 represents a yellow token and a 2 represents a red token:

connect4 = [[0 , 0 , 0 , 0 , 0 , 0 , 0],
      [0 , 0 , 0 , 2 , 0 , 0 , 0],
      [0 , 0 , 0 , 1 , 1 , 0 , 0],
      [0 , 1 , 2 , 2 , 1 , 2 , 1],
      [0 , 2 , 1 , 2 , 2 , 1 , 2],
      [2 , 1 , 2 , 1 , 1 , 1 , 2]]

Web Address

https://www.101computing.net/four-in-a-row-challenge/

Python Code

```
1.   #Four-in-a-row Challenge
2.   import turtle
3.   from random import randint
4.   from time import sleep
5.   YELLOW=1
6.   RED=2
7.
8.   #Draw the grid on screen with all the tokens
9.   def drawGrid(grid):
10.      global RED, YELLOW
11.      #Clear the screen
12.      #myPen.clear()
13.      myPen.setheading(0)
14.      myPen.goto(-150,130)
15.      for row in range (0,6):
16.          for col in range (0,7):
17.              if grid[row][col]==0:
18.                  myPen.fillcolor("#FFFFFF")
19.              elif grid[row][col]==RED:
20.                  myPen.fillcolor("#FF0000")
21.              elif grid[row][col]==YELLOW:
22.                  myPen.fillcolor("#FFFF00")
23.
24.              myPen.begin_fill()
25.              myPen.circle(25)
26.              myPen.end_fill()
```

```
27.
28.                    myPen.penup()
29.                    myPen.forward(50)
30.                    myPen.pendown()
31.              myPen.setheading(270)
32.              myPen.penup()
33.              myPen.forward(50)
34.              myPen.setheading(180)
35.              myPen.forward(50*7)
36.              myPen.setheading(0)
37.              myPen.getscreen().update()
38.
39.    def checkIfWinner(grid, color):
40.        #Check Columns
41.        for row in range(2,0,-1):
42.            for col in range(0,7):
43.                if grid[row][col]>0:
44.                    if grid[row][col]==grid[row+1][col] and
45.                       grid[row][col]==grid[row+2][col] and
46.                       grid[row][col]==grid[row+3][col]:
47.                        return grid[row][col]
48.
49.        #Check Rows
50.        for row in range(0,6):
51.            for col in range(0,3):
52.                if grid[row][col]>0:
53.                    if grid[row][col]==grid[row][col+1] and
54.                       grid[row][col]==grid[row][col+2] and
55.                       grid[row][col]==grid[row][col+3]:
56.                        return grid[row][col]
57.
58.        #check Diagonals
59.        for row in range(2,0,-1):
60.            for col in range(0,3):
61.                if grid[row][col]>0:
62.                    if grid[row][col]==grid[row+1][col+1] and
63.                       grid[row][col]==grid[row+2][col+2] and
64.                       grid[row][col]==grid[row+3][col+3]:
65.                        return grid[row][col]
66.            for col in range(3,7):
67.                if grid[row][col]>0:
68.                    if grid[row][col]==grid[row+1][col-1] and
69.                       grid[row][col]==grid[row+2][col-2] and
70.                       grid[row][col]==grid[row+3][col-3]:
71.                        return grid[row][col]
72.
73.        #No winner yet!
74.        return 0
75.
```

```
76.  #Main Program Starts Here
77.  myPen = turtle.Turtle()
78.  myPen.hideturtle()
79.  myPen.speed(500)
80.  window = turtle.Screen()
81.  window.bgcolor("#2288FF")
82.  myPen.color("#2288FF")
83.  myPen.tracer(0)
84.  myPen.speed(0)
85.
86.  #Initialise empty 6 by 7 connect4 grid
87.  connect4=[]
88.  for row in range(0,6):
89.    connect4.append([])
90.    for col in range(0,7):
91.      connect4[row].append(0)
92.
93.  #Play the game, take it in turn. Up to 42 turns
94.  for turn in range(1,43):
95.    #Randomly pick an column that is not full
96.    column = randint(0,6)
97.    while connect4[0][column]!=0:
98.      #This column is already full, pick another one
99.      column = randint(0,6)
100.
101.   #Make the token slide to the bottom of the grid (Stacked
       on top of any other existing tokens)
102.   row=5
103.   while connect4[row][column]!=0:
104.     row=row - 1
105.
106.   #Find out the colour of the current player (1 or 2)
107.   playerColor = (turn % 2) + 1
108.   #Place the token on the grid
109.   connect4[row][column]=playerColor
110.   #Draw the grid
111.   drawGrid(connect4)
112.
113.   #Check if this token wins the game
114.   winner = checkIfWinner(connect4, playerColor)
115.   if winner==RED:
116.     myPen.penup()
117.     myPen.color("#FF0000")
118.     myPen.goto(-70, -170)
119.     myPen.write("RED Wins!", None, None, "24pt bold")
120.     myPen.getscreen().update()
121.     break   #Stop the game
122.   elif winner==YELLOW:
123.     myPen.penup()
```

```
124.        myPen.color("#FFFF00")
125.        myPen.goto(-80, -170)
126.        myPen.write("Yellow Wins!", None, None, "24pt bold")
127.        myPen.getscreen().update()
128.        break  #Stop the game
129.
130.    sleep(0.2)
```

42. Wordsearch Generator

For this challenge we will write a Python program to randomly generate a wordsearch where a list of keywords will be randomly positioned on the grid and will appear either horizontally, vertically or diagonally.

We will use a few constants to define the width and height of the grid and the list of keywords to include in our grid.

Web Address

https://www.101computing.net/python-wordsearch-generator/

Python Code

```
1.  #Python Wordsearch Generator
2.  import random
3.
4.  ROWS = 12
5.  COLS = 16
6.  words = ["PYTHON","ALGORITHM","CODING","PROGRAM","VARIABLE",
    "INTEGER","STRING"]
7.
8.  #A subroutine to replace all "-
    " (empty characters) with a random letter
9.  def randomFill(wordsearch):
10.   LETTERS="ABCDEFGHIJKLMNOPQRSTUVWXYZ"
11.   for row in range(0,ROWS):
12.     for col in range(0,COLS):
13.       if wordsearch[row][col]=="-":
14.         randomLetter = random.choice(LETTERS)
15.         wordsearch[row][col]=randomLetter
```

```
16.
17. #A subroutine to output the wordsearch on screen
18. def displayWordsearch(wordsearch):
19.   print(" " + ("_"*COLS*2) + "_ ")
20.   print("|" + (" "*COLS*2) + " |")
21.   for row in range(0,ROWS):
22.     line="| "
23.     for col in range(0,COLS):
24.       line = line + wordsearch[row][col] + " "
25.     line = line + "|"
26.     print(line)
27.   print("|" + ("_"*COLS*2) + "_|")
28.
29. #A subroutine to add a word to the wordsearch at a random po
    sition
30. def addWord(word,wordsearch):
31.   placed=False
32.   attempts = 0
33.   while not placed and attempts<100: #Avoid infinite loops i
    f the program can't find a place for a word.
34.     attempts +=1
35.     direction = random.randint(0,5)
36.     #Decide starting row and col position for the first lett
    er of the wor
37.     #Decide horizontal step (hs) and vertical step (vs)
38.
39.     if len(word)>ROWS or len(word)>COLS:
40.       print("Some of your words are too long for this grid.
    Remove long words or resize your grid.")
41.       exit()
42.
43.     if direction==0: #Horizontal Left to Right
44.       row=random.randint(0,ROWS - 1)
45.       col=random.randint(0,COLS - len(word))
46.       hs=1
47.       vs=0
48.     elif direction==1: #Vertical Top To Bottom
49.       row=random.randint(0,ROWS - len(word))
50.       col=random.randint(0,COLS - 1)
51.       hs=0
52.       vs=1
53.     elif direction==2: #Diagonal Top Left -
    To Bottom Right
54.       row=random.randint(0,ROWS - len(word))
55.       col=random.randint(0,COLS - len(word))
56.       hs=1
57.       vs=1
58.     if direction==3: #Horizontal Right to Left
59.       row=random.randint(0,ROWS - 1)
```

```
60.        col=random.randint(len(word)-1,COLS - 1)
61.        hs=-1
62.        vs=0
63.     elif direction==4: #Vertical Bottom To Top
64.        row=random.randint(len(word)-1,ROWS - 1)
65.        col=random.randint(0,COLS - 1)
66.        hs=0
67.        vs=-1
68.     elif direction==5: #Diagonal Bottom Right To Top Left
69.        row=random.randint(len(word)-1,ROWS - 1)
70.        col=random.randint(len(word)-1,COLS - 1)
71.        hs=-1
72.        vs=-1
73.
74.     #Check if word fits without colliding with other letters

75.     collision=False
76.     for i in range(0,len(word)):
77.        if (wordsearch[row+vs*i][col+hs*i]!="-
   " and wordsearch[row+vs*i][col+hs*i]!=word[i]):
78.           collision=True
79.     # No Collision means we can add the word to the gird
80.     if not collision:
81.        for i in range(0,len(word)):
82.           wordsearch[row+vs*i][col+hs*i]=word[i]
83.           placed=True
84.
85.   if not placed:
86.     print("Program aborted. Try again, remove words from you
   r list or increase the size of the grid.")
87.     exit()
88.
89. #Create an empty wordsearch (list of lists)
90. wordsearch = []
91. for row in range(0,ROWS):
92.   wordsearch.append([])
93.   for col in range(0,COLS):
94.     wordsearch[row].append("-")
95.
96. #Adding words to our wordsearch
97. for word in words:
98.   if word != "":
99.     addWord(word,wordsearch)
100.
101.      #All unused spaces in the wordsearch will be replace
   d with a random letter
102.      randomFill(wordsearch)
103.
104.      #Display the fully competed wordseach on screen
```

```
105.        displayWordsearch(wordsearch)
106.
107.        print("\n--- LIST OF WORDS ---\n")
108.        for word in words:
109.            print(" - " + word)
```

43. My Weekly Timetable

A school timetable is displayed as a 2D table consisting of five rows (for each day of the week) and five columns (number of lessons in a day).

Such a table can be stored in a computer program using a two-dimensional array (2D array). In Python, this is done by creating a list of lists.

Each value of a 2D array can then be accessed by proving two indices: the row number and the column number as displayed on the picture below:

My Timetable

	P1	P2	P3	P4	P5
Monday	History	Maths	Computer Science	PE	Music
Tuesday	English	Spanish	Maths	Geography	Art
Wednesday	PE	English	Science	Art	PE
Thursday	Maths	English	Philosophy	Spanish	Music
Friday	Science	Drama	History	Geography	Science

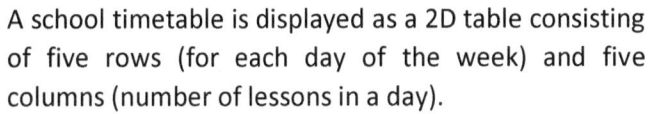

```
timetable[3][0] = "Maths"        timetable[0][2] = "Computer Science"
```

The aim of this challenge is to create three subroutines as follows:

1. whatLesson(day,period)

This function will take two parameters, the day of the week and the period number and will return the corresponding lesson.

2. dailyLessons(day)

This procedure will take one parameter, the day of the week and display all five lessons for the given day. It will be a procedure and not a function as it will not return any value.

3. howManyLessons(subject)

This function will take one parameter, the subject and will count and return the number of lessons for this subject throughout the week.

Web Address

https://www.101computing.net/my-weekly-timetable/

Python Code

```
1.   #My weekly timetable
2.
3.   timetable = []
4.
5.   #Monday
6.   timetable.append(["History","Maths","Computer Science","PE
     ","Music"])
7.   #Tuesday
8.   timetable.append(["English","Spanish","Maths","Geography",
     "Art"])
9.   #Wednesday
10.  timetable.append(["PE","English","Science","Art","PE"])
11.  #Thursday
12.  timetable.append(["Maths","English","Philosohpy","Spanish"
     ,"Music"])
13.  #Friday
14.  timetable.append(["Science","Drama","History","Geography",
     "Science"])
15.
16.  #A function to check what lesson there is on a specific da
     y + period
17.  def whatLesson(day,period):
18.    global timetable
19.    lesson=""
20.    if day=="Monday":
21.      lesson = timetable[0][period-1]
22.    elif day=="Tuesday":
23.      lesson = timetable[1][period-1]
24.    elif day=="Wednesday":
```

```
25.        lesson = timetable[2][period-1]
26.    elif day=="Thursday":
27.        lesson = timetable[3][period-1]
28.    elif day=="Friday":
29.        lesson = timetable[4][period-1]
30.    else:
31.        print("Not a valid week day!")
32.
33.    return lesson
34.
35. #A procedure to display all lessons taking place on a spec
    ific day
36. def dailyLessons(day):
37.    global timetable
38.    lessons=[]
39.    if day=="Monday":
40.        lessons = timetable[0]
41.    elif day=="Tuesday":
42.        lessons = timetable[1]
43.    elif day=="Wednesday":
44.        lessons = timetable[2]
45.    elif day=="Thursday":
46.        lessons = timetable[3]
47.    elif day=="Friday":
48.        lessons = timetable[4]
49.    else:
50.        print("Not a valid week day!")
51.
52.    #OUTPUT
53.    print("Your lessons on this day:")
54.    for lesson in lessons:
55.        print(lesson)
56.
57. #A function to count the nunmber of lessons of a specific
    subject
58. def howManyLessons(subject):
59.    global timetable
60.    count=0
61.    for day in range(0,5):
62.        for period in range(0,5):
63.            if timetable[day][period] == subject:
64.                count+=1
65.    return count
66.
67. #A procedure to display the menu
68. def displayMenu():
69.    print("+-----------------------------")
70.    print("|                             |")
71.    print("|           My Timetable      |")
```

```
72.     print("|                                    |")
73.     print("+-------------------------------")
74.     print("")
75.     print("  1 - What Lesson? ")
76.     print("  2 - Today's Lessons? ")
77.     print("  3 - How Many Lessons? ")
78.     print("  4 - Exit")
79.     print("")
80.
81.  #Main Program Starts Here
82.  displayMenu()
83.  option = input("Choose an option from the menu (1-4):")
84.  while option not in ["1","2","3","4"]:
85.     print("Invalid option")
86.     option = input("Choose an option from the menu (1-
     4):")
87.
88.  if option=="1":
89.     day = input("Day of the week?").title()
90.     period = int(input("Lesson number (1 to 5):"))
91.     while period<1 or period>5:
92.        period = int(input("Lesson number (1 to 5):"))
93.
94.     lesson = whatLesson(day,period)
95.
96.     if lesson!="":
97.        print("On " + day + ", lesson " + str(period) + " you
     have " + lesson + ".")
98.     else:
99.        print("Could not find a lesson for this day/period")
100.
101. elif option=="2":
102.    day = input("Day of the week?").title()
103.    dailyLessons(day)
104.
105. elif option=="3":
106.    subject= input("Enter Subject:")
107.    count = howManyLessons(subject)
108.
109.    if count>1:
110.       print("You have " + str(count) + " " + subject + " les
     sons per week.")
111.    else:
112.       print("You have " + str(count) + " " + subject + " les
     son per week.")
113.
114. elif option=="4":
115.    print("Good bye!")
```

44. Cinema Booking Challenge

For this challenge, you will create a booking system for a cinema which has one main theatre. The theatre consists of 48 seats, organised in six rows of eight seats.

To store information as to whether a seat is booked or available, we will use a 2-dimensional array (in python a list of lists). Each cell of the array will contain the value 1 if the seat is booked or 0 if it is empty:

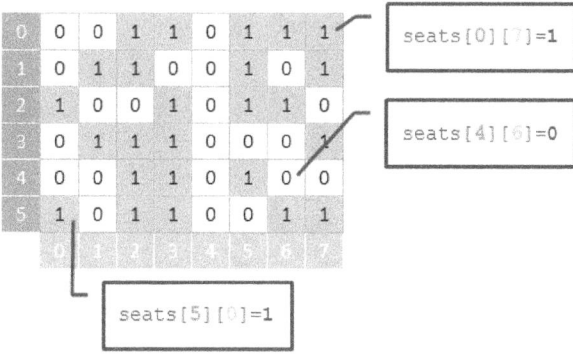

Your booking system will allow the end-user to:

- Book a seat by row/column
- Book a seat close to the front
- Book a seat close to the back
- Reset all bookings
- Save and load bookings using a CSV file

Web Address

https://www.101computing.net/cinema-booking-challenge/

Python Code

```
1.   #Cinema Booking Challenge
2.   seats = []
```

```
3.    seats.append([0,0,0,0,0,0,0,0])
4.    seats.append([0,0,0,0,0,0,0,0])
5.    seats.append([0,0,0,0,0,0,0,0])
6.    seats.append([0,0,0,0,0,0,0,0])
7.    seats.append([0,0,0,0,0,0,0,0])
8.    seats.append([0,0,0,0,0,0,0,0])
9.
10.
11.   def loadBookings():
12.     file = open("seats.csv","r")
13.     row = 0
14.     for line in file:
15.       data = line.split(",")
16.       if len(data)==8: #Only process lines which contain 8 v
      alues
17.         for column in range (0,8):
18.           seats[row][column] = int(data[column])
19.         row = row + 1
20.     file.close()
21.
22.   def saveBookings():
23.     file = open("seats.csv","w")
24.     for row in range(0,6):
25.       line=""
26.       for column in range(0,8):
27.         line = line + str(seats[row][column]) + ","
28.       line = line[:-
      1] + ("\n") #Remove last comma and add a new line
29.       file.write(line)
30.     file.close()
31.
32.
33.   def displayBookings():
34.     #Display Bookings
35.     print("")
36.     print("====================================")
37.     print("")
38.     for row in seats:
39.       print(row)
40.     print("")
41.     print("====================================")
42.
43.   def checkSeat():
44.     row = int(input("Enter a row number (between 0 and 5)"))

45.     column = int(input("Enter a column number (between 0 and
      7)"))
46.
47.     if seats[row][column]==1:
```

```
48.           print("This seat is already booked.")
49.       else:
50.           print("This seat is empty.")
51.
52.    def bookSeat():
53.       print("Booking a Seat by Row/Column")
54.       booked = False
55.       while booked == False:
56.           row = int(input("Enter a row number (between 0 and 5)"
))
57.           column = int(input("Enter a column number (between 0 a
nd 7)"))
58.
59.           if seats[row][column]==1:
60.               print("This seat is already booked.")
61.           else:
62.               print("This seat is empty.")
63.               print("Booking seat...")
64.               seats[row][column]=1
65.               print("We have now booked this seat for you.")
66.               booked=True
67.
68.    def bookSeatAtFront():
69.       print("Booking seat at the front")
70.       for row in range(0,6):
71.           for column in range(0,8):
72.               if seats[row][column]==0:
73.                   print("Booking seat...")
74.                   print("Row: " + str(row))
75.                   print("Column: " + str(column))
76.                   seats[row][column]=1
77.                   print("We have now booked this seat for you.")
78.                   #Stop Searching
79.                   return True
80.       #We scanned the whole theatre without finding an empty s
eat:
81.       print("Sorry the theatre is full -
Cannot make a booking")
82.       return False
83.
84.    def bookSeatAtBack():
85.       print("Booking seat at the back")
86.       for row in range(5,-1,-1):
87.           for column in range(7,-1,-1):
88.               if seats[row][column]==0:
89.                   print("Booking seat...")
90.                   print("Row: " + str(row))
91.                   print("Column: " + str(column))
92.                   seats[row][column]=1
```

```
93.              print("We have now booked this seat for you.")
94.              #Stop Searching
95.              return True
96.     #We scanned the whole theatre without finding an empty s
    eat:
97.     print("Sorry the theatre is full -
        Cannot make a booking")
98.     return False
99.
100. def resetBookings():
101.     print("Reset all bookings to 0")
102.     for row in range(0,6):
103.         for column in range(0,8):
104.             seats[row][column]=0
105.
106.     print("All bookings have now been reset")
107.
108. #Main Program Starts Here
109. #First let's retrieve bookings from the CSV file
110. loadBookings()
111. displayBookings()
112.
113. #Then display a menu of options
114. choice=""
115. while choice!="x":
116.     print("+=============================+")
117.     print("+    CINEMA BOOKING SYSTEM    +")
118.     print("+=============================+")
119.     print("")
120.     print("1 - Book a seat by row/column")
121.     print("2 - Book a seat at the front")
122.     print("3 - Book a seat at the back")
123.     print("4 - Reset bookings")
124.     print("5 - Save all bookings")
125.     print("x - Save & Exit")
126.
127.     choice = input("Your Choice?")
128.
129.     if choice=="1":
130.         bookSeat()
131.         displayBookings()
132.     elif choice=="2":
133.         bookSeatAtFront()
134.         displayBookings()
135.     elif choice=="3":
136.         bookSeatAtBack()
137.         displayBookings()
138.     elif choice=="4":
139.         resetBookings()
```

103

```
140.       displayBookings()
141.    elif choice=="5":
142.       saveBookings()
143.       print("Bookings Saved!")
144.       displayBookings()
145.    else:
146.       print("Invalid Menu Option")
```

45. Airport Code Lookup Check

In this challenge we will implement a small Python program to:

- Ask the user to enter a 3-letter airport code (e.g. LHR) for one of the top 20 busiest airports in the world.
- Output the full name of the airport matching the code.

For this program we will use the official codes from the International Air Transport Association (IATA).

To make our program more robust, we will implement a couple of validation checks used to check if an airport code is valid. Our validation routine will:

- Automatically convert the user input (airport code) to uppercase
- Ensure the airport code provided is exactly 3 characters long (Length Check)
- Ensure the airport code provided is one of the top 20 airport codes (Lookup Check)

To implement our lookup check we will use a dictionary data structure containing all 20 airport codes (keys) and their full names (values).

Web Address

https://www.101computing.net/airport-code-lookup-check/

Python Code

```
1.  #Airport Code Lookup Check
2.
3.  #Define a dictionary of the top 20 busiest airports in the w
    orld (in 2018)
4.  airports = {"ATL":"Hartsfield-
    Jackson Atlanta International Airport",
5.      "PEK":"Beijing Capital International Airport",
6.          "DXB":"Dubai International Airport",
7.          "LAX":"Los Angeles International Airport",
8.          "HND":"Tokyo Haneda Airport",
9.          "ORD":"O'Hare International Airport",
10.         "LHR":"London Heathrow Airport",
11.         "SAR":"Hong Kong International Airport",
12.         "PVG":"Shanghai Pudong International Airport",
13.         "CDG":"Paris-Charles de Gaulle Airport",
14.         "AMS":"Amsterdam Airport Schiphol",
15.         "DEL":"Indira Gandhi International Airport",
16.         "CAN":"Guangzhou Baiyun International Airport",
17.         "FRA":"Frankfurt Airport",
18.         "DFW":"Dallas/Fort Worth International Airport",
19.         "ICN":"Seoul Incheon International Airport",
20.         "IST":"Istanbul Atatürk Airport",
21.         "CGK":"Soekarno-Hatta International Airport",
22.         "SIN":"Singapore Changi Airport",
23.         "DEN":"Denver International Airport",
24.         }
25.
26. code = input("Enter a 3-
    letter airport code:").upper()
27.
28. #Apply a legnth check on the airport code to only accept 3-
    letter codes.
29. while len(code)!=3:
30.   print("Invalid airport code.")
31.   code = input("Enter a 3-
    letter airport code:").upper()
32.
33. #Apply a lookup check to ensure the code is recognised (part
    of the dictionary)
34. while not code in airports:
35.   print("Airpot code not recognised. Please try again with a
    different airport code.")
36.   code = input("Enter a 3-
    letter airport code:").upper()
37.
38. #Output
39. print(airports[code])
40.
41. #Define a dictionary of codes/airlines
```

```
42. airlines = {"AA":"AMERICAN AIRLINES",
43.     "AC":"AIR CANADA",
44.     "AF":"AIR FRANCE",
45.     "AI":"AIR INDIA",
46.     "BA":"BRITISH AIRWAYS",
47.     "DL":"DELTA AIR LINES",
48.     "CA":"AIR CHINA",
49.     "JL":"JAPAN AIRLINES",
50.     "MS":"EGYPTAIR",
51.     "QF":"QANTAS AIRWAYS",
52.     "SQ":"SINGAPORE AIRLINES",
53.     "UA":"UNITED AIRLINES"}
54.
55. airlinecode = input("Enter a 2-
    letter airline code:").upper()
56.
57. #Apply a legnth check on the airline code to only accept 2-
    letter codes.
58. while len(airlinecode)!=2:
59.   print("Invalid airline code.")
60.   airlinecode = input("Enter a 2-
    letter airline code:").upper()
61.
62. #Apply a lookup check to ensure the code is recognised (part
    of the dictionary)
63. while not airlinecode in airlines:
64.   print("Airline code not recognised. Please try again with
    a different airline code.")
65.   airlinecode = input("Enter a 2-
    letter airline code:").upper()
66.
67. #Output
68. print(airlines[airlinecode])
```

46. Chemical Elements Quiz

The aim of this challenge is to create a quiz based on the list of chemical elements of the periodic table based on the following requirements:

- The quiz will include 10 questions.
- Each question will display the name of an element (e.g. Aluminium) and ask the user to enter the symbol of this element (e.g. Al).
- For each correct answer the user will score 2 points and for each incorrect answer, the user will lose 1 point.
- The score cannot go in the negative values.
- A feedback with the correct answer will be given after each question.
- The final score (out of 20) will be displayed at the end of the quiz.

For this challenge, we will use a dictionary data structure to store all the chemical elements of the periodic table using the symbol of each element as the key and the name of the element as the value.

Web Address

https://www.101computing.net/chemical-elements-quiz/

Python Code

```
1.  #Chemical Elements Quiz
2.  import random
3.  score = 0
4.  elements = {"Ac":"Actinium","Ag":"Silver","Al":"Aluminum","A
    m":"Americium",
5.  "Ar":"Argon","As":"Arsenic","At":"Astatine","Au":"Gold","B":
    "Boron","Ba":"Barium",
6.  "Be":"Beryllium","Bh":"Bohrium","Bi":"Bismuth","Bk":"Berkeli
    um","Br":"Bromine",
7.  "C":"Carbon","Ca":"Calcium","Cd":"Cadmium","Ce":"Cerium","Cf
    ":"Californium",
8.  "Cl":"Chlorine","Cm":"Curium","Cn":"Copernicium","Co":"Cobal
    t","Cr":"Chromium",
```

```python
 9.    "Cs":"Cesium","Cu":"Copper","Db":"Dubnium","Ds":"Darmstadtiu
       m","Dy":"Dysprosium",
10.    "Er":"Erbium","Es":"Einsteinium","Eu":"Europium","F":"Fluori
       ne","Fe":"Iron",
11.    "Fl":"Flerovium","Fm":"Fermium","Fr":"Francium","Ga":"Galliu
       m","Gd":"Gadolinium",
12.    "Ge":"Germanium","H":"Hydrogen","He":"Helium","Hf":"Hafnium"
       ,"Hg":"Mercury",
13.    "Ho":"Holmium","Hs":"Hassium","I":"Iodine","In":"Indium","Ir
       ":"Iridium",
14.    "K":"Potassium","Kr":"Krypton","La":"Lanthanum","Li":"Lithiu
       m","Lr":"Lawrencium",
15.    "Lu":"Lutetium","Lv":"Livermorium","Mc":"Moscovium","Md":"Me
       ndelevium",
16.    "Mg":"Magnesium","Mn":"Manganese","Mo":"Molybdenum","Mt":"Me
       itnerium",
17.    "N":"Nitrogen","Na":"Sodium","Nb":"Niobium","Nd":"Neodymium"
       ,"Ne":"Neon",
18.    "Nh":"Nihonium","Ni":"Nickel","No":"Nobelium","Np":"Neptuniu
       m","O":"Oxygen",
19.    "Og":"Oganesson","Os":"Osmium","P":"Phosphorus","Pa":"Protac
       tinium","Pb":"Lead",
20.    "Pd":"Palladium","Pm":"Promethium","Po":"Polonium","Pr":"Pra
       seodymium",
21.    "Pt":"Platinum","Pu":"Plutonium","Ra":"Radium","Rb":"Rubidiu
       m","Re":"Rhenium",
22.    "Rf":"Rutherfordium","Rg":"Roentgenium","Rh":"Rhodium","Rn":
       "Radon",
23.    "Ru":"Ruthenium","S":"Sulfur","Sb":"Antimony","Sc":"Scandium
       ","Se":"Selenium",
24.    "Sg":"Seaborgium","Si":"Silicon","Sm":"Samarium","Sn":"Tin",
       "Sr":"Strontium",
25.    "Ta":"Tantalum","Tb":"Terbium","Tc":"Technetium","Te":"Tellu
       rium","Th":"Thorium",
26.    "Ti":"Titanium","Tl":"Thallium","Tm":"Thulium","Ts":"Tenness
       ine","U":"Uranium",
27.    "V":"Vanadium","W":"Tungsten","Xe":"Xenon","Y":"Yttrium","Yb
       ":"Ytterbium",
28.    "Zn":"Zinc","Zr":"Zirconium"}
29.
30.    print("H-Mg-Ti-O-Au-Ni-Pt-Er-W-Xe-Zn-Li")
31.    print("Pd                              Na")
32.    print("Cu    Chemical Elements Quiz    Fe")
33.    print("Sc                              Te")
34.    print("H-Mg-Ti-O-Au-Ni-Pt-Er-W-Xe-Zn-Li")
35.    print("")
36.
37.    #Select a random element from the dictionary
38.    for q in range(1,11):
```

```
39.    print("Question " + str(q))
40.    symbol = random.choice(elements.keys())
41.    element = elements[symbol]
42.    answer = str(input("What is the chemical symbol of " + ele
   ment + "?")).title()
43.    if answer == symbol:
44.      print("Correct Answer!")
45.      score += 2
46.    else:
47.      print ("Incorrect Answer!")
48.      print ("The correct answer was " + symbol + ".")
49.      score -= 1
50.      if score < 0:
51.        score = 0
52.    print("Your score so far: " + str(score))
53.
54. print ("End of Quiz")
55. print ("Total Score: " + str(score) + " out of 20")
```

47. Food Chain Game

A food chain shows the different organisms that live in a habitat, and what eats what.

A predator is an animal that eats other animals, and the prey is the animal that gets eaten by the predator.

Here is an example of food chain:

```
foodChain = ["Grass" , "Grasshopper" , "Frog", "Snake", "Eagle"]
```

In the food chain above:

- the frog is a predator and the grasshopper is its prey.
- the snake is a predator and the frog is its prey.

109

The program below will randomly pick two organisms from the food chain: One for the player, one for the computer.

The program will find out the positions of these organisms in the given food chain. (This is known as the trophic level of an organism which is the position it holds in a food chain).

The program will compare both positions; the player with the highest position in the food chain will win the game.

Web Address

https://www.101computing.net/food-chain-game-using-python/

Python Code

```
1.  #Food Chain Game Using Python
2.  import random
3.
4.  foodChain = ["Grass" , "Grasshopper" , "Frog", "Snake", "Eag
    le"]
5.  foodChainLength = len(foodChain)
6.
7.  playerPosition = random.randint(0,foodChainLength-1)
8.  playerOrganism = foodChain[playerPosition]
9.  print("Player Organism: " + playerOrganism)
10.
11. computerPosition = random.randint(0,foodChainLength-1)
12. #Pick another position if it is the same as the player posit
    ion
13. while computerPosition == playerPosition:
14.   computerPosition = random.randint(0,foodChainLength-1)
15.
16. computerOrganism = foodChain[computerPosition]
17. print("Computer Organism: " + computerOrganism)
18.
19. #Find out who has the highest position in the food chain
20. if computerPosition>playerPosition:
21.   print(computerOrganism + " has a higher position in the fo
    od chain.")
22.   print("Computer wins!")
23. else:
24.   print(playerOrganism + " has a higher position in the food
    chain.")
25.   print("You win!")
```

48. Food Web Game

When all the food chains in a habitat are joined up together they form a food web. Here is an example of a food web:

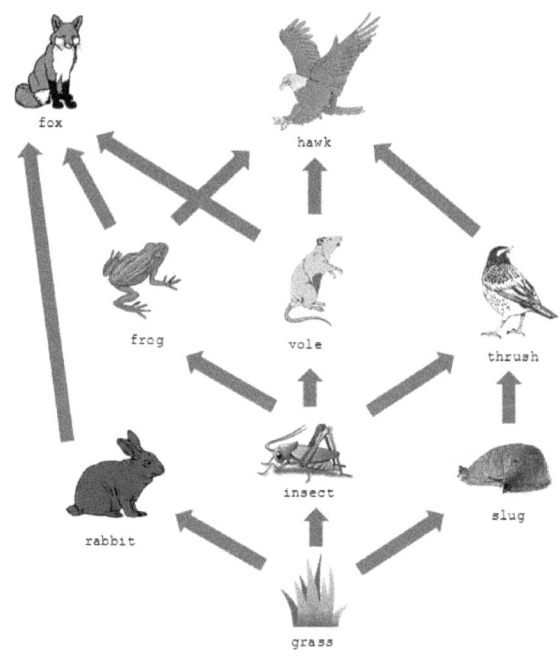

Although it looks complex, it is just several food chains joined together. Here are some of the food chains in this food web:

- grass > insect > vole > hawk
- grass > insect > frog > fox
- grass > insect > vole > fox

To represent a food web we will use a different data structure called a graph.

Most programming languages do not provide direct support for graphs as a data type. Python for instance does not have a graph data structure. However, graphs can be built out of lists and dictionaries as demonstrated in the code provided below.

Web Address

https://www.101computing.net/food-chain-game-using-python/

Python Code

```python
1.  #Food Chain Game Using Python
2.  import random
3.
4.  #A recursive function to find and return a path between two
    nodes if such a path exists.
5.  def findPath(graph, start, end, path=[]):
6.    path = path + [start]
7.    if start == end:
8.      return path
9.    if not graph.has_key(start):
10.     return None
11.   for node in graph[start]:
12.     if node not in path:
13.       newpath = findPath(graph, node, end, path)
14.       if newpath: return newpath
15.   return None
16.
17. organisms = ["grass" , "insect" , "rabbit", "slug", "frog",
    "vole", "thrush", "fox", "hawk"]
18. organismsLength = len(organisms)
19.
20. #Select organism for player
21. playerPosition = random.randint(0,organismsLength-1)
22. playerOrganism = organisms[playerPosition]
23. print("Player Organism: " + playerOrganism)
24.
25. #Select organism for computer
26. computerPosition = random.randint(0,organismsLength-1)
27. #Ensure that the computer organism will be different from th
    e player organism
28. while computerPosition==playerPosition:
29.   computerPosition = random.randint(0,organismsLength-1)
30.
31. computerOrganism = organisms[computerPosition]
32. print("Computer Organism: " + computerOrganism)
```

```
33.
34. #Store the food web as a directed graph
35. foodWeb = {'insect': ['grass'],
36.            'rabbit': ['grass'],
37.            'slug': ['grass'],
38.            'thrush': ['slug','insect'],
39.            'vole': ['insect'],
40.            'frog': ['insect'],
41.            'hawk': ['frog','vole','thrush'],
42.            'fox': ['rabbit','frog','vole']}
43.
44. #Search for a food chain path between both organism
45. if findPath(foodWeb,playerOrganism,computerOrganism):
46.     print(playerOrganism + " is in a foodchain with " + compu
    terOrganism  + " and has a higher position in this chain.")

47.     print("You win!")
48. elif findPath(foodWeb,computerOrganism,playerOrganism):
49.     print(computerOrganism + " is in a foodchain with " + pla
    yerOrganism  + " and has a higher position in this chain.")

50.     print("The computer wins!")
51. else:
52.     print("There is no food chain linking " + playerOrganism
    + " and " + computerOrganism + ".")
```

49. Air Flight Route Planner

For this challenge you will use a graph data structure to create an Air Flight Route Planner for a fictitious airline company offering flights across Europe.

Here is a map showing all the direct flights offered by this airline company:

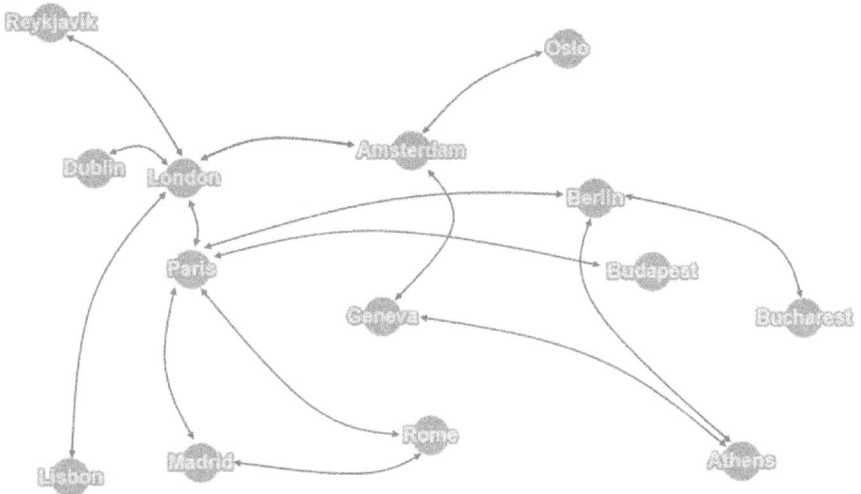

Our task consists of implementing a graph data structure to store all the airports and connections for the above map using Python.

We will then use a program to let the user choose an origin and a destination (e.g. From Dublin to Athens) and our program will:

- Inform the user if there is a direct fight to match the user requirements,
- If not, inform the user of the shortest route between the two airports, indicating all the stops between both airports.

Web Address

https://www.101computing.net/air-flight-route-planner/

Python Code

```
1.  #Air Flight Route Planner
2.
3.  # Create a directed graph data structure using a dictionary
    of lists to list all the airports with their connections
4.  map = {"Amsterdam" : ["Athens","Geneva","London"],
```

114

```
5.          "Athens" : ["Berlin","Geneva"],
6.          "Berlin" : ["Athens","Bucharest","Paris"],
7.          "Budapest" : ["Paris"],
8.          "Bucharest" : ["Berlin"],
9.          "Dublin" : ["London"],
10.         "Geneva" : ["Amsterdam","Athens"],
11.         "Lisbon" : ["London"],
12.         "London" : ["Amsterdam","Dublin","Lisbon","Paris","Rey
    kjavik"],
13.         "Madrid" : ["Paris","Rome"],
14.         "Olso" : ["Amsterdam"],
15.         "Paris" : ["Berlin","Budapest","London","Madrid","Rome
    "],
16.         "Rome" : ["Madrid","Paris"],
17.         "Reykjavik" : ["London"]
18.         }
19.
20. #A backtracking function to find the shortest paths between
    two nodes of a graph
21. def find_shortest_path(graph, start, end, shortestLength=-
    1, path=[]):
22.   path = path + [start]
23.   if start == end:
24.     return path
25.   if not graph.has_key(start):
26.     return None
27.   shortest = None
28.   for node in graph[start]:
29.     if node not in path:
30.       if shortestLength==-1 or len(path)<(shortestLength-
    1):
31.         newpath = find_shortest_path(graph, node, end, short
    estLength, path)
32.         if newpath:
33.           if not shortest or len(newpath) < len(shortest):
34.             shortest = newpath
35.             shortestLength = len(newpath)
36.   return shortest
37.
38. #Retrieve and validating user inputs
39. airportFrom = input("Where will you fly from?").title()
40. while not map.has_key(airportFrom):
41.   print("Airport not recognised. Try again.")
42.   airportFrom = input("Where will you fly from?").title()
43.
44. airportTo=input("Where will you fly to?").title()
45. while not map.has_key(airportTo):
46.   print("Airport not recognised. Try again.")
47.   airportTo = input("Where will you fly to?").title()
```

```
48.
49. print("From: " + airportFrom)
50. print("To: " + airportTo)
51.
52. if airportFrom == airportTo:
53.    print("You need to select two different airports for your
       journey.")
54. else:
55.    print("\nSearching shortest route... \n")
56.    #Find shortest path between two airports
57.    path=find_shortest_path(map,airportFrom,airportTo)
58.
59.    #Output
60.    print("Suggested Route: ")
61.    #Check if there is a direct connection
62.    if len(path)==2:
63.       print("There is a direct connection between " + airportF
          rom + " and " + airportTo + ".")
64.    else:
65.       print("There is no direct connection between " + airport
          From + " and " + airportTo + ".")
66.       print("\nWe recommend the following route:")
67.       for airport in path:
68.          print(airport)
```

A similar approach can be used to find the shortest route between tube stations. We have implemented this algorithm using the London Tube network. You can test it at the web address provided below.

Web Address

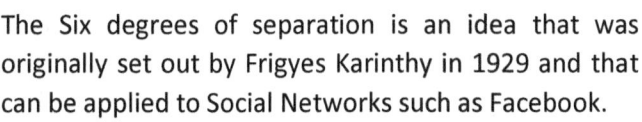

https://www.101computing.net/london-underground-journey-planner/

50. The Social Network

The Six degrees of separation is an idea that was originally set out by Frigyes Karinthy in 1929 and that can be applied to Social Networks such as Facebook.

It is based on the idea that all human beings in the world are six or fewer steps away from each other so that a chain of "a friend of a friend" statements can be made to connect any two people in a maximum of six steps.

In order to verify this concept, we are going to use a graph data structure (in python a list of dictionaries) where all the nodes of the graph will represent the members of a small social network that contains 8 members.

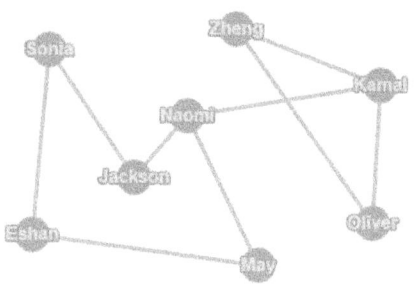

The connections between the nodes will represent the friendship relationships between two members.

We will then write a Python script to ask the end-user to enter two names and use an algorithm to find out the shortest friendship chain between these two members (if it exists).

Note that, to make this challenge more relevant, you will find an implementation of a similar friendship graph with 100 members at the web address provided below.

Web Address

https://www.101computing.net/the-social-network/

Python Code

```
1.  #The Social Network
2.  members = {'Naomi': ['Jackson', 'May', 'Kamal'],
3.  'May': ['Eshan', 'Naomi'],
4.  'Jackson': ['Naomi', 'Sonia'],
5.  'Kamal': ['Oliver', 'Naomi', 'Zheng'],
6.  'Eshan': ['Sonia','May'],
7.  'Sonia': ['Eshan','Jackson'],
```

```
 8. 'Zheng': ['Kamal','Oliver'],
 9. 'Oliver': ['Zheng','Kamal']
10. }
11.
12. #A function to find the shortest path between two nodes
13. def find_shortest_path(graph, start, end, shortestLength=-
    1, path=[]):
14.   path = path + [start]
15.   if start == end:
16.     return path
17.   if not graph.has_key(start):
18.     return None
19.   shortest = None
20.   for node in graph[start]:
21.     if node not in path:
22.       if shortestLength==-1 or len(path)<(shortestLength-
    1):
23.         newpath = find_shortest_path(graph, node, end, short
    estLength, path)
24.         if newpath:
25.           if not shortest or len(newpath) < len(shortest):
26.             shortest = newpath
27.             shortestLength = len(newpath)
28.   return shortest
29.
30. #Main Program Starts Here
31. member1 = input("Name of a member:")
32. member2 = input("Name of another member:")
33. print("\nSearching the shortest friendship chain... \n")
34. path = find_shortest_path(members,member1,member2)
35. print("Friendship Chain: ")
36. print(path)
37. print("Degrees of Separation: ")
38. print(len(path)-1)
```

51. Backtracking Maze – Path Finder

The purpose of this Python challenge is to demonstrate the use of a backtracking algorithm to find the exit path of Maze.

A backtracking algorithm is a recursive algorithm that attempts to solve a given problem by testing all possible paths towards a solution until a solution is found. Each time a path is tested, if a solution is not found, the algorithm backtracks to test another possible path and so on until a solution is found or all paths have been tested.

In this visual demonstration of a backtracking algorithm we are using Python Turtle to display the maze and the paths explored by the computer.

Web Address

https://www.101computing.net/backtracking-maze-path-finder/

Python Code

```python
1.   #Backtracking Maze - Path Finder
2.   import turtle
3.   from random import randint
4.
5.   myPen = turtle.Turtle()
6.   myPen.tracer(0)
7.   myPen.speed(0)
8.   myPen.hideturtle()
9.
10.  def text(message,x,y,size):
11.      FONT = ('Arial', size, 'normal')
12.      myPen.penup()
13.      myPen.goto(x,y)
14.      myPen.write(message,align="left",font=FONT)
15.
16.  # This function draws a box by drawing each side of the square and using the fill function
17.  def box(intDim):
18.      myPen.begin_fill()
19.      # 0 deg.
20.      myPen.forward(intDim)
21.      myPen.left(90)
22.      # 90 deg.
23.      myPen.forward(intDim)
24.      myPen.left(90)
25.      # 180 deg.
26.      myPen.forward(intDim)
27.      myPen.left(90)
28.      # 270 deg.
29.      myPen.forward(intDim)
30.      myPen.end_fill()
31.      myPen.setheading(0)
```

```
32.
33.    palette=["#FFFFFF","#000000","#00ff00","#ff00ff","#AAAAAA"
       ]
34.    #Here is how maze is stored (using a "list of lists")
35.    maze =    [[1,0,1,1,1,1,1,1,1,1,1,1,1,1,1,1]]
36.    maze.append([1,0,1,1,0,0,0,0,0,1,0,0,0,1,0,1])
37.    maze.append([1,0,0,1,0,1,1,1,0,0,0,1,0,1,0,1])
38.    maze.append([1,1,0,1,0,0,0,1,1,0,1,0,0,1,0,1])
39.    maze.append([1,0,0,0,0,1,0,1,0,0,1,0,1,0,0,1])
40.    maze.append([1,0,1,0,1,0,0,1,1,1,1,1,0,1,0,1])
41.    maze.append([1,0,1,1,1,0,1,1,0,0,0,0,0,0,0,1])
42.    maze.append([1,0,0,0,1,1,1,0,0,1,0,1,0,1,1,1])
43.    maze.append([1,0,1,0,1,0,0,0,1,1,0,1,0,1,0,1])
44.    maze.append([1,0,1,0,1,0,1,1,0,0,1,0,0,0,0,1])
45.    maze.append([1,0,1,0,1,0,0,0,1,0,1,1,0,1,1,1])
46.    maze.append([1,0,1,1,1,1,1,0,0,0,1,0,0,0,0,1])
47.    maze.append([1,0,0,0,0,0,1,1,1,0,1,0,1,1,0,1])
48.    maze.append([1,1,1,0,1,0,1,0,1,0,1,0,1,0,0,1])
49.    maze.append([1,0,0,0,1,0,0,0,0,0,1,0,0,1,0,2])
50.    maze.append([1,1,1,1,1,1,1,1,1,1,1,1,1,1,1,1])
51.
52.    def drawMaze(maze):
53.      boxSize = 15
54.      #Position myPen in top left area of the screen
55.      myPen.penup()
56.      myPen.goto(-130,130)
57.      myPen.setheading(0)
58.      for i in range (0,len(maze)):
59.        for j in range (0,len(maze[i])):
60.          myPen.color(palette[maze[i][j]])
61.          box(boxSize)
62.          myPen.penup()
63.          myPen.forward(boxSize)
64.          myPen.pendown()
65.        myPen.setheading(270)
66.        myPen.penup()
67.        myPen.forward(boxSize)
68.        myPen.setheading(180)
69.        myPen.forward(boxSize*len(maze[i]))
70.        myPen.setheading(0)
71.        myPen.pendown()
72.
73.    #A backtracking/recursive function to check all possible p
       aths until the exit is found
74.    def exploreMaze(maze,row,col):
75.      if maze[row][col]==2:
76.        #We found the exit
77.        return True
78.      elif maze[row][col]==0: #Empty path, not explored
```

```
79.          maze[row][col]=3
80.          myPen.clear()
81.          drawMaze(maze)
82.          myPen.getscreen().update()
83.          if row<len(maze)-1:
84.            #Explore path below
85.            if exploreMaze(maze,row+1,col):
86.              return True
87.          if row>0:
88.            #Explore path above
89.            if exploreMaze(maze,row-1,col):
90.              return True
91.          if col<len(maze[row])-1:
92.            #Explore path to the right
93.            if exploreMaze(maze,row,col+1):
94.              return True
95.          if col>0:
96.            #Explore path to the left
97.            if exploreMaze(maze,row,col-1):
98.              return True
99.          #Backtrack
100.         maze[row][col]=4
101.         myPen.clear()
102.         drawMaze(maze)
103.         myPen.getscreen().update()
104.
105. #Main program starts here
106. drawMaze(maze)
107. myPen.getscreen().update()
108.
109. solved = exploreMaze(maze,0,1)
110. if solved:
111.   print("Maze Solved")
112.   text("Maze Solved",-100,-150,20)
113. else:
114.   print("Cannot Solve Maze")
115.   text("Cannot Solve Maze",-130,-150,20)
116.
117. myPen.getscreen().update()
```

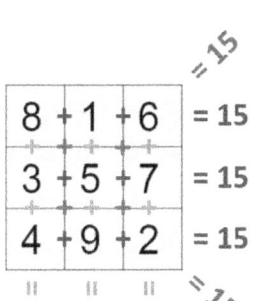

The purpose of this Python challenge is to demonstrate the use of a backtracking algorithm to solve a Magic Square puzzle.

A 3×3 magic square is an arrangement of the numbers from 1 to 9 in a 3 by 3 grid, with each number occurring exactly once, and such that the sum of the entries of any row, any column, or any main diagonal is the same.

A backtracking algorithm is a recursive algorithm that attempts to solve a given problem by testing all possible paths towards a solution until a solution is found. Each time a path is tested, if a solution is not found, the algorithm backtracks to test another possible path and so on until a solution is found or all paths have been tested.

The typical scenario where a backtracking algorithm is used is when you try to find your way out in a maze. Every time you reach a dead-end, you backtrack to try another path until you find the exit or all path have been explored.

Backtracking algorithms can be used for other types of problems such as solving a Magic Square Puzzle or a Sudoku grid.

As you can see in the code below, a backtracking algorithm relies on the use of a recursive function. A recursive function is a function that calls itself until a condition is met.

Web Address

https://www.101computing.net/backtracking-algorithm-magic-square-solver/

Python Code

```
1.    #Backtracking Algorithm - Magic Square Solver
```

```
2.    import turtle
3.    from random import randint
4.    from time import sleep
5.
6.    #initialise empty 3 by 3 grid
7.    grid = []
8.    grid.append([8,0,0])
9.    grid.append([0,0,7])
10.   grid.append([0,9,0])
11.
12.   SUM=15 #Each Row, Column and Diagonal will add up to 15
13.
14.   myPen = turtle.Turtle()
15.   myPen.tracer(0)
16.   myPen.speed(0)
17.   myPen.color("#000000")
18.   myPen.hideturtle()
19.   topLeft_x=-150
20.   topLeft_y=150
21.
22.   def text(message,x,y,size):
23.       FONT = ('Arial', size, 'normal')
24.       myPen.penup()
25.       myPen.goto(x,y)
26.       myPen.write(message,align="left",font=FONT)
27.
28.   #A procedure to draw the grid on screen using Python Turtl
      e
29.   def drawGrid(grid):
30.     intDim=100
31.     for row in range(0,4):
32.       myPen.penup()
33.       myPen.goto(topLeft_x,topLeft_y-row*intDim)
34.       myPen.pendown()
35.       myPen.goto(topLeft_x+3*intDim,topLeft_y-row*intDim)
36.     for col in range(0,4):
37.       myPen.penup()
38.       myPen.goto(topLeft_x+col*intDim,topLeft_y)
39.       myPen.pendown()
40.       myPen.goto(topLeft_x+col*intDim,topLeft_y-3*intDim)
41.
42.     for row in range (0,3):
43.         for col in range (0,3):
44.             if grid[row][col]!=0:
45.                 text(grid[row][col],topLeft_x+col*intDim+25,topL
      eft_y-row*intDim-intDim+25,50)
46.
47.   #A function to check if the grid is a magic square
48.   def checkGrid(grid):
```

```
49.     global SUM
50.     for row in range(0,3):
51.         for col in range(0,3):
52.             if grid[row][col]==0:
53.                 return False
54.     for row in range(0,3):
55.         if (grid[row][0]+grid[row][1]+grid[row][2])!=SUM:
56.             return False
57.     for col in range(0,3):
58.         if (grid[0][col]+grid[1][col]+grid[2][col])!=SUM:
59.             return False
60.     if (grid[0][0]+grid[1][1]+grid[2][2])!=SUM:
61.         return False
62.     if (grid[0][2]+grid[1][1]+grid[2][0])!=SUM:
63.         return False
64.
65.     #We have a magic square!
66.     return True
67.
68.  #A backtracking/recursive function to check all possible c
     ombinations of numbers until a solution is found
69.  def solveGrid(grid):
70.      #Find next empty cell
71.      for i in range(0,9):
72.          row=i//3
73.          col=i%3
74.          if grid[row][col]==0:
75.              for value in range (1,10):
76.                  #Can only use numbers that have not been used yet

77.                  if not(value in grid[0] or value in grid[1] or val
     ue in grid[2]):
78.                      grid[row][col]=value
79.                      #sleep(0.0001)
80.                      myPen.clear()
81.                      drawGrid(grid)
82.                      myPen.getscreen().update()
83.                      if checkGrid(grid):
84.                          print("Grid Complete and Checked")
85.                          return True
86.                      else:
87.                          if solveGrid(grid):
88.                              return True
89.              break
90.      print("Backtrack")
91.      grid[row][col]=0
92.
93.  drawGrid(grid)
94.  myPen.getscreen().update()
```

```
 95.  sleep(1)
 96.
 97.  solved = solveGrid(grid)
 98.  if solved:
 99.     print("Magic Square Solved")
100.     text("Magic Square Solved",-130,-180,20)
101.  else:
102.     print("Cannot Solve Magic Square")
103.     text("Cannot Solve Magic Square",-150,-180,20)
104.
105.  myPen.getscreen().update()
```

53. Sudoku Solver

The purpose of this Python challenge is to demonstrate the use of a backtracking algorithm to solve a Sudoku puzzle.

The objective of a Sudoku puzzle is to fill a 9×9 grid with digits so that each column, each row, and each of the nine 3×3 subgrids that compose the grid (also called "boxes") contains all of the digits from 1 to 9. A Sudoku puzzle is a partially completed grid, which for a well-posed puzzle has a single solution.

To solve this challenge, we have used a similar approach to the approach used to solve the previous challenge (magic square) applying the rules of Sudoku to our backtracking algorithm.

Web Address

https://www.101computing.net/backtracking-algorithm-sudoku-solver/

Python Code

```
1.  #Backtracking Algorithm - Sudoku Solver
2.  import turtle
3.  from random import randint
4.  from time import sleep
5.
6.  #initialise empty 9 by 9 grid
```

```
7.  grid = []
8.  grid.append([3, 0, 6, 5, 0, 8, 4, 0, 0])
9.  grid.append([5, 2, 0, 0, 0, 0, 0, 0, 0])
10. grid.append([0, 8, 7, 0, 0, 0, 0, 3, 1])
11. grid.append([0, 0, 3, 0, 1, 0, 0, 8, 0])
12. grid.append([9, 0, 0, 8, 6, 3, 0, 0, 5])
13. grid.append([0, 5, 0, 0, 9, 0, 6, 0, 0])
14. grid.append([1, 3, 0, 0, 0, 0, 2, 5, 0])
15. grid.append([0, 0, 0, 0, 0, 0, 0, 7, 4])
16. grid.append([0, 0, 5, 2, 0, 6, 3, 0, 0])
17.
18. myPen = turtle.Turtle()
19. myPen.tracer(0)
20. myPen.speed(0)
21. myPen.color("#000000")
22. myPen.hideturtle()
23. topLeft_x=-150
24. topLeft_y=150
25.
26. def text(message,x,y,size):
27.     FONT = ('Arial', size, 'normal')
28.     myPen.penup()
29.     myPen.goto(x,y)
30.     myPen.write(message,align="left",font=FONT)
31.
32. #A procedure to draw the grid on screen using Python Turtle

33. def drawGrid(grid):
34.   intDim=35
35.   for row in range(0,10):
36.     if (row%3)==0:
37.       myPen.pensize(3)
38.     else:
39.       myPen.pensize(1)
40.     myPen.penup()
41.     myPen.goto(topLeft_x,topLeft_y-row*intDim)
42.     myPen.pendown()
43.     myPen.goto(topLeft_x+9*intDim,topLeft_y-row*intDim)
44.   for col in range(0,10):
45.     if (col%3)==0:
46.       myPen.pensize(3)
47.     else:
48.       myPen.pensize(1)
49.     myPen.penup()
50.     myPen.goto(topLeft_x+col*intDim,topLeft_y)
51.     myPen.pendown()
52.     myPen.goto(topLeft_x+col*intDim,topLeft_y-9*intDim)
53.
54.   for row in range (0,9):
```

126

```
55.        for col in range (0,9):
56.            if grid[row][col]!=0:
57.                text(grid[row][col],topLeft_x+col*intDim+9,topLeft
    _y-row*intDim-intDim+8,18)
58.
59.
60. #A function to check if the grid is full
61. def checkGrid(grid):
62.   for row in range(0,9):
63.       for col in range(0,9):
64.           if grid[row][col]==0:
65.               return False
66.
67.   #We have a complete grid!
68.   return True
69.
70. #A backtracking/recursive function to check all possible com
    binations of numbers until a solution is found
71. def solveGrid(grid):
72.   #Find next empty cell
73.   for i in range(0,81):
74.       row=i//9
75.       col=i%9
76.       if grid[row][col]==0:
77.           for value in range (1,10):
78.               #Check that this value has not already be used on th
    is row
79.               if not(value in grid[row]):
80.                   #Check that this value has not already be used on
    this column
81.                   if not value in (grid[0][col],grid[1][col],grid[2]
    [col],grid[3][col],grid[4][col],grid[5][col],grid[6][col],gr
    id[7][col],grid[8][col]):
82.                       #Identify which of the 9 squares we are working
    on
83.                       square=[]
84.                       if row<3:
85.                           if col<3:
86.                               square=[grid[i][0:3] for i in range(0,3)]
87.                           elif col<6:
88.                               square=[grid[i][3:6] for i in range(0,3)]
89.                           else:
90.                               square=[grid[i][6:9] for i in range(0,3)]
91.                       elif row<6:
92.                           if col<3:
93.                               square=[grid[i][0:3] for i in range(3,6)]
94.                           elif col<6:
95.                               square=[grid[i][3:6] for i in range(3,6)]
96.                           else:
```

```
97.                         square=[grid[i][6:9] for i in range(3,6)]
98.                 else:
99.                     if col<3:
100.                         square=[grid[i][0:3] for i in range(
    6,9)]
101.                     elif col<6:
102.                         square=[grid[i][3:6] for i in range(
    6,9)]
103.                     else:
104.                         square=[grid[i][6:9] for i in range(
    6,9)]
105.                     #Check that this value has not already b
    e used on this 3x3 square
106.                     if not value in (square[0] + square[1] +
    square[2]):
107.                         grid[row][col]=value
108.                         myPen.clear()
109.                         drawGrid(grid)
110.                         myPen.getscreen().update()

111.                         if checkGrid(grid):
112.                             print("Grid Complete and Checked")
113.                             return True
114.                         else:
115.                             if solveGrid(grid):
116.                                 return True
117.                 break
118.         print("Backtrack")
119.         grid[row][col]=0
120.
121.
122.     drawGrid(grid)
123.     myPen.getscreen().update()
124.     sleep(1)
125.
126.     solved = solveGrid(grid)
127.     if solved:
128.         print("Sudoku Grid Solved")
129.         text("Sudoku Grid Solved",-110,-190,20)
130.     else:
131.         print("Cannot Solve Sudoku Grid")
132.         text("Cannot Solve Sudoku Grid",-130,-190,20)
133.
134.     myPen.getscreen().update()
```

Your task is to design an algorithm used to create a Sudoku Grid. The generated Sudoku grid should have enough clues (numbers in cells) to be solvable resulting in a unique solution.

A Sudoku game is number-placement puzzle. The objective is to fill a 9×9 grid with digits so that each column, each row, and each of the nine 3×3 subgrids that compose the grid (also called "boxes", "blocks", or "regions") contain all of the digits from 1 to 9. The puzzle setter provides a partially completed grid, which for a well-posed puzzle has a single solution.

Our aim for this challenge is not to generate a Sudoku solver algorithm but instead to create an algorithm to be used by a puzzle setter to produce a well-posed Sudoku grid: a grid with a unique solution. For instance the output of our algorithm could be a grid such as this one.

3		6	5		8	4		
5	2							
	8	7					3	1
		3		1			8	
9			8	6	3			5
	5			9		6		
1	3					2	5	
							7	4
		5	2		6	3		

Our solution is based on 5 steps:

1. Generate a full grid of numbers (fully filled in). This step is more complex as it seems as we cannot just randomly generate numbers to fill in the grid. We have to make sure that these numbers are positioned on the grid following the Sudoku rules. To do so will use a Sudoku solver algorithm (backtracking algorithm) that we will apply to an empty grid. We will add a random element to this solver algorithm to make sure that a new grid is generated every time we run it.

2. From our full grid, we will then remove 1 value at a time.

3. Each time a value is removed we will apply a Sudoku solver algorithm to see if the grid can still be solved and to count the number of solutions it leads to.

4. If the resulting grid only has one solution we can carry on the process from step 2. If not we will have to put the value we took away back in the grid.
5. We can repeat the same process (from step 2) several times using a different value each time to try to remove additional numbers, resulting in a more difficult grid to solve. The number of attempts we will use to go through this process will have an impact on the difficulty level of the resulting grid.

Web Address

https://www.101computing.net/sudoku-generator-algorithm/

Python Code

```
1.   #Sudoku Generator Algorithm
2.   import turtle
3.   from random import randint, shuffle
4.   from time import sleep
5.
6.   #initialise empty 9 by 9 grid
7.   grid = []
8.   grid.append([0, 0, 0, 0, 0, 0, 0, 0, 0])
9.   grid.append([0, 0, 0, 0, 0, 0, 0, 0, 0])
10.  grid.append([0, 0, 0, 0, 0, 0, 0, 0, 0])
11.  grid.append([0, 0, 0, 0, 0, 0, 0, 0, 0])
12.  grid.append([0, 0, 0, 0, 0, 0, 0, 0, 0])
13.  grid.append([0, 0, 0, 0, 0, 0, 0, 0, 0])
14.  grid.append([0, 0, 0, 0, 0, 0, 0, 0, 0])
15.  grid.append([0, 0, 0, 0, 0, 0, 0, 0, 0])
16.  grid.append([0, 0, 0, 0, 0, 0, 0, 0, 0])
17.
18.  myPen = turtle.Turtle()
19.  myPen.tracer(0)
20.  myPen.speed(0)
21.  myPen.color("#000000")
22.  myPen.hideturtle()
23.  topLeft_x=-150
24.  topLeft_y=150
25.
26.  def text(message,x,y,size):
27.      FONT = ('Arial', size, 'normal')
28.      myPen.penup()
```

```
29.        myPen.goto(x,y)
30.        myPen.write(message,align="left",font=FONT)
31.
32.    #A procedure to draw the grid on screen using Python Turtl
       e
33.    def drawGrid(grid):
34.       intDim=35
35.       for row in range(0,10):
36.          if (row%3)==0:
37.             myPen.pensize(3)
38.          else:
39.             myPen.pensize(1)
40.          myPen.penup()
41.          myPen.goto(topLeft_x,topLeft_y-row*intDim)
42.          myPen.pendown()
43.          myPen.goto(topLeft_x+9*intDim,topLeft_y-row*intDim)
44.       for col in range(0,10):
45.          if (col%3)==0:
46.             myPen.pensize(3)
47.          else:
48.             myPen.pensize(1)
49.          myPen.penup()
50.          myPen.goto(topLeft_x+col*intDim,topLeft_y)
51.          myPen.pendown()
52.          myPen.goto(topLeft_x+col*intDim,topLeft_y-9*intDim)
53.
54.       for row in range (0,9):
55.          for col in range (0,9):
56.             if grid[row][col]!=0:
57.                text(grid[row][col],topLeft_x+col*intDim+9,topLe
       ft_y-row*intDim-intDim+8,18)
58.
59.
60.    #A function to check if the grid is full
61.    def checkGrid(grid):
62.       for row in range(0,9):
63.          for col in range(0,9):
64.             if grid[row][col]==0:
65.                return False
66.
67.       #We have a complete grid!
68.       return True
69.
70.    #A backtracking/recursive function to check all possible c
       ombinations of numbers until a solution is found
71.    def solveGrid(grid):
72.       global counter
73.       #Find next empty cell
74.       for i in range(0,81):
```

```
75.        row=i//9
76.        col=i%9
77.        if grid[row][col]==0:
78.          for value in range (1,10):
79.             #Check that this value has not already be used on
      this row
80.             if not(value in grid[row]):
81.                #Check that this value has not already be used o
      n this column
82.                if not value in (grid[0][col],grid[1][col],grid[
      2][col],grid[3][col],grid[4][col],grid[5][col],grid[6][col
      ],grid[7][col],grid[8][col]):
83.                   #Identify which of the 9 squares we are workin
      g on
84.                   square=[]
85.                   if row<3:
86.                     if col<3:
87.                       square=[grid[i][0:3] for i in range(0,3)]

88.                     elif col<6:
89.                       square=[grid[i][3:6] for i in range(0,3)]

90.                     else:
91.                       square=[grid[i][6:9] for i in range(0,3)]

92.                   elif row<6:
93.                     if col<3:
94.                       square=[grid[i][0:3] for i in range(3,6)]

95.                     elif col<6:
96.                       square=[grid[i][3:6] for i in range(3,6)]

97.                     else:
98.                       square=[grid[i][6:9] for i in range(3,6)]

99.                   else:
100.                    if col<3:
101.                      square=[grid[i][0:3] for i in range(6,9)]

102.                    elif col<6:
103.                      square=[grid[i][3:6] for i in range(6,9)]

104.                    else:
105.                      square=[grid[i][6:9] for i in range(6,9)]

106.                  #Check that this value has not already be used
      on this 3x3 square
107.                  if not value in (square[0] + square[1] + squar
      e[2]):
```

```
108.                  grid[row][col]=value
109.                  if checkGrid(grid):
110.                      counter+=1
111.                      break
112.                  else:
113.                      if solveGrid(grid):
114.                          return True
115.          break
116.      grid[row][col]=0
117.
118.  numberList=[1,2,3,4,5,6,7,8,9]
119.  #shuffle(numberList)
120.
121.  #A backtracking/recursive function to check all possible c
      ombinations of numbers until a solution is found
122.  def fillGrid(grid):
123.    global counter
124.    #Find next empty cell
125.    for i in range(0,81):
126.      row=i//9
127.      col=i%9
128.      if grid[row][col]==0:
129.        shuffle(numberList)
130.        for value in numberList:
131.          #Check that this value has not already be used on
      this row
132.          if not(value in grid[row]):
133.            #Check that this value has not already be used o
      n this column
134.            if not value in (grid[0][col],grid[1][col],grid[
      2][col],grid[3][col],grid[4][col],grid[5][col],grid[6][col
      ],grid[7][col],grid[8][col]):
135.              #Identify which of the 9 squares we are workin
      g on
136.              square=[]
137.              if row<3:
138.                if col<3:
139.                  square=[grid[i][0:3] for i in range(0,3)]

140.                elif col<6:
141.                  square=[grid[i][3:6] for i in range(0,3)]

142.                else:
143.                  square=[grid[i][6:9] for i in range(0,3)]

144.              elif row<6:
145.                if col<3:
146.                  square=[grid[i][0:3] for i in range(3,6)]
```

```
147.              elif col<6:
148.                square=[grid[i][3:6] for i in range(3,6)]

149.              else:
150.                square=[grid[i][6:9] for i in range(3,6)]

151.            else:
152.              if col<3:
153.                square=[grid[i][0:3] for i in range(6,9)]

154.              elif col<6:
155.                square=[grid[i][3:6] for i in range(6,9)]

156.              else:
157.                square=[grid[i][6:9] for i in range(6,9)]

158.              #Check that this value has not already be used
     on this 3x3 square
159.              if not value in (square[0] + square[1] + squar
     e[2]):
160.                grid[row][col]=value
161.                if checkGrid(grid):
162.                  return True
163.                else:
164.                  if fillGrid(grid):
165.                    return True
166.        break
167.    grid[row][col]=0
168.
169. #Generate a Fully Solved Grid
170. fillGrid(grid)
171. drawGrid(grid)
172. myPen.getscreen().update()
173. sleep(1)
174.
175.
176. #Start Removing Numbers one by one
177.
178. #A higher number of attempts will end up removing more num
     bers from the grid
179. #Potentially resulting in more difficiult grids to solve!

180. attempts = 5
181. counter=1
182. while attempts>0:
183.    #Select a random cell that is not already empty
184.    row = randint(0,8)
185.    col = randint(0,8)
186.    while grid[row][col]==0:
```

```
187.        row = randint(0,8)
188.        col = randint(0,8)
189.    #Remember its cell value in case we need to put it back

190.    backup = grid[row][col]
191.    grid[row][col]=0
192.
193.    #Take a full copy of the grid
194.    copyGrid = []
195.    for r in range(0,9):
196.        copyGrid.append([])
197.        for c in range(0,9):
198.            copyGrid[r].append(grid[r][c])
199.
200.    #Count the number of solutions that this grid has (using
       a backtracking approach implemented in the solveGrid() fu
   nction)
201.    counter=0
202.    solveGrid(copyGrid)
203.    #If the number of solution is different from 1 then we n
   eed to cancel the change by putting the value we took away
   back in the grid
204.    if counter!=1:
205.        grid[row][col]=backup
206.        #We could stop here, but we can also have another atte
   mpt with a different cell just to try to remove more numbe
   rs
207.        attempts -= 1
208.
209.    myPen.clear()
210.    drawGrid(grid)
211.    myPen.getscreen().update()
212.
213. print("Sudoku Grid Ready")
```

Chapter #6: String Manipulation Techniques

In nearly all of the challenges we have completed so far we have used variables to store **string** values. We have already used some string manipulation techniques such as **string concatenation** (joining strings together) and **string casting** (e.g. casting an integer or float to a string and vice-versa). Remember a string is a collection (list) of **characters**. So using a string is similar to using a list. You can hence reuse some of the techniques covered in the previous chapter to your string variables.

Other techniques can be used to change the **case** of a string (lower case, upper case, title case), extract characters from a string (in python this is called **slicing**), loop through all the characters of a string one at a time, convert characters of a string using the **ASCII code** and concatenate (join) two strings together.

The next few challenges will help you further improve your string manipulation techniques including:

- String Concatenation,
- String Casting,
- Changing the Case of a String,
- Slicing Strings,
- Using the ASCII Code.

55. Text Alignment Challenge

This challenge focuses on the use of string manipulation techniques in order to format the output when printing a list of keywords on the screen. We will create three procedures to align the content of our list to the left, to the centre and to the right of a banner as follows:

```
 _____      _____      _____
|                |    |                |    |                |
| Amsterdam      |    |    Amsterdam   |    |      Amsterdam |
| Berlin         |    |     Berlin     |    |         Berlin |
| London         |    |     London     |    |         London |
| Madrid         |    |     Madrid     |    |         Madrid |
| Oslo           |    |      Oslo      |    |           Oslo |
| Paris          |    |     Paris      |    |          Paris |
| Rome           |    |      Rome      |    |           Rome |
| Stockholm      |    |    Stockholm   |    |      Stockholm |
| Vienna         |    |     Vienna     |    |         Vienna |
|_____|    |_____|    |_____|
```

Web Address

https://www.101computing.net/text-alignment-challenge/

Python Code

```python
1.  #Text Alignment Challenge
2.
3.  #A procedure to print the content of a list aligned to the left
4.  def leftAlign(list):
5.      print("_____")
6.      print("|                   |")
7.
8.      for item in list:
9.          itemLength = len(item)
10.         spaces = " " * (15 - itemLength)
11.         print("| " + item + spaces + " |")
12.     print("|_____|")
13.
14. #A procedure to print the content of a list aligned to the left
15. def rightAlign(list):
16.     print("_____")
```

```
17.    print("|                    |")
18.
19.    for item in list:
20.       itemLength = len(item)
21.       spaces = " " * (15 - itemLength)
22.       print("| " + spaces + item + " |")
23.    print("|_____|")
24.
25. #A procedure to print the content of a list, aligned to the center
26. def centerAlign(list):
27.    print("_____")
28.    print("|                    |")
29.
30.    for item in list:
31.       itemLength = len(item)
32.       left = (15 - itemLength) // 2
33.       right = (15 - itemLength) - left
34.       leftSpaces = " " * left
35.       rightSpaces= " " * right
36.       print("| " + leftSpaces + item + rightSpaces + " |")
37.    print("|_____|")
38.
39. ### MAIN PROGRAM STARTS HERE ####
40. capitals = ["Paris","Amsterdam","Oslo","London","Berlin","Vienna","Rome","Stockholm","Madrid"]
41. capitals.sort()
42.
43. leftAlign(capitals)
44. rightAlign(capitals)
45. centerAlign(capitals)
```

56. Tally Marks Counter

Tally marks are a form of numeral system used for counting. They are most useful in counting or tallying ongoing results, such as the score in a game or sport, as no intermediate results need to be erased or discarded.

For this challenge we will write a Python script that:

- Asks the user to enter a number,

- Converts the user input to an integer,
- Translates this number into tally marks,
- Displays the tally marks on screen.

Web Address

https://www.101computing.net/tally-marks-counter/

Python Code

```
1.  # Tally Marks Counter
2.
3.  #Retrieve number form end-user
4.  number = int(input("Input a positive number:"))
5.
6.  #Find out how many blocks of 5 tallies: ||||- to include
7.  quotient = number // 5
8.  #Find out how many tallies are remaining
9.  remainder = number % 5
10.
11. tallyMarks = "||||-    " * quotient + "|" * remainder
12.
13. #Output
14. print(tallyMarks)
```

57. Word Unscramble

In this challenge, we will create a Word Unscramble quiz where the computer will randomly pick up words from a given list, scramble the letters of the word, output the scrambled word (anagram) and ask the user to guess the original word. For each correct answer, the user will be given 1 point.

The flowchart for this challenge is given at the web address provided below.

Web Address

https://www.101computing.net/word-unscramble-challenge/

```
1.  #Word Unscramble Challenge
2.  from random import shuffle
3.
4.  #A function to scramble a word!
5.  def scramble(word):
6.    #Convert word from a string to a list of letters
7.    letters=list(word)
8.    #Shuffle list
9.    shuffle(letters)
10.   #convert list back to a string
11.   scrambledWord = "".join(letters)
12.   return scrambledWord
13.
14.
15. #Main Program Starts Here
16. words = ["mouse","keyboard","monitor","printer","harddrive",
    "speakers"]
17.
18. #Display welcome banner
19. print("ABCDEFGHIJKLMNOPQRSTUVWXYZ")
20. print("A                          Z")
21. print("A      Word Unscramble     Z")
22. print("A       Input, Output      Z")
23. print("A    & Storage Devices     Z")
24. print("A                          Z")
25. print("ABCDEFGHIJKLMNOPQRSTUVWXYZ")
26.
27. #Initialise key variables
28. score = 0
29. total = 0
30.
31. #Iterate through the list of words
32. for i in range(0,len(words)):
33.   word = words[i]
34.   scrambledWord = scramble(word)
35.   print("\nScrambled Word: " + scrambledWord)
36.
37.   #Retrieve user input
38.   userGuess = input("Unscrambled word?").lower()
39.   total += 1
40.
41.   if userGuess == word:
42.     print("Correct Answer!")
43.     score += 1
44.   else:
45.     print("Wrong Answer!")
```

```
46.
47.    #Display score so far
48.    print("Your score: " + str(score) + " out of " + str(total
       ))
49.
50. print("End of Quiz!")
```

58. The Rail Fence Cipher

The rail fence cipher (sometimes called zigzag cipher) is a transposition cipher that jumbles up the order of the letters of a message using a basic algorithm.

The rail fence cipher works by writing your message on alternate lines across the page, and then reading off each line in turn.

For example, let's consider the plaintext "This is a secret message".

```
Plaintext       T H I S I S A S E C R E T M E S S A G E
```

To encode this message we will first write over two lines (the "rails of the fence") as follows:

Rail Fence	T		I		I		A		E		R		T		E		S		G	
Encoding		H		S		S		S		C		E		M		S		A		E

Note that all white spaces have been removed from the plain text.

The ciphertext is then read off by writing the top row first, followed by the bottom row:

```
Ciphertext      T I I A E R T E S G H S S S C E M S A E
```

For this challenge, we will have to write two python programs, one to encrypt a message (plaintext to ciphertext) and one to decrypt an encoded message (ciphertext to plaintext). The flowcharts of both the encoder and the decoder algorithms are available at the web address provided below.

141

https://www.101computing.net/the-rail-fence-cipher/

Python Code for the Rail Fence Encoder

```
1.  #The Rail Fence Cipher - Encoder
2.
3.  plaintext = input("Type a message to encode:")
4.  #Convert plaintext to UPPERCASE
5.  plaintext = plaintext.upper()
6.  #Remove white spaces from plaintext
7.  plaintext = plaintext.replace(" ", "")
8.
9.  #Apply Cipher Text Encoding Algorithm
10. ciphertext=""
11.
12. for i in range( 0,len(plaintext),2):
13.   ciphertext=ciphertext + plaintext[i]
14. for i in range( 1,len(plaintext),2):
15.   ciphertext=ciphertext + plaintext[i]
16.
17. #Output ciphertext:
18. print ciphertext
```

Python Code for the Rail Fence Decoder

```
1.  #The Rail Fence Cipher - Decoder
2.
3.  ciphertext = input("Enter a message to decode:")
4.
5.  #Ensure the ciphertext contains an even number of characters
    .
6.  if len(ciphertext)%2 != 0:
7.    ciphertext=ciphertext + " "
8.
9.  #Apply the Rail Fence Decoding Algorithm
10. midpoint=len(ciphertext) //2
11. plaintext=""
12. for i in range(0,midpoint):
13.   plaintext= plaintext + ciphertext[i]+ ciphertext[i+midpoin
      t]
14.
15. #Ouptut plaintext
16. print plaintext
```

59. Random Password Generator

For this challenge, we will use a Python script to generate a random password of 8 characters. Each time the program is run, a new password will be generated randomly. The passwords generated will be 8 characters long and will have to include the following characters in any order:

- 2 uppercase letters from A to Z,
- 2 lowercase letters from a to z,
- 2 digits from 0 to 9,
- 2 punctuation signs such as !, ?, ", # etc.

To solve this challenge we will have to generate random characters and to do so we will need to use the ASCII code.

Web Address

https://www.101computing.net/random-password-generator/

Python Code

```
1.  #Random Password Generator
2.  import random
3.
4.  #A function do shuffle all the characters of a string
5.  def shuffle(string):
6.      tempList = list(string)
7.      random.shuffle(tempList)
8.      return ''.join(tempList)
9.
10. #Main program starts here
11. #Generate a random characters based on their ASCII code valu
    es
12. uppercaseLetter1=chr(random.randint(65,90)) #Uppercase lette
    r A to Z
13. uppercaseLetter2=chr(random.randint(65,90)) #Uppercae letter
     A to Z
14. lowercaseLetter1=chr(random.randint(97,122)) #Lowercase lett
    er a to z
15. lowercaseLetter2=chr(random.randint(97,122)) #Lowercase lett
    er a to z
16. digit1=chr(random.randint(48,57)) #Digit 0 to 9
```

```
17. digit2=chr(random.randint(48,57))  #Digit 0 to 9
18. punctuationSign1=chr(random.randint(33,47))  #Punctuation sig
n
19. punctuationSign2=chr(random.randint(58,64))  #Punctuation sig
n
20.
21. #Generate password using all the characters, in random order

22. password = uppercaseLetter1 + uppercaseLetter2 + lowercaseLe
tter1 + lowercaseLetter2 + digit1 + digit2 + punctuationSign
1 + punctuationSign2
23. password = shuffle(password)
24.
25. #Ouput
26. print(password)
```

60. Pascal Triangle

In mathematics, one of the most interesting number patterns is Pascal's Triangle. It is named after Blaise Pascal (1623 – 1662), a famous French Mathematician and Philosopher.

To build a Pascal Triangle we start with a "1" at the top. We then place numbers below each number in a triangular pattern: Each number is the result of adding the two numbers directly above it. (See animation)

For this challenge we will use a Python script to output a Pascal Triangle after a fixed number of iterations (rows).

```
                1
              1   1
            1   2   1
          1   3   3   1
        1   4   6   4   1
      1   5  10  10   5   1
    1   6  15  20  15   6   1
```

Web Address

https://www.101computing.net/pascal-triangle/

144

```
1.  #Pascal Triangle
2.
3.  def formatNumber(number):
4.      if number<10:
5.          return "  "+str(number) + " "
6.      else:
7.          return " " + str(number) + " "
8.
9.  #First Row
10. row = [1]
11. print("   " * 8 + formatNumber(row[0]))
12.
13. #We will now workout any extra rows using a for loop...
14. for i in range(1,8):
15.     newRow=[1]
16.     for j in range(1,len(row)):
17.         newRow.append(row[j-1] + row[j])
18.     newRow.append(1)
19.
20.     #Display new row
21.     line = "   " * (8 - i)
22.     for value in newRow:
23.         line = line + formatNumber(value)
24.     print(line)
25.
26.     row = newRow
```

61. Boarding Pass Validation

In this challenge we are writing a computer program for an airline company. The program will be used at a check-in desk to generate and print custom boarding passes.

The program will capture several user inputs before generating the pass. In order to make our program more robust, we have added validation routines so that any invalid input is detected and automatically rejected by the program. The program performs the following validation checks:

- The firstname and lastname of the passenger cannot be left blank,
- The airport codes (departure and arrival) have to be exactly 3 characters long,
- The airport codes (departure and arrival) should be automatically converted to UPPERCASE,
- The program should ask whether or not a QR code will be printed on the boarding pass. Only a "Yes" or a "No" answer should be accepted,
- The gate number has to be based on the following format: 1 uppercase letter + 2-digit number,
- The flight number has to be based on the following format: 2 uppercase letters + 4-digit number,
- The departure and arrival times must be in the 12:60 AM/PM format,
- The date must be in the DD/MM/YYYY format.

Note that, to implement the last two validation checks to validate date & time inputs, we are using a function called *strptime()* from the *time* library. If you are completing this challenge online using trinket.io you will need to use a Python 3 trinket available at the web address provided below.

Web Address
https://www.101computing.net/boarding-pass-validation/

Python 3 – Trinket.io
https://trinket.io/python3

Python Code

```
1.   #Boarding Pass Validation
2.   import time
3.
4.   print(">->->->->->->->->->->->->->->->->->")
5.   print(">                                 >")
6.   print(">     BOARDING PASS VALIDATION     >")
7.   print(">                                 >")
8.   print(">->->->->->->->->->->->->->->->->->")
```

```
9.    print("")
10.
11.   #Firstname
12.   firstname=input("Passenger Firstname?").strip()
13.   while firstname=="":
14.     print("Firstname must be filled in.")
15.     firstname=input("Passenger Firstname?")
16.
17.   #Lastname
18.   lastname=input("Passenger Lastname?").strip()
19.   while lastname=="":
20.     print("Lastname must be filled in.")
21.     lastname=input("Passenger Lastname?")
22.
23.   #Departure Code
24.   departureCode=input("Departure Airport Code?").upper()
25.   while len(departureCode)!=3:
26.     print("Airport Code must be 3 characters long.")
27.     departureCode=input("Departure Airport Code?").upper()
28.
29.   #Arrival Code
30.   arrivalCode=input("Arrival Airport Code?").upper()
31.   while len(arrivalCode)!=3:
32.     print("Airport Code must be 3 characters long.")
33.     arrivalCode=input("Arrival Airport Code?").upper()
34.
35.   #QR Code?
36.   answer = input("Would you like to print a QR code?").upper
      ()
37.   while (answer!="YES" and answer!="NO"):
38.     answer = input("Would you like to print a QR code?").upp
      er()
39.
40.   UPPERCASE = "ABCDEFGHIJKLMNOPQRSTUVWXYZ"
41.   DIGIT = "0123456789"
42.
43.   #Gate Number
44.   valid = False
45.   while valid == False:
46.     gate = input("Gate Number?").upper()
47.     if len(gate)==3:
48.       if gate[0] in UPPERCASE and gate[1] in DIGIT and gate[
      2] in DIGIT:
49.           valid=True
50.
51.   #Flight Number
52.   valid = False
53.   while valid == False:
54.     flight = input("Flight Number?").upper()
```

```
55.    if len(flight)==6:
56.        if flight[0] in UPPERCASE and flight[1] in UPPERCASE
    and flight[2] in DIGIT and flight[3] in DIGIT and flight[4
    ] in DIGIT and flight[5] in DIGIT: .
57.            valid=True
58.
59.  #Departure Time
60.  timeFormat = "%I:%M %p"
61.  valid = False
62.  while valid == False:
63.    departureTime = input("Departure Time? ")
64.    try:
65.      validtime = time.strptime(departureTime, timeFormat)
66.      valid=True
67.    except ValueError:
68.      print("Invalid Time Format. Try again.")
69.
70.  #Arrival Time
71.  valid = False
72.  while valid == False:
73.    arrivalTime = input("Arrival Time? ")
74.    try:
75.      validtime = time.strptime(arrivalTime, timeFormat)
76.      valid=True
77.    except ValueError:
78.      print("Invalid Time Format. Try again.")
79.
80.  #Departure Date
81.  dateFormat = "%d/%m/%Y"
82.  valid = False
83.  while valid == False:
84.    departureDate = input("Departure Date? ")
85.    try:
86.      validdate = time.strptime(departureDate, dateFormat)
87.      valid = True
88.    except ValueError:
89.      print("Invalid Time Format. Try again.")
90.
91.
92.  #Printing Boarding Pass
93.  print(" _____ ")
94.  print("|                                   |")
95.  print("|  Passenger Details:               |")
96.  print("|   Firstname:                      |")
97.  print("|    >  " + firstname)
98.  print("|   Lastname:                       |")
99.  print("|    >  " + lastname)
100. print("|                                   |")
101. print("|  Flight Details:                  |")
```

148

```
102. print("|                                          |")
103. print("|     Departure Airport Code:              |")
104. print("|     >  " + departureCode)
105. print("|     Arrival Airpot Code:                 |")
106. print("|     >  " + arrivalCode)
107. print("|     Gate:                                |")
108. print("|     >  " + gate)
109. print("|     Flight Number:                       |")
110. print("|     >  " + flight)
111. print("|     QR Code?                             |")
112. print("|     >  " + answer)
113. print("|     Departure Date:                      |")
114. print("|     >  " + departureDate)
115. print("|     Departure Time:                      |")
116. print("|     >  " + departureTime)
117. print("|     Arrival Time:                        |")
118. print("|     >  " + arrivalTime)
119. print("|_____|")
```

62. Luhn Algorithm

In this challenge we will use the **Luhn Algorithm** to check if a debit card or credit card number is a valid card number.

This method is used every time you scan or enter your credit card number (e.g. when paying online) to check if your card number is a valid credit card number. This method can be used to quickly detect credit card numbers that have been mistyped or to detect when someone is trying to enter a fake/made up credit card number. Note that it's not 100% efficient, so is only used a as a pre-check to deter some invalid card numbers. If this first test passes, additional more robust checks will be performed for the online transaction to be approved.

The Luhn Algorithm consists of 4 key steps.

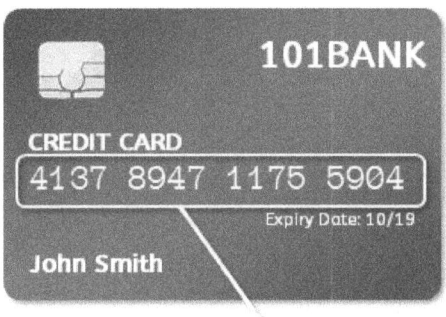

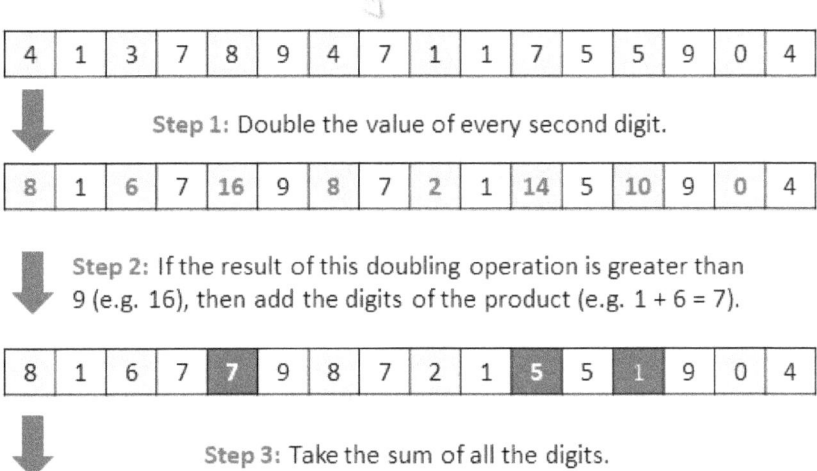

80 ends with a **0** ➡ Valid **Card Number**

Our program will ask the end-user to enter a 16-digit card number and will then apply the Luhn algorithm to decide and output whether or not this card number is valid.

Web Address

https://www.101computing.net/is-my-credit-card-valid/

```
1.  #Is My Credit Card Number Valid?
2.
3.  cardNumber = input("Enter a 16-digit card number:")
4.
5.  #Remove spaces
6.  cardNumber = cardNumber.replace(" ","")
7.
8.  #Length check to only accept 16 digits card numbers
9.  while len(cardNumber)!=16:
10.   print("Invlid card number. A valid card number should be 1
      6 digits long.")
11.   cardNumber = input("Enter a 16-digit card number:")
12.
13. #Applying Luhn Algorithm
14. total = 0
15. for i in range(0,len(cardNumber)):
16.    digit = int(cardNumber[i])
17.
18.    if i%2==0: # Even Position
19.        #Step 1:
20.        digit = digit*2
21.        #Step 2:
22.        if digit>=10:
23.           digit = 1 + (digit-10)
24.
25.    #Step 3:
26.    total = total + digit
27.
28. #step 4:
29. if total%10 == 0:
30.   print("This is a valid card number.")
31. else:
32.   print("This is an invalid card number.")
```

63. Recursive vs. Iterative Palindrome Check

A palindrome is a word, phrase, or sequence that reads the same backwards as forwards, e.g. madam.

For this challenge we will investigate two algorithms used to find out if a word is a palindrome or not. The first algorithm will use an iterative approach; the second algorithm will use a recursive approach.

Iterative Approach:

An iterative approach is based around the use of a loop which can be:

- A count-controlled loop (e.g. FOR loop)
- A condition-controlled loop (e.g. WHILE loop or REPEAT UNTIL loop)

For our iterative palindrome check algorithm, we will use a loop to check all the letters in the first half of the word and compare them with the letters in the second half of the word (in reverse order). If they all match then the word is a palindrome.

Web Address

https://www.101computing.net/recursive-vs-iterative-palindrome-check/

Python Code: Iterative Approach

```
1.  #Iterative Palindrome Check - Iterative Approach
2.
3.  def isPalindrome(word):
4.    midPoint = len(word)//2
5.    palindrome = True
6.    for i in range(0,midPoint):
7.      left = word[i]
8.      right = word[len(word)-i-1]
9.      if left!=right:
10.       palindrome=False
11.       break
12.   return palindrome
13.
14.
15. word = input("Enter a word or sentence:")
16. #Length check - we need a word of at least 2 characters
17. while len(word)<2:
18.   word = input("Try again -
      Enter a word or sentence with at least 2 characters.")
19.
20. if isPalindrome(word):
```

```
21.    print("This is a palindrome.")
22. else:
23.    print("This is not a palindrome.")
```

Recursive Appoarch:

A recursive function is a function that:

* Includes a call to itself,
* Has a stopping condition to stop the recursion.

For our recursive palindrome check algorithm, we will use a function that:

* Checks that the word is at least two characters long:
    o If the word is less than two characters then the function will stop the recursion (stopping condition) and Return True as the word is a palindrome.
    o If the word is two or more characters long, the function will check that the first and last letter of the word are the same:
        ▪ If they are the same, the function will extract the word in the middle (remove the first and the last letter) and call itself with this new shortest word.
        ▪ If they are different, then the word is not a palindrome. The function will stop the recursion here (stopping condition) and return False.

Python Code: Recursive Approach

```
1.  #Recursive Palindrome Check - Recursive Approach
2.
3.  def isPalindrome(word):
4.      if len(word)<2:
5.          return True    # Stop the recursion
6.      else:
7.          firstLetter = word[0]
8.          lastLetter = word[len(word)-1]
9.          if firstLetter == lastLetter:
10.             middleWord = word[1:len(word)-1]
11.             print(firstLetter + "==" + lastLetter)
12.             print("Now checking if '" + middleWord + "' is a palin
    drome.")
```

```
13.        return isPalindrome(middleWord)   #recursive call
14.    else:
15.        print(firstLetter + "!=" + lastLetter)
16.        return False    # Stop the recursion
17.
18. word = input("Enter a word or sentence:")
19. #Length check - we need a word of at least 2 characters
20. while len(word)<2:
21.    word = input("Try again -
       Enter a word or sentence with at least 2 characters.")
22.
23. if isPalindrome(word):
24.    print("This is a palindrome.")
25. else:
26.    print("This is not a palindrome.")
```

64. Enigma Daily Settings Generator

Before attempting this challenge, you should familiarise yourself with the Enigma machine by completing the Enigma Mission X challenge accessible using the web address provided below.

Web Address: Enigma Mission X

https://www.101computing.net/enigma-mission-x-challenge/

Code Books were used by the Germans to list all the settings needed to set up the Enigma machines before starting to encrypt or decrypt messages. The Germans used to change the Enigma settings very regularly (e.g. once a day) so that if the Allies managed to break their code (find out the Enigma settings) they would only be able to use them for that day and would have to find the new settings every day. Code books were highly confidential documents as if a codebook was captured or reconstructed, messages could easily be decrypted.

An Enigma code book would have one page per month. The page would include all the settings for each day of the month with the first day of the month at the bottom of the page so that once used, a setting could be torn off the page.

The settings would indicate which rotors to use and in which order to connect them. Initially the Enigma machine came with a box of five rotors to choose from. On an Enigma M3, three out of the five rotors were connected. The M4 Enigma used four rotors chosen from a box of up to eight rotors.

The settings would also include the wheel settings (how to connect the rotors) and their initial position. Finally the settings would indicate which letters to connect by plugging cables on the plugboard.

The aim of this challenge is to write a piece of Python code to generate a full code book of Enigma daily settings for the Enigma M3 series (which consists of three rotors to choose from a collection of five unique rotors).

The code book should include 30 or 31 set of randomly generated daily settings (one for each day of the month) displayed in a table as follows:

Each set of daily settings should include:

- The date (number between 1 and 30/31, listed in reverse order)
- The choice of three rotors (e.g. IV I III)
- The ring settings (e.g. ABC)
- The plugboard permutations (e.g. AF CK EW MT SV XY)
- The initial rotor positions (e.g. DEF)

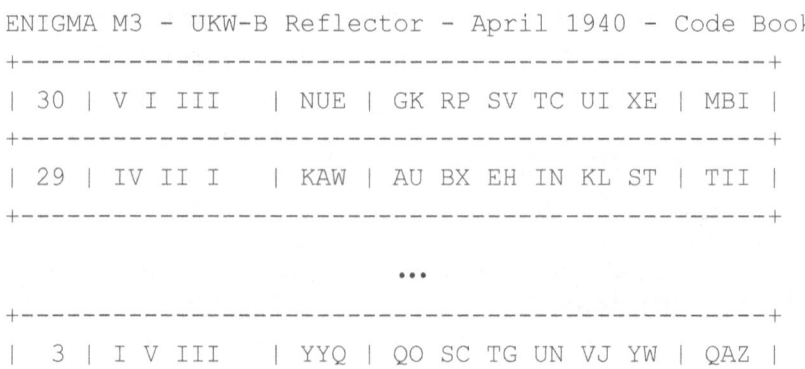

```
ENIGMA M3 - UKW-B Reflector - April 1940 - Code Book
+---------------------------------------------------+
| 30 | V I III   | NUE | GK RP SV TC UI XE | MBI |
+---------------------------------------------------+
| 29 | IV II I   | KAW | AU BX EH IN KL ST | TII |
+---------------------------------------------------+


                        ...


+---------------------------------------------------+
|  3 | I V III   | YYQ | QO SC TG UN VJ YW | QAZ |
```

```
+--------------------------------------------------------+
|  2 | II III V   | ARV | AT BV EK HD PN YJ | ERC |
+--------------------------------------------------------+
|  1 | V I II     | OZH | AQ FX JT LM RB WK | PSP |
+--------------------------------------------------------+
```

Web Address
https://www.101computing.net/enigma-daily-settings-generator/

Python Code

```
1.  #Enigma Daily Settings / Code Book Generator
2.  from random import randint
3.
4.  TITLE = "ENIGMA M3 - UKW-B Reflector - April 1940 -
    Code Book"
5.  NUMBER_OF_DAYS = 30
6.
7.  def rotor_selection(numberOfRotors):
8.      rotors = ["I","II","III","IV","V"]
9.      alphabet = "ABCDEFGHIJKLMNOPQRSTUVWXYZ"
10.     i = randint(0, numberOfRotors-1)
11.     ii = randint(0, numberOfRotors-1)
12.     while ii==i:
13.         ii = randint(0, numberOfRotors-1)
14.     iii = randint(0, numberOfRotors-1)
15.     while iii==i or iii==ii:
16.         iii = randint(0, numberOfRotors-1)
17.
18.     rotor_i = rotors[i]
19.     rotor_ii = rotors[ii]
20.     rotor_iii = rotors[iii]
21.
22.     settings = rotor_i +  " " + rotor_ii + " " + rotor_iii
23.     settings = settings + (" "*(9-len(settings)))
24.     return settings
25.
26. def ring_settings(numberOfRotors):  # returns ring settings

27.     alphabet = "ABCDEFGHIJKLMNOPQRSTUVWXYZ"
28.     settings = ""
29.     for i in range(numberOfRotors):
30.         rotor = randint(0, 25)
31.         settings = settings + alphabet[rotor]
```

156

```
32.        return settings
33.
34. def plugboard_settings(numberOfPermutations):   # Plugboard s
    teckering
35.        alphabet = "ABCDEFGHIJKLMNOPQRSTUVWXYZ"
36.        settings = ""
37.        stecksA = []
38.        stecksB= []
39.
40.        for i in range(numberOfPermutations):
41.          a = randint(0, 25)
42.          while a in stecksA:
43.            a = randint(0, 25)
44.          stecksA.append(a)
45.
46.        for i in range(numberOfPermutations):
47.          b = randint(0, 25)
48.          while b in stecksA or b in stecksB:
49.            b = randint(0, 25)
50.          stecksB.append(b)
51.
52.        stecksA.sort()
53.
54.        settings=""
55.        for i in range(numberOfPermutations):
56.            settings = settings + alphabet[stecksA[i]] + alphabet
    [stecksB[i]] + " "
57.
58.
59.        settings = settings[:-1]
60.        return settings
61.
62. def rotor_positions(numberOfRotors):   # Rotor position
63.        alphabet = "ABCDEFGHIJKLMNOPQRSTUVWXYZ"
64.        settings = ""
65.        for i in range(numberOfRotors):
66.          rotor = randint(0, 25)
67.          settings = settings + alphabet[rotor]
68.        return settings
69.
70.
71. def generateCodeBook(title, numberOfDays):
72.        print(title)
73.        for day in range(numberOfDays,0,-1):
74.            print('+-----------------------------------------
    ----+')
75.            if day<10:
76.              settings = "|   " + str(day) + " | "
77.            else:
```

```
78.          settings = "| " + str(day) + " | "
79.          settings = settings  + rotor_selection(5) + " | "
80.          settings = settings + ring_settings(3) + " | "
81.          settings = settings + plugboard_settings(6) + " | "

82.          settings = settings + rotor_positions(3) + " |"
83.          print(settings)
84.
85.      print('+------------------------------------------------
    +')
86.
87. generateCodeBook(TITLE, NUMBER_OF_DAYS)
```

65. Enigma Crib Analysis

During World War II, Enigma machines were used by the Germans to encrypt and decrypt military radio communications. An Enigma machine consists of a complex sets of interconnected rotors used to performs substitution and transposition ciphers to encrypt data. The Germans would change the enigma settings every day making it extremely difficult for the allies to break the Enigma code.

In order to crack the Enigma code, the allies decided to set up a team of code breakers (cryptanalysts) at Bletchley Park, UK. Amongst these, Alan Turing and Dillwyn Knox rapidly identified that the best approach to crack the Enigma code was to find a method to identify the Enigma settings used by the German on that day. This is due to the fact that the same settings can be used to both encrypt a plaintext to cypher text and to decrypt a cipher text back to its original plaintext. In other words the Enigma machine is used to implement a symmetric encryption: knowing the key (Enigma settings) enables you to both encrypt and decrypt messages.

The method they identified to work out the Enigma settings relied on the use of cribs. The term crib was used at Bletchley Park to denote any known plaintext or suspected plaintext at some point in an enciphered message. Effectively code breakers realised that the Germans were regularly sending Weather reports (in German Wetter Vorhersage) and could identify the ciphertext containing these words (based on the time of the day these reports were sent). Another message that Germans often used was the message "Nothing to report" (in German Keine besonderen Ereignisse) which was also used to identify useful cribs.

So let's consider the following encrypted message:

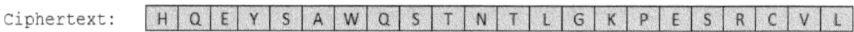

Now let's assume that we know (or strongly suspect) that this message contains the expression "SECRET MESSAGE", but we are not sure at which position in the text this might be.

It could be that the plain text message starts with "SECRETMESSAGE" in this case the crib would be:

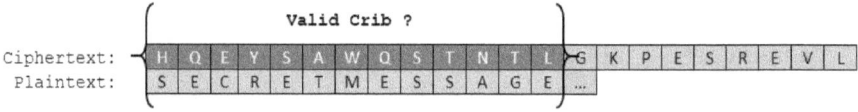

However it could be that the expression "SECRETMESSAGE" is within the ciphertext at a different position. (Not necessary at the very start of the message). E.g. If it was at position 5 the crib would then be:

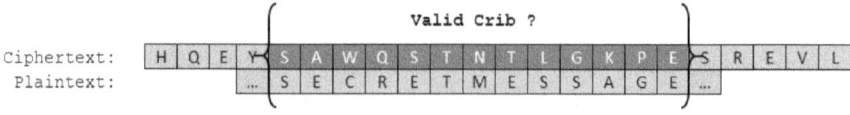

So when an encrypted message was intercepted and the code breakers suspected it may contain a crib, one of their first tasks was to identify the possible starting position of the crib to get a full crib (plaintext with matching ciphertext). To do so cryptanalysts exploited the property of the Enigma machine which ensured that it never encoded a letter as itself. So any crib that contained at least one letter encoded as itself could be automatically discarded. This hugely reduced the number of potential cribs that could then be exploited to try to work out the Enigma settings.

Using our initial ciphertext, you can see how most crib positions can be discarded, resulting in only two possible cribs:

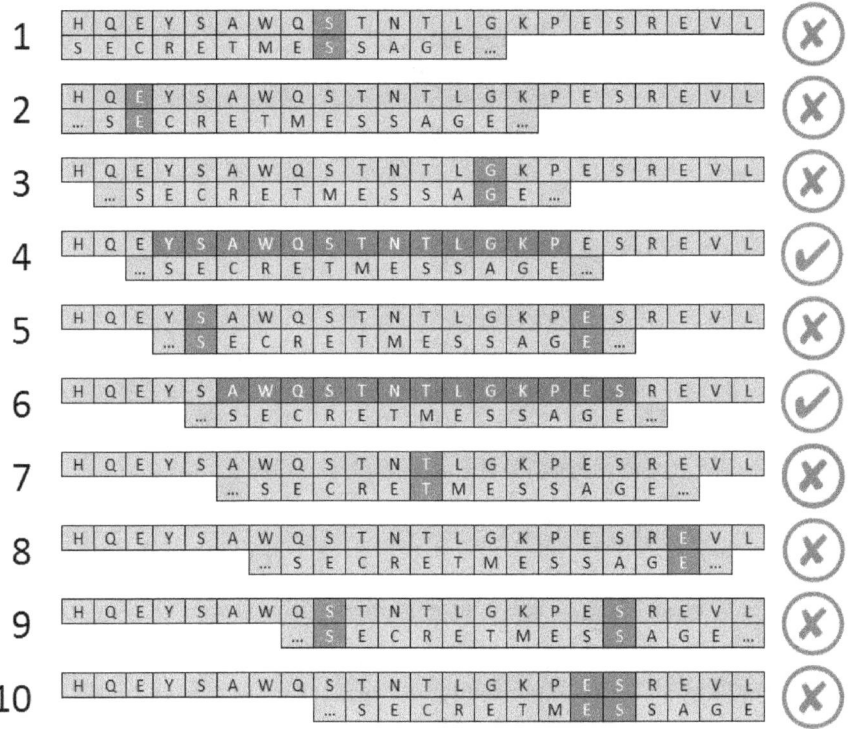

In this challenge we will write a computer program to help cryptanalyst identify potential cribs from a ciphertext. Our program will use to inputs: a plaintext crib (e.g. SECRETMESSAGE) and a full cypher text. The program will then work out and return all potential cribs by investigating all possible positions of the crib in the cipher text and discarding invalid cribs (cribs containing a letter that would be encoded as itself).

Web Address

https://www.101computing.net/enigma-crib-analysis/

```
1.  #Enigma Crib Analysis
2.
3.  ciphertext = "HQEYSAWQSTNTLGKPESREVL"
4.  plaintext  = "SECRETMESSAGE"
5.
6.  cipherLength = len(ciphertext)
7.  plainLength = len(plaintext)
8.  counter =  0
9.
10. print("### Enigma Crib Analysis ###\n")
11. print("Ciphertext: " + ciphertext)
12. print("Plaintext:  " + plaintext)
13.
14. print("\nIdentifying valid cribs based on the characteristic
    of the enigma machine: a letter will never be encrypted as
    itslef.")
15.
16. if (plainLength > cipherLength):
17.    print("\nCannot identify valid cribs. The ciphertext need
    s to be longer or the same length than the plaintext.")
18. else:
19.
20.   for i in range(0,cipherLength-plainLength):
21.     validCrib = True
22.     for j in range(0,plainLength):
23.       if (ciphertext[i+j]==plaintext[j]):
24.         validCrib = False
25.
26.     if validCrib:
27.       counter+=1
28.       print("\nValid Cipher at position " + str(i))
29.       print("Cipher Crib: " + ciphertext[i:i+plainLength])
30.       print("Plaintext:   " + plaintext)
31.
32.   if (counter==0):
33.     print("\nCould not identify any valid crib!")
```

66. Enigma Encoder

The Enigma machines are a series of electro-mechanical rotor cipher machines. The first machines were invented at the end of World War I by German engineer Arthur Scherbius and were mainly used to protect commercial, diplomatic and military communication. Enigma machines became more and more complex and were heavily used by the German army during World War II to encrypt radio signals.

The Enigma machine was used to both encrypt and decrypt Enigma messages (Enigma encryption is symmetric, which means that the same settings can be used to both encrypt or decrypt a message).

In this challenge we will create an enigma encoder program to encrypt and decrypt messages using specific Enigma settings. But before doing so we need to gain a better understanding of how the Enigma machine actually works. To do so you can read more about the Enigma using the web addresses provided below and use our online Enigma emulator to start encoding or decoding secret messages.

Web Address

https://www.101computing.net/enigma-encoder/

Web Address: Online Enigma Machine

https://www.101computing.net/enigma-M3/

Python Code

```
1.   #Enigma Encoder
2.
3.   # ---------------- Enigma Settings ----------------
4.   rotors = ("I","II","III")
5.   reflector = "UKW-B"
6.   ringSettings ="ABC"
7.   ringPositions = "DEF"
8.   plugboard = "AT BS DE FM IR KN LZ OW PV XY"
9.   # ------------------------------------------------
10.
```

```
11.  def caesarShift(str, amount):
12.      output = ""
13.      for i in range(0,len(str)):
14.          c = str[i]
15.          code = ord(c)
16.          if ((code >= 65) and (code <= 90)):
17.              c = chr(((code - 65 + amount) % 26) + 65)
18.          output = output + c
19.      return output
20.
21.  def encode(plaintext):
22.      global rotors, reflector,ringSettings,ringPositions,plug
     board
23.      #Enigma Rotors and reflectors
24.      rotor1 = "EKMFLGDQVZNTOWYHXUSPAIBRCJ"
25.      rotor1Notch = "Q"
26.      rotor2 = "AJDKSIRUXBLHWTMCQGZNPYFVOE"
27.      rotor2Notch = "E"
28.      rotor3 = "BDFHJLCPRTXVZNYEIWGAKMUSQO"
29.      rotor3Notch = "V"
30.      rotor4 = "ESOVPZJAYQUIRHXLNFTGKDCMWB"
31.      rotor4Notch = "J"
32.      rotor5 = "VZBRGITYUPSDNHLXAWMJQOFECK"
33.      rotor5Notch = "Z"
34.
35.      rotorDict = {"I":rotor1,"II":rotor2,"III":rotor3,"IV":ro
     tor4,"V":rotor5}
36.      rotorNotchDict = {"I":rotor1Notch,"II":rotor2Notch,"III"
     :rotor3Notch,"IV":rotor4Notch,"V":rotor5Notch}
37.
38.      reflectorB = {"A":"Y","Y":"A","B":"R","R":"B","C":"U","U
     ":"C","D":"H","H":"D","E":"Q","Q":"E","F":"S","S":"F","G":
     "L","L":"G","I":"P","P":"I","J":"X","X":"J","K":"N","N":"K
     ","M":"O","O":"M","T":"Z","Z":"T","V":"W","W":"V"}
39.      reflectorC = {"A":"F","F":"A","B":"V","V":"B","C":"P","P
     ":"C","D":"J","J":"D","E":"I","I":"E","G":"O","O":"G","H":
     "Y","Y":"H","K":"R","R":"K","L":"Z","Z":"L","M":"X","X":"M
     ","N":"W","W":"N","Q":"T","T":"Q","S":"U","U":"S"}
40.
41.      alphabet = "ABCDEFGHIJKLMNOPQRSTUVWXYZ"
42.      rotorANotch = False
43.      rotorBNotch = False
44.      rotorCNotch = False
45.
46.      if reflector=="UKW-B":
47.          reflectorDict = reflectorB
48.      else:
49.          reflectorDict = reflectorC
50.
```

```
51.     #A = Left,  B = Mid,  C=Right
52.     rotorA = rotorDict[rotors[0]]
53.     rotorB = rotorDict[rotors[1]]
54.     rotorC = rotorDict[rotors[2]]
55.     rotorANotch = rotorNotchDict[rotors[0]]
56.     rotorBNotch = rotorNotchDict[rotors[1]]
57.     rotorCNotch = rotorNotchDict[rotors[2]]
58.
59.     rotorALetter = ringPositions[0]
60.     rotorBLetter = ringPositions[1]
61.     rotorCLetter = ringPositions[2]
62.
63.     rotorASetting = ringSettings[0]
64.     offsetASetting = alphabet.index(rotorASetting)
65.     rotorBSetting = ringSettings[1]
66.     offsetBSetting = alphabet.index(rotorASetting)
67.     rotorCSetting = ringSettings[2]
68.     offsetCSetting = alphabet.index(rotorASetting)
69.
70.     rotorA = caesarShift(rotorA,offsetASetting)
71.     rotorB = caesarShift(rotorB,offsetBSetting)
72.     rotorC = caesarShift(rotorC,offsetCSetting)
73.
74.     if offsetASetting>0:
75.        rotorA = rotorA[26-offsetASetting:] + rotorA[0,26-
    offsetASetting]
76.     if offsetBSetting>0:
77.        rotorB = rotorB[26-offsetBSetting:] + rotorB[0,26-
    offsetBSetting]
78.     if offsetCSetting>0:
79.        rotorC = rotorC[26-offsetCSetting:] + rotorC[0,26-
    offsetCSetting]
80.
81.     ciphertext = ""
82.
83.     #Converplugboard settings into a dictionary
84.     plugboardConnections = plugboard.upper().split(" ")
85.     plugboardDict = {}
86.     for pair in plugboardConnections:
87.        if len(pair)==2:
88.          plugboardDict[pair[0]] = pair[1]
89.          plugboardDict[pair[1]] = pair[0]
90.
91.     plaintext = plaintext.upper()
92.     for letter in plaintext:
93.        encryptedLetter = letter
94.
95.        if letter in alphabet:
```

```
96.         #Rotate Rotors -
        This happens as soon as a key is pressed, before encrypti
        ng the letter!
97.         rotorTrigger = False
98.         #3rd rotor rotates by 1 for every key being pressed
99.         if rotorCLetter == rotorCNotch:
100.           rotorTrigger = True
101.         rotorCLetter = alphabet[(alphabet.index(rotorCLetter
    ) + 1) % 26]
102.         #Check if rotorB needs to rotate
103.         if rotorTrigger:
104.           rotorTrigger = False
105.           if rotorBLetter == rotorBNotch:
106.             rotorTrigger = True
107.           rotorBLetter = alphabet[(alphabet.index(rotorBLett
    er) + 1) % 26]
108.
109.           #Check if rotorA needs to rotate
110.           if (rotorTrigger):
111.             rotorTrigger = False
112.             rotorALetter = alphabet[(alphabet.index(rotorALe
    tter) + 1) % 26]
113.
114.         else:
115.             #Check for double step sequence!
116.           if rotorBLetter == rotorBNotch:
117.             rotorBLetter = alphabet[(alphabet.index(rotorBLe
    tter) + 1) % 26]
118.             rotorALetter = alphabet[(alphabet.index(rotorALe
    tter) + 1) % 26]
119.
120.         #Implement plugboard encryption!
121.         if letter in plugboardDict.keys():
122.           if plugboardDict[letter]!="":
123.             encryptedLetter = plugboardDict[letter]
124.
125.         #Rotors & Reflector Encryption
126.         offsetA = alphabet.index(rotorALetter)
127.         offsetB = alphabet.index(rotorBLetter)
128.         offsetC = alphabet.index(rotorCLetter)
129.
130.         # Wheel 3 Encryption
131.         pos = alphabet.index(encryptedLetter)
132.         let = rotorC[(pos + offsetC)%26]
133.         pos = alphabet.index(let)
134.         encryptedLetter = alphabet[(pos - offsetC +26)%26]
135.
136.         # Wheel 2 Encryption
137.         pos = alphabet.index(encryptedLetter)
```

```
138.        let = rotorB[(pos + offsetB)%26]
139.        pos = alphabet.index(let)
140.        encryptedLetter = alphabet[(pos - offsetB +26)%26]
141.
142.        # Wheel 1 Encryption
143.        pos = alphabet.index(encryptedLetter)
144.        let = rotorA[(pos + offsetA)%26]
145.        pos = alphabet.index(let)
146.        encryptedLetter = alphabet[(pos - offsetA +26)%26]
147.
148.        # Reflector encryption!
149.        if encryptedLetter in reflectorDict.keys():
150.            if reflectorDict[encryptedLetter]!="":
151.                encryptedLetter = reflectorDict[encryptedLetter]
152.
153.        #Back through the rotors
154.        # Wheel 1 Encryption
155.        pos = alphabet.index(encryptedLetter)
156.        let = alphabet[(pos + offsetA)%26]
157.        pos = rotorA.index(let)
158.        encryptedLetter = alphabet[(pos - offsetA +26)%26]
159.
160.        # Wheel 2 Encryption
161.        pos = alphabet.index(encryptedLetter)
162.        let = alphabet[(pos + offsetB)%26]
163.        pos = rotorB.index(let)
164.        encryptedLetter = alphabet[(pos - offsetB +26)%26]
165.
166.        # Wheel 3 Encryption
167.        pos = alphabet.index(encryptedLetter)
168.        let = alphabet[(pos + offsetC)%26]
169.        pos = rotorC.index(let)
170.        encryptedLetter = alphabet[(pos - offsetC +26)%26]
171.
172.        #Implement plugboard encryption!
173.        if encryptedLetter in plugboardDict.keys():
174.            if plugboardDict[encryptedLetter]!="":
175.                encryptedLetter = plugboardDict[encryptedLetter]
176.
177.      ciphertext = ciphertext + encryptedLetter
178.    return ciphertext
179.
180. #Main Program Starts Here
181. print("  ##### Enigma Encoder #####")
182. print("")
183. plaintext = input("Enter text to encode or decode:\n")
184. ciphertext = encode(plaintext)
185.
186. print("\nEncoded text: \n " + ciphertext)
```

Chapter #7: Date & Time Manipulation Techniques

When writing programs we sometimes have to manipulate **dates and times**. The operations we can do on these can be trickier than the usual arithmetic operations we have used so far. For instance we sometimes have to find the difference in days between two dates or add a specific amount of time to a date and time to find out what will be the resulting date and time.

Date and time information also needs to be formatted to be presented in a human readable format. To make things even more complex, not all countries use the same **date and time format**. For instance, while in the UK dates use the DD/MM/YYYY format, in the US they use the MM/DD/YYYY format!

The next few challenges will explore:

- Formatting Dates and Times,
- Performing Calculations based on Dates and Times.

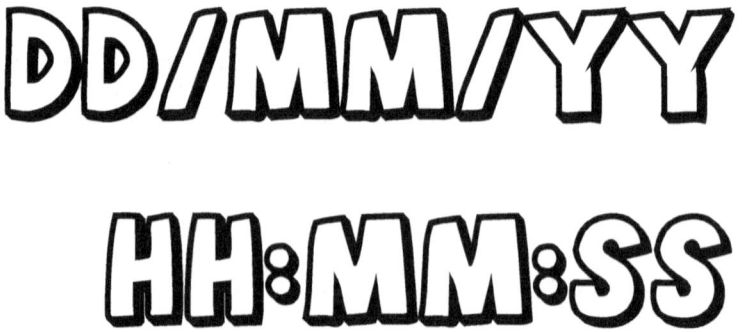

For this challenge we will create a program to measure how long it will take the end-user to type the entire alphabet from a to z.

Once the user has typed the alphabet, the program will check that they typed it correctly. If not the user should try again until they type it right.

The program should then output:

- How many attempts the user had,
- How long it took them in total,
- How long it took them on average per attempt,
- How long it took them on their last attempt (which is when they got it correct).

Web Address

https://www.101computing.net/fast-typing-test/

Python Code

```
1.  #Fast Typing Test Challenge
2.  import time
3.
4.  print("><><><><><><><><><><><><")
5.  print("> Reaction Time Tester <")
6.  print("><><><><><><><><><><><><")
7.  #Pause of 1 second
8.  time.sleep(1)
9.
10. alphabet = "abcdefghijklmnopqrstuvwxyz"
11. numberOfAttempts = 0
12. attemptsDuration = []
13. text=""
14.
15. #Record duration of very attempt till the user gets it right
16. startingTime=time.time()
17. while text!=alphabet:
18.     start = time.time()
19.     text = input("Type the whole alphabet as fast as you can?")
    )
```

```
20.    end = time.time()
21.    numberOfAttempts += 1
22.
23.    duration = round(end - start,2)
24.    attemptsDuration.append(duration)
25.
26.    if text!=alphabet:
27.       print("Wrong alphabet. Try again!")
28.
29. #Output key statistics:
30. overallDuration = round(end-startingTime)
31. print("Overall Duration: " + str(overallDuration) + " second
    s.")
32. print("Number of attempts: " + str(numberOfAttempts))
33. print("Last attempt: " + str(duration) + " seconds.")
34. print("Average in: " + str(round(overallDuration / numberOfA
    ttempts,2)) + " seconds.")
```

68. Time Guessing Game

For this challenge, we will create a game where the user is given a random number between 1 and 10. The program will display the number on screen and ask the user to wait for this number of seconds before pressing the return key. Once the user has done so, the program will calculate how long they waited for and give the user a score as follows:

- If the user waited for more than the given time, they went bust: 0 points,
- If the user presses the return key at the right time or up to 1/2 second earlier: 50pts,
- If the user presses the return key between 1 second to 1/2 second earlier: 25pts,
- If the user presses the return key between 2 seconds to 1 second earlier: 10pts,
- If the user presses the return key more than 2 seconds earlier: 0pts.

https://www.101computing.net/time-guessing-game/

```
1.  #Fast Typing Test Challenge
2.  import time
3.  from random import randint
4.
5.  print("><><><><><><><><><><><><<")
6.  print("> Time Guessing Game <")
7.  print("><><><><><><><><><><><><<")
8.  #Pause of 1 second
9.  time.sleep(1)
10.
11. duration = randint(1,10)
12.
13. start=time.time()
14. text = input("Press the return key in " + str(duration) + "
    seconds?")
15. end = time.time()
16.
17. userDuration = round(end - start,2)
18. print("You waited for: " + str(userDuration) + " seconds.")
19.
20. #Calculate Score:
21. if userDuration > duration:
22.    print("You went bust. Score: 0!")
23. else:
24.    timeDifference = duration - userDuration
25.    if timeDifference<=0.50:
26.      print("Your Score: 50pts!")
27.    elif timeDifference<=1:
28.      print("Your Score: 25pts!")
29.    elif timeDifference<=2:
30.      print("Your Score: 10pts!")
31.    else:
32.      print("Your Score: 0pt!")
```

The Unix epoch (or Unix time or POSIX time or Unix timestamp) is the number of seconds that have elapsed since January 1, 1970 (midnight GMT).

This explains how date & time values are actually stored on computers: using an integer value representing the number of seconds since 01/01/1970 00:00:00 GMT. Note that a negative value would represent a date prior to 01/01/1970.

You can check the Unix Epoch Timestamp of the current date and time at the web address provided below.

Web Address

https://www.101computing.net/epochunix-timestamp-converter/

Human Readable Date to Epoch Date Converter:

Our first challenge is to write a Python script to convert a date entered in a human readable format e.g. DD/MM/YYYY HH:MM:SS as an input and output the date using the Epoch/Unix Timestamp.

To do so you will need to calculate the number of seconds elapsed between the date given and 01/01/1970 00:00:00.

To simplify our calculations we will make the following assumptions:

- There are 365.25 days in a year.
- There are 30.44 days in a month (on average).
- There are 24 hours in a day.
- There are 60 minutes in an hour.
- There are 60 seconds in a minute.

```
1.  #Epoch/Unix - Timestamp Converter
2.
3.  datetime = input("Enter a date in the DD/MM/YYYY HH:MM:SS")
4.
5.  dateandtime = datetime.split(" ")
6.  date = dateandtime[0]
7.  time = dateandtime[1]
8.
9.  yearmonthday = date.split("/")
10. day = int(yearmonthday[0])
11. month = int(yearmonthday[1])
12. year = int(yearmonthday[2])
13.
14. hoursminutesseconds = time.split(":")
15. hours = int(hoursminutesseconds[0])
16. minutes = int(hoursminutesseconds[1])
17. seconds = int(hoursminutesseconds[2])
18.
19. #Caculate the UNIX Epoch timestamp (number of seconds since
    01/01/1970)
20. #Without using the datetime library!
21. timestamp = seconds
22. timestamp += minutes * 60
23. timestamp += hours * 3600
24. timestamp += (day-1) * 24 * 3600
25. timestamp += (month-1) * 30.44 * 24 * 3600
26. timestamp += (year-1970) * 365.25 * 24 * 3600
27.
28. print("Timestamp approximation: " + str(int(timestamp)))
```

Epoch Date to Human Readable Date Converter

Our second challenge is to work out and output an actual date in the DD/MM/YYYY HH:MM:SS format from an Epoch timestamp.

```
1.  #Epoch/Unix - Timestamp Converter -
    www.101computing.net/epochunix-timestamp-converter/
2.
3.  timestamp = int(input("Enter UNIX timestamp:"))
4.
```

```
5.  #Convert the UNIX timestamp is a DD/MM/YYYY HH:MM:SS format

6.  #Without using the datetime library
7.
8.  years = int(1970 + timestamp // (365.25 * 24 * 3600))
9.  remainder = timestamp % (365.25 * 24 * 3600)
10.
11. months = int(1 + remainder // (30.44 * 24 * 3600))
12. remainder = remainder % (30.44 * 24 * 3600)
13.
14. days = int(1 + remainder // (24 * 3600))
15. remainder = remainder % (24 * 3600)
16.
17. hours = int(remainder // 3600)
18. remainder = remainder % 3600
19.
20. minutes = int(remainder // 60)
21. seconds = int(remainder % 60)
22.
23. datetime = str(days) + "/" + str(months) + "/" + str(years)
    + " " + str(hours) + ":" + str(minutes) + ":" + str(seconds)

24. print(datetime)
```

Chapter #8: File Handling Operations

Though variables and data structures such as lists and dictionaries are useful to temporary store values within our code, we sometimes need to access or save values into **external files**. This allows us to split the data from the actual code and to save data that will still be there even if the user quits the program. One approach to do this is to use a **text file**. The next few challenges will focus on:

- Reading, writing and appending data from/to a text file,
- Using CSV (Comma separated Values) files,
- Implementing a Linear Search and a Binary Search through a CSV file.

There have been 66 monarchs of England and Britain spread over a period of 1500 years.

For this Python challenge we will use a text file listing all of these monarchs in chronological order. We will then write a Python program to prompt the user to enter a year (between 757 and 2019) and our program will look up for the name of the monarch of England at the given date.

The text file this challenge is based on, is a CSV file (Comma separated Values) and contains one line per monarch. On each line it stores the year the reign started, the year it ended and the name of the monarch as follows:

StartYear,EndYear,Name

The text file is available at the web address provided below.

Our program will display the name of the monarch matching the year entered, and will also mention who was the previous monarch and the next monarch.

For instance the output of the program could be:

In 1192, the monarch of England was Richard I. His predecessor was Henry II up until 1189 and his successor was John whose reign started in 1199.

Web Address

https://www.101computing.net/kings-queens-of-england/

Python Code

```
1.  #Kings & Queens of England
2.
3.  print("*****************************")
4.  print("*      Kings & Queens      *")
5.  print("*        of England        *")
6.  print("*****************************")
7.  print("")
8.
```

```
 9. year=int(input("Enter a year between 757 and 2017:"))
10.
11. file = open("Monarchs-of-England.csv","r")
12.
13. monarch =""
14. predecessor = ""
15. successor = ""
16. findSuccessor = False
17. monarchFound = False
18.
19. #Linear search through each line of the text file
20. for line in file:
21.    #Extract the data
22.    fields = line.split(",")
23.    startOfReign = int(fields[0])
24.    endOfReign = int(fields[1])
25.    monarch = fields[2]
26.
27.    if findSuccessor == True:
28.       print("Their successor was " + monarch + " from " + str(
       startOfReign) + ".")
29.       findSuccessor = False #Carry on searching in case there
       are more than one monarch on that year
30.
31.    if startOfReign <= year and endOfReign >= year:
32.       monarchFound = True
33.       findSuccessor = True
34.
35.       print("In " + str(year) + " the monarch of England was "
       + monarch + ".")
36.       if predecessor!="":
37.          print("Their predecesor was " + predecessor + " up unt
       il " + str(startOfReign) + ".")
38.
39.    predecessor=monarch
40.
41. if not monarchFound:
42.    print("There was no monarch at this date")
43.
44. file.close()
```

71. Leaderboard

The aim of this challenge is to add a leaderboard functionality to one of our existing games or quizzes in order to:

- Store the player score at the end of the game,
- Add an option for the player to view the leaderboard showing the ten highest scores sorted in descending order.

For this challenge we will create a leaderboard using a text file. The leaderboard.txt file will use the following format:

player_name;score;

The code provided below consists of two procedures that can be used with any existing games with a basic scoring system.

Web Address

https://www.101computing.net/leaderboard/

Python Code

```
1.  #Leaderboard Challenge
2.
3.  #A function to add/store a user's score in a leaderboard.txt
    file
4.  def storeScore(username,score):
5.      file = open("leaderboard.txt","a")
6.      file.write(username + ";"+str(score)+";"+"\n")
7.      file.close()
8.
9.  #A function to display the top 10 scores from a leaderboard.
    txt file
10. def displayLeaderboard():
11.     file = open("leaderboard.txt","r")
12.     #Prepare the list (empty list to start with)
13.     scores = []
14.
15.     #Read through the text file line by line
16.     for eachLine in file:
17.         #Extract the data from the text file
```

```
18.              splitData=eachLine.split(";")
19.              if len(splitData)==3:
20.                  username = splitData[0]
21.                  userscore = int(splitData[1])
22.              #Append this data to the list of scores
23.                  scores.append([username,userscore])
24.
25.       file.close()
26.
27.       #Sort the list of scores in DESCENDING order
28.       sortedScores = sorted(scores,key=lambda sort: sort[1], r
          everse=True)
29.
30.       #only keep the top 10 scores:
31.       del sortedScores[10:]
32.
33.          #Output top 10 scores
34.       for score in sortedScores:
35.          print(score[0] + ": " + str(score[1]))
36.
37. #Testing both functions
38. storeScore("Jack", 12)
39. displayLeaderboard()
```

72. Football Results Tracker

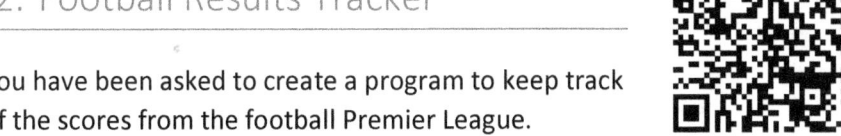

You have been asked to create a program to keep track of the scores from the football Premier League.

Your program will store match results in a text file using the following format:

home team;away team;home score;away score;

For instance, after a few games your text file may contain the following information:

Chelsea;Everton;2;0;
Liverpool;Arsenal;4;0;
Crystal Palace;Swansea City;0;2;
Newcastle United;West Ham United;3;0;

Manchester United;Leicester City;2;0;
Manchester City;Everton;1;1;
Swansea City;Manchester United;0;4;
Liverpool;Crystal Palace;1;0;

Your program will include three options to choose from:

Option 1: Adding new scores

Your program should include an option to input and append a new line / match score to the text file. To do so the program will:

- Ask the user to input the name of the Home team,
- Ask the user to input the name of the Away team,
- Ask the user to input the Home Score (number of goals scored by the home team.),
- Ask the user to input the Away Score (number of goals scored by the away team.),
- Append all this information at the end of the text file.

Option 2: Display all results

Create another option where the program will display all the scores on screen using the following format:

Home Team – Home Score:Away Score – Away Team

Option 3: Search for a team and display its results and total league points:

The program will:

- Allow the user to enter a team name to display all the results of this team.
- Calculate and display the number of points of a team; knowing that a team scores 3 points for a win, 1 point for a draw and 0 points for a loss.

Web Address

https://www.101computing.net/football-results-tracker/

```
1.  #Football Results Tracker
2.  def displayBanner():
3.    print("  _____  ")
4.    print("  |                       |  ")
5.    print("  |     Premier League    |  ")
6.    print("  |     Results Tracker   |  ")
7.    print("  |                       |  ")
8.    print("__|_____|___")
9.    print("")
10.
11. def displayMenu():
12.   print("")
13.   print(" > Option 1: Add a new match score")
14.   print(" > Option 2: Display all scores")
15.   print(" > Option 3: Search all scores of a team")
16.   print(" > Option 4: Exit")
17.   print("")
18.
19. def addScore():
20.   print("\n--- Adding New Score ---\n")
21.   homeTeam = input("Type the name of the home team:")
22.   awayTeam = input("Type the name of the away team:")
23.   homeScore = input("How many goals for " + homeTeam + "?")

24.   awayScore = input("How many goals for " + awayTeam + "?")

25.
26.   #Append data at the end of the text file
27.   file = open("results.txt","a")
28.   file.write("\n" + homeTeam + ";" + awayTeam + ";" + homeSc
      ore + ";" + awayScore + ";")
29.   file.close()
30.   print("Your match score has now been added.")
31.
32. def displayResults():
33.   #Output all scores stored in the text file
34.   print("\n--- All Scores ---\n")
35.   file = open("results.txt","r")
36.   for line in file:
37.     data = line.split(";")
38.     homeTeam = data[0]
39.     awayTeam = data[1]
40.     homeScore = data[2]
41.     awayScore = data[3]
42.     print(homeTeam + " -
      " + homeScore + ":" + awayScore + " - " + awayTeam)
```

180

```
43.    file.close()
44.
45. def displayTeamPoints():
46.    print("\n--- Team Scores ---\n")
47.    team = input("Type the name of a team:")
48.    points = 0
49.    numberOfGamesPlayed = 0
50.
51.    #Display all scores of a given team using a linear search
52.    file = open("results.txt","r")
53.    for line in file:
54.      data = line.split(";")
55.      homeTeam = data[0]
56.      awayTeam = data[1]
57.      if team == homeTeam or team==awayTeam:
58.        numberOfGamesPlayed += 1
59.        homeScore = int(data[2])
60.        awayScore = int(data[3])
61.        print(homeTeam + " -
    " + str(homeScore) + ":" + str(awayScore) + " -
    " + awayTeam)
62.        if homeScore == awayScore: #It's a draw
63.          points += 1
64.        elif homeScore>awayScore and team == homeTeam: #It's a
    win at home!
65.          points += 3
66.        elif awayScore>homeScore and team == awayTeam: #It's a
    win against the home team!
67.          points += 3
68.    file.close()
69.    print(team + " played " + str(numberOfGamesPlayed) + " gam
    e(s).")
70.    print(team + " has " + str(points) + " point(s) so far.")
71.
72. #Main Program Starts Here
73. displayBanner()
74. displayMenu()
75.
76. while True:
77.    choice = input("\nChoose an option between 1 and 4.")
78.    if choice == "1":
79.      addScore()
80.    elif choice == "2":
81.      displayResults()
82.    elif choice == "3":
83.      displayTeamPoints()
84.    elif choice == "4":
85.      print("Good bye!")
86.      break
```

181

73. Italian Takeaway Ordering System

An Italian takeaway is asking us to write a computer program to facilitate the ordering process and automatically calculate the total cost of an order.

They have stored their menu and all prices into a text file which you will find at the web address provided below. The file contains the following information:

Code;Description;Price;

When a customer orders food, they give the lists of codes they would like to order. For instance a customer could order the following:

S4,P3,P7,X2,D4,C1,W2

Our program should allow the customer to order as many options from the menu as they need. For each option, it should look up the price in the text file provided. It should then calculate and output the total cost of the order.

Web Address

https://www.101computing.net/italian-takeaway-ordering-system/

Python Code

```
1.  #Italian Takeaway Ordering System
2.  print(" ~~~~~~~~~~~~~~~~~~~~~~~~~~ ")
3.  print("|    Italian Takeway       |")
4.  print("|    Ordering System       |")
5.  print(" ~~~~~~~~~~~~~~~~~~~~~~~~~~ ")
6.  print("")
7.  print("Welcome to our takeway ordering system.")
8.  print("Type X to exit.")
9.
10. code = input("Enter the option code you would like to order:
    (e.g.P1)")
11.
12. file = open("food-menu.txt","r")
13.
14. totalCost = 0
```

```
15. while (code!="X"):
16.     #Start Linear search through the text file
17.     itemFound=False
18.     for line in file:
19.         #Extract the data stored on this line
20.         data = line.split(";")
21.         itemCode = data[0]
22.         itemDescription = data[1]
23.         itemPrice = float(data[2])
24.
25.         #Is this the item we are looking for?
26.         if itemCode == code:
27.             itemFound=True
28.             print(itemCode + " - " + itemDescription + " -
    £" + str(itemPrice))
29.             totalCost = totalCost + itemPrice
30.
31.     if not itemFound:
32.         print("Item code does not exist.")
33.     code = input("Enter another code or X to exit.")
34.
35. print("Total cost of your order: £" + str(totalCost))
36. print("Good bye!")
37.
38. file.close()
```

74. London Bus Timetable

For this challenge, we will write a Python script to extract relevant information from a bus timetable to help end-users plan their journey. The timetable is saved as a text file available at the web address provided below.

Bus Stops	Day Times						
St Paul's Cathedral	08:34	10:00	11:45	13:45	14:30	16:30	18:36
Tower Of London	08:46	10:12	11:57	13:57	14:42	16:42	18:48
Tower Bridge	08:48	10:14	11:59	13:59	14:44	16:44	18:50
The Shard	08:56	10:22	12:07	14:07	14:52	16:52	18:58
Tate Modern	09:03	10:29	12:14	14:14	14:59	16:59	19:05
London Eye	09:12	10:38	12:23	14:23	15:08	17:08	19:14
Westminster	09:17	10:43	12:28	14:28	15:13	17:13	19:19
Downing Street	09:23	10:49	12:34	14:34	15:19	17:19	19:25
Buckingham Palace	09:30	10:56	12:41	14:41	15:26	17:26	19:32
Hyde Park	09:38	11:04	12:49	14:49	15:34	17:34	19:40
Oxford Circus	09:45	11:11	12:56	14:56	15:41	17:41	19:47
Piccadilly Circus	09:51	11:17	13:02	15:02	15:47	17:47	19:53
Covent Garden	10:03	11:29	13:14	15:14	15:59	17:59	20:05

Our program will

- Ask the user for the bus station they will take the bus from,
- Ask the user at what time they will be at the bus station,
- Ask the user where do they want to go,
- Load the content of the above timetable into a two-dimensional array (list of lists in Python) called timetable.
- Find out and output the earliest time the user can reach their destination.

Web Address

https://www.101computing.net/london-bus-timetable/

Python Code

```
1.  #London Bus Timetable - Journey Planner
2.
3.  timetable = []
4.  file = open("bus-timetable.csv","r")
5.  for line in file:
6.      #Remove New Line Character
7.      line = line[:-1]
8.      #Split the line into a list of values
9.      stationTimes = line.split(",")
```

```
10.    #Append this data to our timetable 2D list
11.    timetable.append(stationTimes)
12.
13. file.close()
14.
15. #Retrieve user Inputs (From / To Stations, Departure time)
16. stationFrom = input("Departure Station:")
17. stationTo = input("Arrival Station:")
18. startTime = input("Depart after (enter a time e.g. 9:30):")

19. startTimeHours = int(startTime.split(":")[0])
20. startTimeMinutes = int(startTime.split(":")[1])
21.
22. stationFromFound = False
23. stationToFound = False
24. timeFound = False
25.
26. #Retrieve departure and arrival time
27. column = 0
28. for station in timetable:
29.   if stationFrom == station[0]:
30.       stationFromFound = True
31.       departTime = ""
32.       for i in range(1,len(station)):
33.           timeHours = int(station[i].split(":")[0])
34.           timeMinutes = int(station[i].split(":")[1])
35.           if timeFound==False:
36.              departTime = station[i]
37.              column = i
38.              if timeHours<startTimeHours:
39.                 timeFound = False
40.              elif timeHours==startTimeHours and timeMinutes<=
    startTimeMinutes:
41.                 timeFound = False
42.              else:
43.                 timeFound=True
44.
45.   if stationTo == station[0] and column>0:
46.     stationToFound = True
47.     arriveTime = station[column]
48.
49. #Output findings
50. if stationFromFound==False:
51.   print("Departure station not found!")
52. else:
53.   if stationToFound==False:
54.     print("Arrival station not found!")
55.   else:
56.     if timeFound==False:
```

185

```
57.        print("There is no more bus leaving " + stationFrom +
    " at this time of the day.")
58.    else:
59.        print("Your Journey:")
60.        print("Depart from " + stationFrom + " at " + departTi
    me)
61.        print("Arrive at " + stationTo + " at " + arriveTime)
```

75. Professor Snape's Magic Potions

In this challenge we will use file handling techniques to read through and access the content of different text files.

We have saved three recipes for the following three magic potions using one text file per recipe:

- **Invisibility Potion:** A potion that makes you invisible for a short period of time.
- **Aging Potion:** A potion which causes the drinker to temporarily become older. The more of the potion is drunk, the larger the aging which occurs.
- **Poison Antidote:** A potion which counteracts ordinary poisons, such as creature bites and stings

The three text files for these potions are available at the web address provided below.

Our program will display a menu to let the user decide which potion to display on screen. Based on the user's choice, the program will open the relevant text file and display the recipe on screen.

Web Address

https://www.101computing.net/professor-snape-s-magic-potions/

```
1.  #Professor Snape's Magic Potions
2.
3.  print("#~~~~~~~~~~~~~~~~~~~~~~~~~~~~~~~~#")
4.  print("#          Magic Potions        #")
5.  print("#             Recipes           #")
6.  print("#~~~~~~~~~~~~~~~~~~~~~~~~~~~~~~~~#")
7.  print("")
8.
9.  def readPotionFile(filename):
10.   #Open text file in read mode
11.   file = open(filename,"r")
12.
13.   step=1
14.   #Read and display each line one by one
15.   for line in file:
16.     print("Step " + str(step) + ":")
17.     print("    " + line)
18.     step = step + 1
19.
20.   #Close the text file
21.   file.close()
22.
23. ##########################################
24. #          Main Program Starts Here         #
25. ##########################################
26. print("1 - Invisibilty Potion")
27. print("2 - Poison Antidote")
28. print("3 - Aging Potion")
29. option = input("Which potion would you like to display: 1 -
    3? ")
30.
31. if option=="1":
32.   print("#~~~ Invisibility Potion ~~~#")
33.   readPotionFile("invisibility-potion.txt")
34. elif option=="2":
35.   print("#~~~ Poison antidote ~~~#")
36.   readPotionFile("poison-antidote.txt")
37. elif option=="3":
38.   print("#~~~ Aging Potion ~~~#")
39.   readPotionFile("aging-potion.txt")
40. else:
41.   print("Invalid option!")
```

76. US Presidents Quiz

Since the establishment of the United States of America, in 1789, 45 people have served as president, the first one being George Washington.

For this challenge we will use a text file listing all of these US presidents in chronological order. (The text file is available at the web address provided below). We will then write a Python program to randomly pick two presidents from this list of 45 presidents. Our program will display the name of both presidents and ask the end-user who is the most recent president amongst the two presidents being displayed. For instance the program will output the following question:

Who was the most recent president?
A) John F. Kennedy or B) Richard Nixon.

The game carries on as long as the user is correct. For each correct answer the user will score 10 points. The game ends once the user gets a wrong answer.

Web Address

https://www.101computing.net/us-presidents-quiz/

Python Code

```
1.  #US Presidents Quiz
2.  import random
3.
4.  print("xxxxxxxxxxxxxxxxxxxxxxxxxxxxxxx")
5.  print("x      US Presidents      x")
6.  print("x         Quiz            x")
7.  print("xxxxxxxxxxxxxxxxxxxxxxxxxxxxxxx")
8.  print("")
9.
10. file=open("us-presidents.csv")
11. #Stores all the content of the text file into a list
12. listOfPresidents = file.readlines()
13. file.close()
14.
15. round=1
```

```
16. score=0
17. while True:
18.    print("Round " + str(round) + ":")
19.    #Pick a president from the list, at random
20.    line = random.choice(listOfPresidents)
21.    #Split the fields
22.    president=line.split(",")
23.    number1 = president[0]
24.    name1 = president[1]
25.    dateFrom1 = president[2]
26.    dateTo1 = president[3]
27.
28.    #Now let's pick a second president, ensuring it's not the
   same as the first one!
29.    number2=number1
30.    while number2==number1:
31.       line = random.choice(listOfPresidents)
32.       #Split the fields
33.       president=line.split(",")
34.       number2 = president[0]
35.       name2 = president[1]
36.       dateFrom2 = president[2]
37.       dateTo2 = president[3]
38.
39.    #Ask the question to the end-user
40.    print("Who was the most recent president?")
41.    answer = input("A - " + name1 + " or B -
   " + name2).upper()
42.
43.    print(name1 + " was president from " + dateFrom1 + " to "
   + dateTo1 + ".")
44.    print(name2 + " was president from " + dateFrom2 + " to "
   + dateTo2 + ".")
45.
46.    #Check if the user is right
47.    if answer=="A" and dateFrom1>dateFrom2:
48.       print("You are correct!")
49.       score+=10
50.       print("Your Score: " + str(score))
51.    elif answer=="B" and dateFrom1<dateFrom2:
52.       print("You are correct!")
53.       score+=10
54.       print("Your Score: " + str(score))
55.    elif answer=="A" and dateFrom1==dateFrom2 and dateTo1>date
   To2:
56.       print("You are correct!")
57.       score+=10
58.       print("Your Score: " + str(score))
```

189

```
59.    elif answer=="B" and dateFrom1==dateFrom2 and dateTo1<date
       To2:
60.        print("You are correct!")
61.        score+=10
62.        print("Your Score: " + str(score))
63.    else:
64.        print("Wrong guess!")
65.        break
66.
67. print("Game Over!")
68. print("Your Final Score: " + str(score))
```

77. Monopoly Quiz

For this challenge we will create a quiz based on the game of Monopoly.

The computer will randomly display a street name from the list of streets used in the game and the user will have to guess the colour used in the game for the selected street.

The user will score one point per correct answer and will be asked to guess the colour of ten different streets, one at a time. At the end the user will be given their score out of ten.

Our game will also include a menu option at the beginning to ask the user if they want to play with the UK, US or French Monopoly.

When the quiz is over our program will also ask the user to enter their name and store their name and final score in a leaderboard text file.

You will find at the web address provided below three text files containing all the street names and colours based on the UK, US and French game of monopoly.

Web Address

https://www.101computing.net/monopoly-quiz/

```
1.  #Monopoly Quiz
2.  import random
3.
4.  def quiz(file):
5.      #Extract all the data from the text file
6.      file = open(file,"r")
7.      lines = file.readlines()
8.      file.close
9.
10.     score = 0
11.     #Repeat 10 times
12.     for round in range(1,11):
13.         print("Round " + str(round) + ":")
14.         #Select a random line from the file
15.         randomLine = random.choice(lines)
16.         #Split the two pieces of data, streetname and colour usi
    ng the ; as separator
17.         data = randomLine.split(";")
18.         streetName = data[0]
19.         colour = data[1].lower()
20.
21.         #Ask the user to answer a question
22.         userGuess=input("What colour is " + streetName + "?").lo
    wer()
23.
24.         #Complete the code here to check if the user guess is co
    rrect.
25.         if userGuess==colour:
26.             score+=1
27.             print("Correct")
28.         else:
29.             print("Incorrect")
30.
31.     print("Game Over")
32.     print("Final Score: " + str(score) + "ouf of 10")
33.     #Append Score to leaderboard file:
34.     username = input("Enter your name:")
35.     file = open("leaderboard.txt","a")
36.     file.write(username + ";" + str(score) + ";")
37.     file.close()
38.
39. #Main Program Starts Here
40. print("$-$-$-$-$-$-$-$-$-$-$")
41. print("$                   $")
42. print("$    Monopoly Quiz   $")
43. print("$                   $")
```

```
44. print("$-$-$-$-$-$-$-$-$-$-$")
45. print("")
46.
47. option=""
48. while option not in ["UK","US","French"]:
49.    option = input("Would like to play with a UK, US or French
       monopoly?")
50.
51. if option=="UK":
52.    quiz("UK-monopoly.txt")
53. elif option=="US":
54.    quiz("US-monopoly.txt")
55. elif option=="French":
56.    quiz("French-monopoly.txt")
```

78. Real-Time ISS Tracker

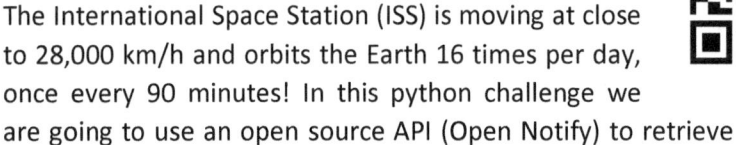

The International Space Station (ISS) is moving at close to 28,000 km/h and orbits the Earth 16 times per day, once every 90 minutes! In this python challenge we are going to use an open source API (Open Notify) to retrieve some real-time data from NASA about the location of the ISS.

We will first make a call to the API to retrieve the current location (longitude and latitude) of the ISS.

Then we will use the API to retrieve and display the date and time of the next five passes of the ISS over Paris, France (longitude: 45.51° N, latitude: 2.20° E).

You can read more about the API on: http://open-notify.org/Open-Notify-API/

Web Address

https://www.101computing.net/real-time-iss-tracker/

Web Address: Open Notify API

http://open-notify.org/Open-Notify-API/

```
1.  #Real Time ISS Tracker
2.  import json, urllib.request, time
3.
4.  #A first JSON request to retrieve the current longitude and
    latitude of the IIS space station (real time)
5.  url = "http://api.open-notify.org/iss-now.json"
6.  response = urllib.request.urlopen(url)
7.  result = json.loads(response.read())
8.
9.  #Let's extract the required information
10. location =result["iss_position"]
11. lat = location["latitude"]
12. lon = location["longitude"]
13.
14. #Output informationon screen
15. print("Current Position of the ISS:")
16. print("Latitude: " + str(lat))
17. print("Longitude: " +str(lon))
18.
19. #Paris Location
20. latitude = 48.8
21. longitude = 2.20
22.
23. url = "http://api.open-notify.org/iss-
    pass.json?lat=" + str(latitude) + "&lon=" + str(longitude) +
    "&n=5"
24. response = urllib.request.urlopen(url)
25. result = json.loads(response.read())
26. passes = result["response"]
27.
28. print("The ISS will pass above Paris on:")
29. for p in passes:
30.     risetime = p["risetime"]
31.     duration = p["duration"]
32.     minutes = duration//60
33.     seconds = duration%60
34.     datetime = time.strftime('%A, %Y-%m-
    %d %H:%M:%S', time.localtime(risetime))
35.     print(datetime + " for " + str(minutes) + " minutes and "
    + str(seconds) + " seconds.")
```

79. Currency Converter

Our aim is to create a currency converter to help us convert a sum of money from one currency to another.

Currency exchange rates are constantly changing which is why we have decided against the idea of storing all the exchanges rates in our code are these would not remain up-to-date. Instead we will retrieve up-to-date currency exchange rates by making calls to an API that provides the current rates.

To do so we will use the "Currency Converter API" to retrieve up-to-date exchange rates. You can read more about this API on: https://currencyconverterapi.com/. For the purpose of this blog post we will use the free version of this API.

Note that the Open Notify API uses JSON to format the data. JSON (JavaScript Object Notation) is a popular lightweight data-interchange format. Its main benefit is that it is easy for humans to read and write and it is easy for machines to parse and generate as you can see in the code provided below. You can read more about JSON on https://www.json.org/

Web Address

https://www.101computing.net/currency-converter/

Python Code

```
1.  #Currency Converter
2.  import json, urllib.request
3.
4.  #See full lists of valid currencies on https://free.currency
    converterapi.com/api/v6/currencies
5.  validCurrencies = []
6.
7.  #Display banner and list of valid currencies
8.  print("$£¥€$£¥€$£¥€$£¥€$£¥€$£¥€$£¥€$£¥€$£¥€")
9.  print("$£¥€                            $£¥€")
10. print("$£¥€      Currency Converter     $£¥€")
11. print("$£¥€                            $£¥€")
12. print("$£¥€$£¥€$£¥€$£¥€$£¥€$£¥€$£¥€$£¥€$£¥€")
```

```
13. print("")
14. print("List of currencies: ")
15. url = "https://free.currencyconverterapi.com/api/v6/currenci
    es"
16. response = urllib.request.urlopen(url)
17. result = json.loads(response.read())
18. currencies = result["results"]
19. for currency in currencies:
20.   print(currencies[currency]["id"] + " -
      " + currencies[currency]["currencyName"])
21.   validCurrencies.append(currency)
22. print("")
23.
24. #Initialise key variables
25. currencyFrom = ""
26. currencyTo = ""
27. amount = 0
28.
29. #Retrieve user inputs
30. while not currencyFrom in validCurrencies:
31.   currencyFrom = input("Enter Currency to convert From: (e.g
      . GBP)").upper()
32.
33. while not currencyTo in validCurrencies:
34.   currencyTo = input("Enter Currency to convert To: (e.g. EU
      R)").upper()
35.
36. amount = float(input("Enter amount to convert: (e.g. 10.00)"
    ))
37.
38. #A JSON request to retrieve the required exchange rate
39. url = "https://free.currencyconverterapi.com/api/v6/convert?
    q="+currencyFrom + "_" + currencyTo +"&compact=y"
40. response = urllib.request.urlopen(url)
41. result = json.loads(response.read())
42.
43. #Let's extract the required information
44. exchangeRate=result[currencyFrom + "_" + currencyTo]
45. rate = exchangeRate["val"]
46.
47. #Output exchange rate and converted amount
48. print("")
49. print("Exchange rate: 1 " + currencyFrom + " = " + str(rate)
      + " " + currencyTo)
50. print(str(amount) + " " + currencyFrom + " = " + ("{0:.2f}".
      format(amount*rate)) + " " + currencyTo)
```

80. Break Even Point

In Business or Economics the Break Even Point (BEP) is the point at which the total of fixed and variable costs of a business becomes equal to its total revenue. At this point, a business neither earns any profit nor suffers any loss. The following graph explains all the concepts used to find out the break even point:

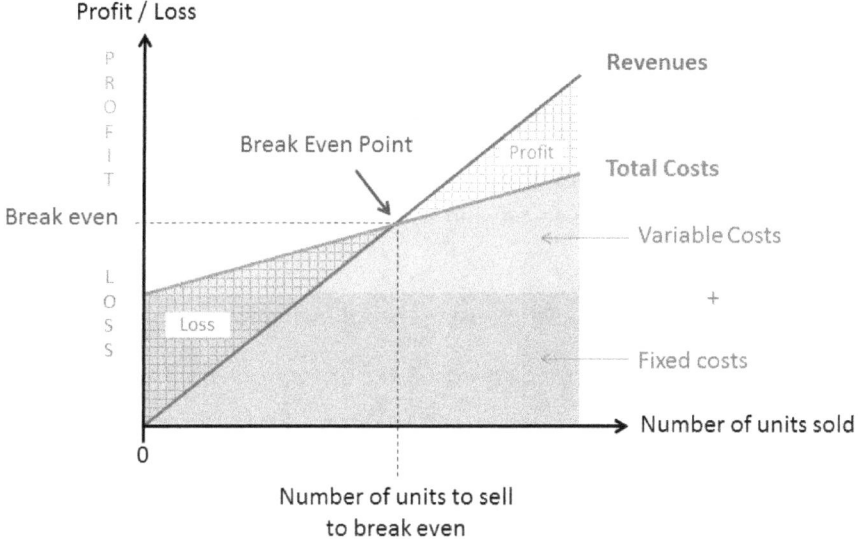

Let's consider an online bakery that specialises in selling Birthday Cakes online. The owner of the bakery has estimated all the costs involved and grouped them into two categories:

- Fixed Costs: These costs will remain the same and do not vary depending on the number of cakes being sold. They include:
  o The rent,
  o Purchasing Cooking Equipment,
  o Utility Bills,
  o Website (Setup and maintenance/hosting).
- Variable Costs: These costs will vary depending on the number of cakes being sold. They include:

- o Ingredients,
- o Packaging,
- o Delivery Fees.

The total costs of this online bakery consist of the fixed costs plus the variable costs and can be calculated using the following formula:

Total Costs = fixed costs + (variable costs x number of cakes sold)

The revenues of this online bakery consist of the money received when selling cakes. They can be calculated using the following formula:

Revenues = average cake price x number of cakes sold

The question we are trying to answer is as follows:

What is the break even point of this online bakery? In other words, how many cakes will need to be sold to cover all the costs and start making a profit?

We can answer this question using the following formula:

Number of Cakes to break even = Fixed Costs / (Average Price – Variable Costs)

For this challenge, we have listed all the costs of our online bakery, both fixed and variable into a text file that you will find at the web address provided below. The text file we will use contains one line per cost as follows:

Description;Type of cost (fixed cost or variable cost);Value (in pounds);

The average price per cake is £16.00.

We will use a Python program to extract the relevant information from the text file in order to:

- Calculate the sum of all fixed costs.
- Calculate the sum of all variable costs.

- Find out the break even point for this business: how many cakes will need to be sold to cover all the costs and start making a profit?

Web Address

https://www.101computing.net/break-even-point/

Python Code

```
1.  #Break Even Point
2.
3.  print("****************************")
4.  print("*      Break Even Point    *")
5.  print("*         Calculator       *")
6.  print("****************************")
7.  print("")
8.
9.  #Initialise key variables
10. averageCakePrice = 16
11. fixedCosts = 0
12. variableCosts = 0
13.
14. #Retrieve all costs from the text file
15. file = open("costs.txt","r")
16.
17. for line in file:
18.    data = line.split(";")
19.    if data[1]=="fixed cost":
20.       fixedCosts += float(data[2])
21.    elif data[2]=="variable cost":
22.       variableCosts += float(data[2])
23.
24. file.close()
25.
26. #Calculate Break Even Point
27. breakEvenPoint = int(fixedCosts / (averageCakePrice -
    variableCosts))
28.
29. #Output Findings:
30. print("Fixed Costs: £" + str(fixedCosts))
31. print("Variable Costs: £" + str(variableCosts))
32. print("Average Cake Price: £" + str(averageCakePrice))
33. print("To break even, the bakery will need to sell " + str(b
    reakEvenPoint) + " cakes.")
```

Chapter #9: 2D and 3D Representation

Most of our challenges so far have been based on a text-based interface. At this stage you are most likely longing to create your own programs or video games based on a Graphical User Interface. Before doing so though we recommend you to gain a very good understanding of how **(x,y) and (x,y,z) coordinates** can be used within a Python program to draw 2D or 3D shapes on the screen. The following challenges will help you investigate the following concepts:

- Python Turtle,
- (x,y) Coordinates,
- (x,y,z) Coordinates.

Challenges 81 to 98 are based on the **Python Turtle library**, included per default in the Python package.

Challenges 99 and 100 are based on the **Processing library** which enables to work on 2D/3D projects with Python. You can find out more about the Processing library for Python on:
http://py.processing.org/

81. The Honeycomb Challenge

Honeycomb is a structure of hexagonal cavities (cells of wax), made by bees to store honey and eggs.

In this challenge we will use a set of iterative algorithms to draw a honeycomb pattern.

First, we will create a function to draw a single hexagonal cavity. Our function called *drawCavity()* will take three parameters:

- x – the x coordinates to position the hexagon.
- y – the x coordinates to position the hexagon.
- edgeLength – the length in pixels of an edge of the hexagon.

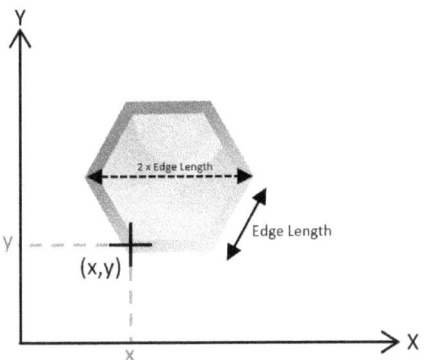

We will then need to use some nested for loops in order to tessellate the hexagonal cell to recreate a 2D honeycomb pattern.

Web Address

https://www.101computing.net/honeycomb-challenge/

Python Code

```
1.  #The honeycomb challenge
2.  import turtle
3.  myPen = turtle.Turtle()
4.  myPen.shape("arrow")
5.
```

```
6.  mypen.color("#a86f14")
7.  mypen.fillcolor("#efb456")
8.  mypen.pensize(2)
9.  mypen.tracer(0)
10. mypen.speed(0)
11.
12. #A Procedue to draw a pentagonal cavity at a given (x,y) pos
    ition.
13. def drawCavity(x,y,edgeLength):
14.   mypen.penup()
15.   mypen.goto(x,y)
16.   mypen.pendown()
17.   mypen.begin_fill()
18.   for i in range(0,6):
19.       mypen.forward(edgeLength)
20.       mypen.left(60)
21.   mypen.end_fill()
22.
23.
24. #Main Program Starts Here
25. #Comlpete this code to draw a full honeycomb pattern
26. for y in range(150,-150,-int(20*3**0.5)):
27.   for x in range(-150,150,60):
28.       drawCavity(x,y,20)
29.       drawCavity(x+30,y-10*3**0.5,20)
30.
31. mypen.hideturtle()
32. mypen.getscreen().update()
```

82. The Pizzaiolo's Puzzle

A pizzaiolo (a man who makes pizza) has been asked to produce a very large pizza, to sprinkle some Parmesan cheese evenly on the pizza and to spread a full jar of black olives (approximately 80 olives) on the pizza.

He has decided to find a method to evenly spread the olives on the pizza to ensure that:

- the olives cover the entire pizza,
- the olives are relatively equidistant from each other.

After doing some research online, our pizzaiolo came across the following webpage about Fermat's Spiral, and was captivated to find out about how the Vogel's model could be used to calculate the polar coordinates of each olive to be added to his pizza:

$$r = c \sqrt{n}$$

$$\theta = 137.508\,n$$

Vogel's Model

- Where θ is the angle,
- r is the radius or distance from the centre,
- n is the index number of the olive,
- c is a constant scaling factor,
- The angle 137.508° is the golden angle which is approximated by ratios of Fibonacci numbers.

In this challenge we are using Python Turtle to draw a pizza and we are applying Vogel's model to evenly spread olives, pepperoni slices and parmesan cheese on our pizza.

Web Address

https://www.101computing.net/the-pizzaiolos-puzzle/

Python Code

```
1.  #The Pizzaiolo's Puzzle
2.  import turtle
3.  import math
4.  from random import randint
5.
6.  myPen = turtle.Turtle()
7.  myPen.tracer(0)
8.  myPen.speed(0)
9.  screen = turtle.Screen()
10. screen.bgcolor("#FFFFFF")
11. myPen.penup()
12. myPen.goto(0,0)
```

```
13.
14. def drawPizza(x,y,radius):
15.    myPen.penup()
16.    myPen.goto(x,y-radius)
17.    myPen.pendown()
18.    myPen.color("#f4c542")
19.    myPen.pensize(6)
20.    myPen.fillcolor("#c42513")
21.    myPen.begin_fill()
22.    myPen.circle(radius)
23.    myPen.end_fill()
24.
25. def drawOlive(x,y,radius):
26.    myPen.pensize(1)
27.    myPen.penup()
28.    myPen.goto(x,y-radius)
29.    myPen.pendown()
30.    myPen.color("#000000")
31.    myPen.fillcolor("#000000")
32.    myPen.begin_fill()
33.    myPen.circle(radius)
34.    myPen.end_fill()
35.
36. def drawParmesan(x,y,radius):
37.    myPen.pensize(1)
38.    myPen.penup()
39.    myPen.goto(x,y-radius)
40.    myPen.pendown()
41.    myPen.color("#f1f94d")
42.    myPen.fillcolor("#f1f94d")
43.    myPen.begin_fill()
44.    myPen.circle(radius)
45.    myPen.end_fill()
46.
47. def drawPepperoni(x,y,radius):
48.    myPen.pensize(1)
49.    myPen.penup()
50.    myPen.goto(x,y-radius)
51.    myPen.pendown()
52.    myPen.pensize(1)
53.    myPen.color("#700313")
54.    myPen.fillcolor("#8c091d")
55.    myPen.begin_fill()
56.    myPen.circle(radius)
57.    myPen.end_fill()
58.
59. #Draw the Pizza
60. drawPizza(0,0,180)
61.
```

```
62. c=26 #scaling factor
63. for n in range(40):
64.    #Generate Polar Coordinates using Vogel's Model
65.    r = c*(n**0.5)
66.    teta = n*137.508
67.    #Convert polar coordinates to Cartesian coordinates using
       trigonometric formulas (SOHCAHTOA)
68.    x = r*math.cos(math.radians(teta))
69.    y = r*math.sin(math.radians(teta))
70.    drawPepperoni(x,y,14)
71.
72. c=18 #scaling factor
73. for n in range(80):
74.    #Generate Polar Coordinates using Vogel's Model
75.    r = c*(n**0.5)
76.    teta = n*137.508
77.    #Convert polar coordinates to Cartesian coordinates using
       trigonometric formulas (SOHCAHTOA)
78.    x = r*math.cos(math.radians(teta))
79.    y = r*math.sin(math.radians(teta))
80.    drawOlive(x,y,4)
81.
82. c=10 #scaling factor
83. for n in range(300):
84.    #Generate Polar Coordinates using Vogel's Model
85.    r = c*(n**0.5)
86.    teta = n*137.508
87.    #Convert polar coordinates to Cartesian coordinates using
       trigonometric formulas (SOHCAHTOA)
88.    x = r*math.cos(math.radians(teta))
89.    y = r*math.sin(math.radians(teta))
90.    drawParmesan(x,y,1)
91.
92. myPen.hideturtle()
93. myPen.getscreen().update()
```

83. Darts Scoring Algorithm

The following diagram explains how a dart is allocated a score in a game of darts:

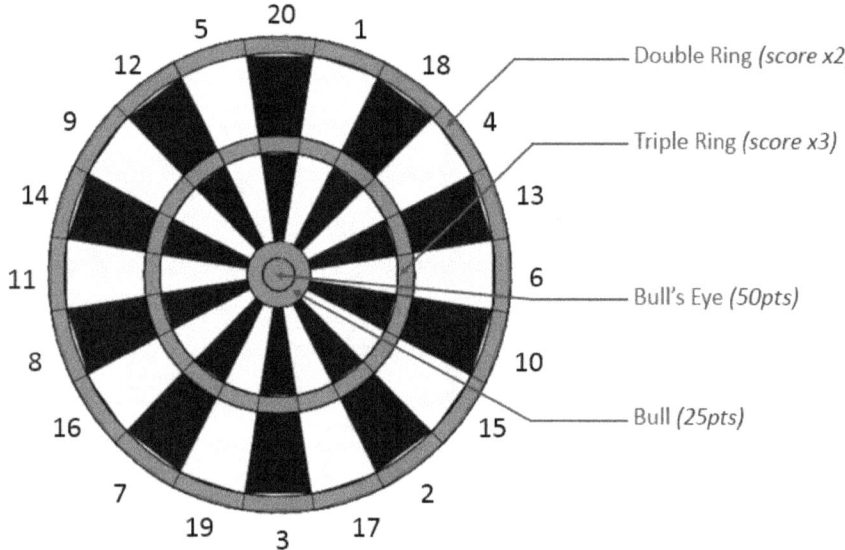

The code provided below uses Python Turtle to display a dartboard and to throw an arrow by generating random (x,y) coordinates. It then calculates both the distance from the centre of the board and the angle of the arrow based on its (x,y) coordinates. Finally, it uses this information to find out the actual score of the arrow.

Web Address

https://www.101computing.net/darts-scoring-algorithm/

Python Code

```
1.  #Darts Scoring Algorithm
2.  import turtle
3.  import random
4.  import math
5.
6.  def drawLayer(radius, color1, color2):
```

```
7.      angle = 18
8.      initialAngle=angle
9.      myPen.penup()
10.     myPen.setheading(180)
11.     myPen.goto(0,radius)
12.     myPen.circle(radius, angle//2) #move along arc
13.     myPen.pendown()
14.     i=0
15.
16.     while i <= 20 :
17.       myPen.begin_fill()
18.       myPen.circle(radius, angle) #move along arc
19.       myPen.left(90)
20.       myPen.forward(radius) # turtle now at centre
21.       myPen.left(180-initialAngle)
22.       myPen.forward(radius) # back on edge of circle
23.       myPen.left(90)
24.       myPen.speed(0)
25.       angle = initialAngle*2 # moves turtle to begin next pie
    shape
26.       i = i + 1
27.       if i %2 == 0 :
28.            myPen.fillcolor(color1)    # this conditional creat
    es the alernating pattern
29.       else :
30.            myPen.fillcolor(color2)
31.       myPen.end_fill()
32.
33. def drawTarget():
34.     drawLayer(144,"#FF0000","#099909")
35.     drawLayer(134,"#111111","#FFFFAA")
36.     drawLayer(84,"#FF0000","#099909")
37.     drawLayer(74,"#111111","#FFFFAA")
38.
39.     #Outer Bull
40.     myPen.fillcolor("#099909")
41.     myPen.penup()
42.     myPen.setheading(180)
43.     myPen.goto(0,20)
44.     myPen.begin_fill()
45.     myPen.pendown()
46.     myPen.circle(20)
47.     myPen.end_fill()
48.
49.     #Bull's Eye
50.     myPen.fillcolor("#FF0000")
51.     myPen.penup()
52.     myPen.setheading(180)
53.     myPen.goto(0,10)
```

```
54.    myPen.begin_fill()
55.    myPen.pendown()
56.    myPen.circle(10)
57.    myPen.end_fill()
58.
59. def drawCross(color, size, x, y):
60.    myPen.pensize(3)
61.    myPen.color(color)
62.    myPen.penup()
63.    myPen.goto(x-size,y-size)
64.    myPen.pendown()
65.    myPen.goto(x+size,y+size)
66.    myPen.penup()
67.    myPen.goto(x-size,y+size)
68.    myPen.pendown()
69.    myPen.goto(x+size,y-size)
70.
71. def writeScore(text):
72.    myPen.penup()
73.    myPen.goto(-80, 170)
74.    myPen.color("#000000")
75.    myPen.write(text, None, None, "16pt bold")
76.
77. def calculateScore(arrowx,arrowy):
78.    score = 0
79.    distance = 0
80.    #Add code here using Pythagoras formula to calculate the d
       istance to the centre.
81.    distance = (arrowx**2 + arrowy**2)**0.5
82.
83.    #Use SOCATOA to calculate the angle matching the arrow pos
       ition
84.    angle = math.degrees(math.atan2(arrowy,arrowx))
85.    if angle<0:
86.      angle+=360
87.
88.    #Use a collection of IF statements to calculate the score
       of the arrow based on the distance and angle
89.    if distance<=10: #Bull's Eyes
90.      score = 50
91.    elif distance<=20: #Bull
92.      score = 225
93.    elif distance>144: #Off target
94.      score = 0
95.    else: #On target
96.      if angle<=9 or angle>351:
97.        score = 6
98.      elif angle<=27:
99.        score = 13
```

207

```
100.              elif angle<=45:
101.                  score = 4
102.              elif angle<=63:
103.                  score = 18
104.              elif angle<=81:
105.                  score = 1
106.              elif angle<=99:
107.                  score = 20
108.              elif angle<=117:
109.                  score = 5
110.              elif angle<=135:
111.                  score = 12
112.              elif angle<=153:
113.                  score = 9
114.              elif angle<=171:
115.                  score = 14
116.              elif angle<=189:
117.                  score = 11
118.              elif angle<=207:
119.                  score = 8
120.              elif angle<=225:
121.                  score = 16
122.              elif angle<=243:
123.                  score = 7
124.              elif angle<=261:
125.                  score = 19
126.              elif angle<=279:
127.                  score = 3
128.              elif angle<=297:
129.                  score = 17
130.              elif angle<=315:
131.                  score = 2
132.              elif angle<=333:
133.                  score = 15
134.              elif angle<=351:
135.                  score = 10
136.
137.              if distance>=74 and distance<=84: #Triple ring
138.                  score = score * 3
139.              elif distance>=134 and distance<=144: #Double ri
     ng
140.                  score = score * 2
141.
142.          return score
143.
144.      ##########################################
145.      #        MAIN PROGRAM STARTS HERE        #
146.      ##########################################
147.      myPen = turtle.Turtle()
```

```
148.        mypen.tracer(0)
149.        mypen.speed(0)
150.        mypen.color("#FF0000")
151.
152.        mypen.shape('arrow')
153.        mypen.pensize(1)
154.        mypen.pencolor('black')
155.
156.        drawTarget()
157.        #Shooting the arrow
158.        arrowx= random.randint(-150,150)
159.        arrowy= random.randint(-150,150)
160.        drawCross("#00FFFF",10,arrowx,arrowy)
161.
162.        #Calculate and display score
163.        score = calculateScore(arrowx,arrowy)
164.        writeScore("Your Score: + " + str(score))
165.
166.        #Hide the pen
167.        mypen.penup()
168.        mypen.goto(-300,-300)
169.
170.        mypen.getscreen().update()
```

84. Confetti Ring Challenge

For the next three challenges we will produce on screen artwork by randomly positioning confetti on different shapes of canvas. Our code will use Python Turtle to draw the canvas and the confetti. We will also create a colour palette based on a gradient of colours. You will find at the web address provided below the code used to randomly position each confetti within the boundaries of a square and of a disc. The following code will randomly position each confetti within the boundaries of ring/doughnut shape.

Web Address

https://www.101computing.net/confetti-artwork-challenges/

Python Code

```
1.  #Confetti Artwork Challenge - Ring Shape
2.  import turtle
3.  import random
4.  from math import cos, sin, radians
5.
6.  #Initialise Python Turtle
7.  myPen = turtle.Turtle()
8.  myPen.hideturtle()
9.  myPen.tracer(0)
10. myPen.speed(0)
11. window = turtle.Screen()
12. window.bgcolor("#EEEEEE")
13.
14. #A function to draw the Canvas
15. def drawCanvas(x,y,radius1, radius2):
16.    myPen.penup()
17.    myPen.goto(x,y-radius1)
18.    myPen.pensize(4)
19.    myPen.color("#333333")
20.    myPen.pendown()
21.    myPen.circle(radius1)
22.    myPen.penup()
23.    myPen.goto(x,y-radius2)
24.    myPen.pensize(4)
25.    myPen.color("#333333")
26.    myPen.pendown()
27.    myPen.circle(radius2)
28.    myPen.pensize(1)
29.
30. #A function to draw a confetti
31. def drawConfetti(x,y,radius,color):
32.    myPen.penup()
33.    myPen.goto(x,y-radius)
34.    myPen.pendown()
35.    myPen.fillcolor(color)
36.    myPen.color(color)
37.    myPen.begin_fill()
38.    myPen.circle(radius)
39.    myPen.end_fill()
40.
41. #Main Program Starts Here
42. innerRadius = 80
43. outerRadius = 150
44. drawCanvas(0,0,innerRadius,outerRadius)
45.
46. for confetti in range(0,2000):
47.    radius = random.randint(5,12)
48.
49.    distance = random.randint(innerRadius,outerRadius)
```

```
50.    angle = radians(random.randint(0,360))
51.
52.    x = distance * cos(angle)
53.    y = distance * sin(angle)
54.
55.    #Generate a random orange colour!
56.    color = (random.randint(180,255),random.randint(0,210),0)
57.
58.    #Draw Confetti
59.    drawConfetti(x,y,radius,color)
60.
61. myPen.getscreen().update()
```

Note that, though the approach used below covers the whole ring shape it does not produce a uniform distribution of confetti per square inch of the ring shape. The code could be changed to produce such an even distribution (see approach used in the "Lunar Craters" challenge).

85. Confetti Diamond Challenge

Using a similar approach to the previous challenge, the following code will randomly position each confetti within the boundaries of a diamond shape.

Web Address

https://www.101computing.net/confetti-artwork-challenges/

Python Code

```
1.  #Confetti Artwork Challenge - Diamond shape
2.  import turtle
3.  import random
4.  from math import cos, sin, radians
5.
6.  #Initialise Python Turtle
7.  myPen = turtle.Turtle()
8.  myPen.hideturtle()
9.  myPen.tracer(0)
10. myPen.speed(0)
11. window = turtle.Screen()
```

```
12.  window.bgcolor("#EEEEEE")
13.
14.  #A function to draw the Canvas
15.  def drawCanvas(x,y,width):
16.     myPen.penup()
17.     myPen.goto(x-width/2,0)
18.     myPen.pensize(4)
19.     myPen.pendown()
20.     myPen.goto(0,y+width/2)
21.     myPen.goto(x+width/2,0)
22.     myPen.goto(0,y-width/2)
23.     myPen.goto(x-width/2,0)
24.
25.  #A function to draw a confetti
26.  def drawConfetti(x,y,radius,color):
27.     myPen.penup()
28.     myPen.goto(x,y-radius)
29.     myPen.pendown()
30.     myPen.fillcolor(color)
31.     myPen.color(color)
32.     myPen.begin_fill()
33.     myPen.circle(radius)
34.     myPen.end_fill()
35.
36.  #Main Program Starts Here
37.  width = 300
38.  drawCanvas(0,0,width)
39.
40.  for confetti in range(0,2000):
41.     radius = random.randint(5,12)
42.
43.     x = random.randint(-width//2,width//2)
44.     if x>=0:
45.       y = random.randint(-width//2+x,width//2-x)
46.     else:
47.       y = random.randint(-width//2-x,width//2+x)
48.
49.     #Generate a random colour!
50.     color = (random.randint(0,255),random.randint(0,255),rando
     m.randint(0,255))
51.
52.     #Draw Confetti
53.     drawConfetti(x,y,radius,color)
54.
55.  myPen.getscreen().update()
```

Note that, though the approach used below covers the whole diamond shape it does not produce a uniform distribution of confetti per square inch of the diamond shape. The code could be changed to produce such an even distribution (see approach used in the next challenge).

86. Confetti Triangle Challenge

Using a similar approach to the previous challenge, the following code will randomly position each confetti within the boundaries of an equilateral triangle. Note that the approach used below is slightly more advanced than the approach used in the previous challenges as it produces a uniform distribution of confetti per square inch of the triangle.

Web Address

https://www.101computing.net/confetti-artwork-challenges/

Python Code

```
1.  #Confetti Artwork Challenge - Triangle Shape
2.  import turtle
3.  import random
4.
5.  #Initialise Python Turtle
6.  myPen = turtle.Turtle()
7.  myPen.hideturtle()
8.  myPen.tracer(0)
9.  myPen.speed(0)
10. window = turtle.Screen()
11. window.bgcolor("#EEEEEE")
12.
13. #A function to draw the Canvas
14. def drawCanvas(x,y,width):
15.     myPen.penup()
16.     myPen.goto(x,y)
17.     myPen.pensize(4)
18.     myPen.pendown()
19.     for side in range(0,3):
20.         myPen.forward(width)
21.         myPen.left(120)
22.
23. #A function to draw a confetti
```

```
24. def drawConfetti(x,y,radius,color):
25.    myPen.penup()
26.    myPen.goto(x,y-radius)
27.    myPen.pendown()
28.    myPen.fillcolor(color)
29.    myPen.color(color)
30.    myPen.begin_fill()
31.    myPen.circle(radius)
32.    myPen.end_fill()
33.
34. #Main Program Starts Here
35. width = 300
36. height = int(width*(3**0.5)/2)
37. drawCanvas(-width//2,-height//2,width)
38.
39. for confetti in range(0,2000):
40.    radius = random.randint(5,12)
41.
42.    x = random.randint(-width//2,width//2)
43.    y = random.randint(0,height)
44.    if x>0:
45.       #Only keep confettis which are below the right side of t
   he triangle
46.       while y>height*(1-
   x/(width/2)): #Based on the linear equation of the right han
   d side
47.          x = random.randint(0,width//2)
48.          y = random.randint(0,height)
49.    elif x<0:
50.       #Only keep confettis which are below the left side of th
   e triangle
51.       while y>height*(1+x/(width/2)): #Based on the linear equ
   ation of the left hand side
52.          x = random.randint(-width//2,0)
53.          y = random.randint(0,height)
54.
55.    #Final translation: (triangle is in the center of the scre
   en)
56.    y = y - height//2
57.
58.    #Generate a random grey colour!
59.    grey = random.randint(0,255)
60.    color = (grey,grey,grey)
61.
62.    #Draw Confetti
63.    drawConfetti(x,y,radius,color)
64.
65. myPen.getscreen().update()
```

In this challenge we will write a script to randomly draw confetti of different sizes on a square canvas while ensuring that none of the confetti overlap with each other!

Our algorithm will use a collision detection algorithm based on Pythagoras' theorem used to calculate the distance between two confetti as explained below:

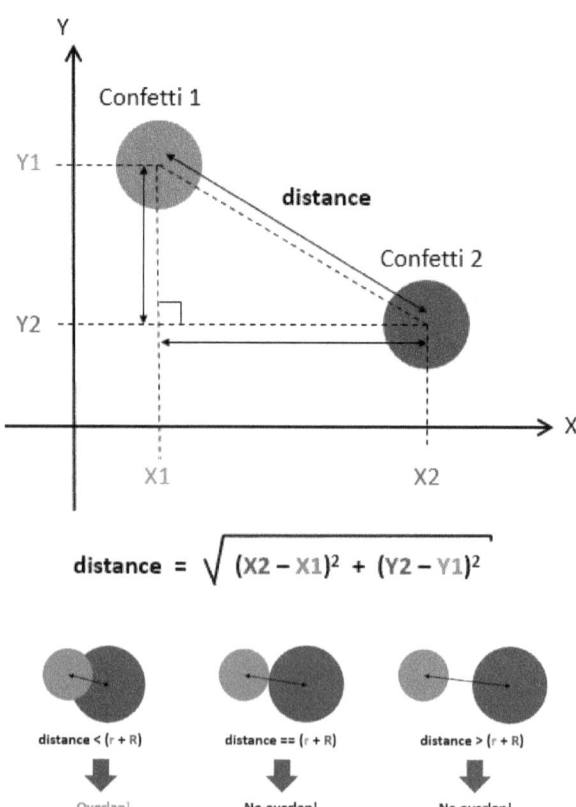

$$distance = \sqrt{(X2 - X1)^2 + (Y2 - Y1)^2}$$

```
1.  #Confetti Challenge
2.  import turtle
3.  import random
4.
5.  numberOfConfetti = 60
6.
7.  myPen = turtle.Turtle()
8.  myPen.hideturtle()
9.  myPen.speed(0)
10. window = turtle.Screen()
11. window.bgcolor("#000000")
12.
13. #Draw the Canvas
14. myPen.penup()
15. myPen.goto(-180,-182)
16. myPen.pensize(4)
17. myPen.color("#FF00FF")
18. myPen.pendown()
19. for side in range(0,4):
20.     myPen.forward(360)
21.     myPen.left(90)
22.
23. myPen.pensize(1)
24. list = []
25.
26. #Add Confetti
27. for confetti in range(0,numberOfConfetti):
28.     overlap = True
29.     while overlap:
30.         radius = random.randint(10,30)
31.         x = random.randint(-180+radius,180-radius)
32.         y = random.randint(-180+radius,180-radius)
33.         #Check if new confetti overlap with any existing confett
    i
34.         overlap = False
35.         for confetti in list:
36.             #Use Pythagoras Formula to calculate the distance betw
    een two confetti
37.             distance = ((confetti[0] - x)**2 + (confetti[1] -
    y)**2)**0.5
38.             #If two confetti are too close to each other, then the
    y will overlap!
39.             if distance<=(radius+confetti[2]) + 2:
40.                 overlap = True
41.
42.     list.append([x,y,radius])
```

216

```
43.
44.    #Generate a random purple colour!
45.    color = (random.randint(50,255),0,random.randint(50,255))

46.    myPen.penup()
47.    myPen.goto(x,y-radius)
48.    myPen.pendown()
49.    myPen.fillcolor(color)
50.    myPen.color(color)
51.    myPen.begin_fill()
52.    myPen.circle(radius-2)
53.    myPen.end_fill()
54.    print(str(len(list)) + " confetti")
55.
56. print("The end")
```

88. Intersection Point

The aim of this challenge is to write a script that allows the user to input the equation of two straight lines (Line 1: y=ax+b, Line 2: y=cx+d). The program will then calculate the coordinates of the intersection point if such a point exists!

Web Address

https://www.101computing.net/intersection-point/

Python Code

```
1.  #Intersection point of two lines
2.
3.  #Retrieve user inputs
4.  print("Line 1: y = ax + b")
5.  a = float(input("a?"))
6.  b = float(input("b?"))
7.
8.  print("y = " + str(a) + "x" + " + " + str(b))
9.
10. print("Line 2: y = cx + d")
11. c = float(input("c?"))
12. d = float(input("d?"))
13.
```

```
14. print("y = " + str(c) + "x" + " + " + " + str(d))
15.
16. #Are both lines parallel?
17. if a==c:
18.    print("Both lines are parallel: no intersection point!")
19. else:
20.    #Calculate (x,y) coordinates of the intersection point
21.    x = (d-b)/(a-c)
22.    y = a*x + b
23.    print("Intersection point: (" + str(x) + "," + str(y) + ")
    ")
```

89. The Pentagram Challenge

A polygon is a plane shape (2D) with straight lines. It consists of vertices and edges.

A polygon is regular when all angles are equal and all sides are equal. For instance a regular pentagon consists of 5 vertices and 5 edges of equal size. The vertices of a regular pentagon are equally spread on a circle. This outside circle is called a circumcircle, and it connects all vertices (corner points) of the polygon. The radius of the circumcircle is also the radius of the polygon. We can use the trigonometric formulas to work out the (x,y) coordinates of each vertex of a regular pentagon. (See picture on the right).

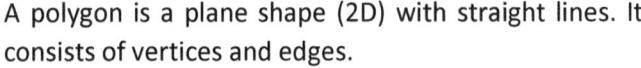

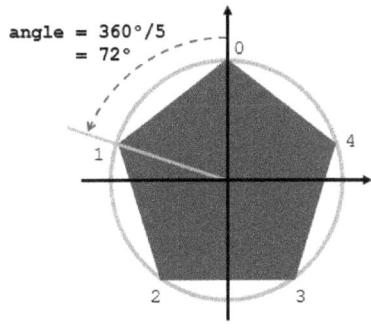

$$x_n = R.\cos(90 + 72n)$$

$$y_n = R.\sin(90 + 72n)$$

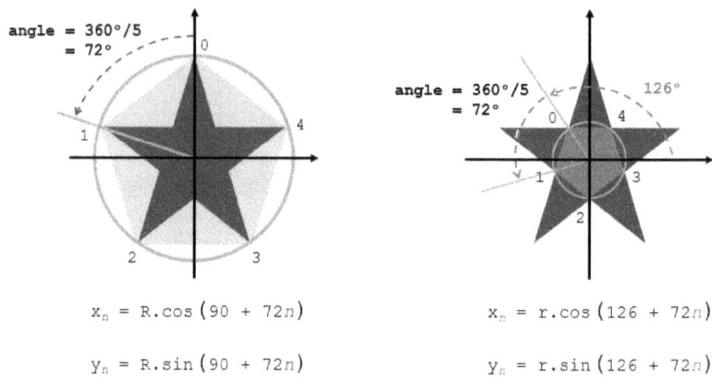

$$x_n = R.\cos(90 + 72n)$$

$$y_n = R.\sin(90 + 72n)$$

$$x_n = r.\cos(126 + 72n)$$

$$y_n = r.\sin(126 + 72n)$$

A pentagram is a polygon that looks like a 5-pointed star. The outer vertices (points of the stars) form a regular pentagon. The inner vertices of the star also form a smaller "inner" regular pentagon.

We can hence use a similar approach to calculates the (x,y) coordinates of both "outer" and "inner" vertices of our pentagram.

Finally, using Python Turtle we can uses our list of vertices / coordinates to draw our pentagram on screen.

Web Address

https://www.101computing.net/pentagram-challenge/

Python Code

```
1.  #Pentagram Challenge
2.  import turtle, math
3.  myPen = turtle.Turtle()
4.  myPen.shape("arrow")
5.  myPen.pencolor("purple")
6.  myPen.pensize(2)
7.  myPen.speed(1000)
8.
9.  #A Procedure to draw a polygon from a list of vertices.
10. def drawPolygon(polygon):
11.   myPen.penup()
12.   myPen.goto(polygon[0][0],polygon[0][1])
13.   myPen.pendown()
14.
15.   for i in range(1,len(polygon)):
```

```
16.      myPen.goto(polygon[i][0],polygon[i][1])
17.
18.  myPen.goto(polygon[0][0],polygon[0][1])
19.
20.
21. #A polygon is can be stored as a list of vertices
22. pentagram=[]
23. R = 150
24. r = 57
25. for n in range(0,5):
26.    x = R*math.cos(math.radians(90+n*72))
27.    y = R*math.sin(math.radians(90+n*72))
28.    pentagram.append([x,y])
29.    x = r*math.cos(math.radians(126+n*72))
30.    y = r*math.sin(math.radians(126+n*72))
31.    pentagram.append([x,y])
32.
33. drawPolygon(pentagram)
34. myPen.hideturtle()
```

90. Python Turtle Morphing Algorithm

Tweening/Morphing effects are often used in computer animations to change the shape of an object by morphing an object from one shape into another.

In tweening, key frames are provided and "in-between" frames are calculated to make a smooth looking animation.

In this blog post we will implement a tweening algorithm to morph a letter of the alphabet (e.g. "A" into another letter "Z") using a linear interpolation.

We will consider a letter as being a list of connected nodes (dots) where each dot has its own set of (x,y) coordinates.

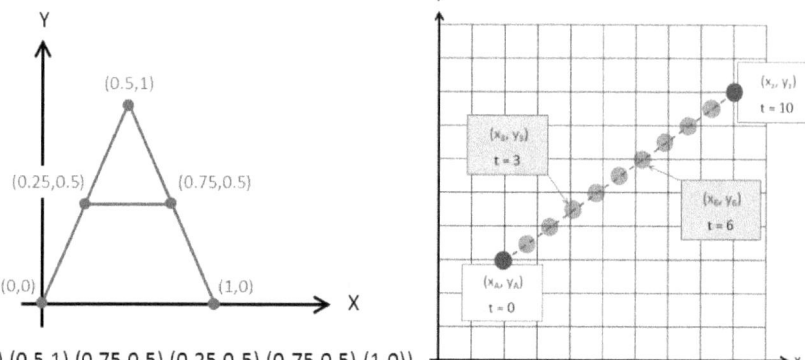

"A" : ((0,0),(0.5,1),(0.75,0.5),(0.25,0.5),(0.75,0.5),(1,0))

Using the following linear interpolation formulas we can calculate the (x,y) coordinates of each dot for any "in-between" frame.

$x(t) = x_A + (x_Z - x_A) * t / 10$

$y(t) = y_A + (y_Z - y_A) * t / 10$

- "t" represents the time: in other words the frame number (e.g. between 0 and 10)
- (x_A, y_A) the coordinates of a node/dot from the starting letter (e.g. A)
- (x_Z, y_Z) the coordinates of a node/dot from the ending letter (e.g. Z)

In this challenge we have created a tweening animation going through all the letters of your firstname. (e.g. J -> A -> M -> E -> S).

Web Address

https://www.101computing.net/python-turtle-morphing-algorithm/

Python Code

```
1.    #Python Turtle - Morphing Algorithm
2.    import turtle
3.    import random
4.    from time import sleep
```

```
5.
6.    alphabet = {
7.        'A': [(0,0),(0.5,1),(0.75,0.5),(0.25,0.5),(0.75,0.5),(
      1,0)],
8.        'B': [(0,0),(0,1),(0.625 ,1),(0.75,0.875),(0.75,0.625)
      ,(0.625,0.5),(0,0.5),(0.625,0.5),(0.75,0.375),(0.75,0.125)
      ,(0.625,0),(0,0)],
9.        'C': [(0.75,0.125),(0.625,0),(0.125,0),(0,0.125),(0,0.
      875),(0.125,1),(0.625,1),(0.75,0.875)],
10.        'D': [(0,0),(0,1),(0.625 ,1),(0.75,0.875),(0.75,0.125)
      ,(0.625,0),(0,0)],
11.        'E': [(0.75,0),(0,0),(0,0.5),(0.75,0.5),(0,0.5),(0,1),
      (0.75,1)],
12.        'F': [(0,0),(0,0.5),(0.75,0.5),(0,0.5),(0,1),(0.75,1)]
      ,
13.        'G': [(0.75,0.5),(0.625,0.5),(0.75,0.5),(0.75,0.125),(
      0.625,0),(0.125,0),(0,0.125),(0,0.875),(0.125,1),(0.625,1)
      ,(0.75,0.875)],
14.        'H': [(0,0),(0,1),(0,0.5),(0.75,0.5),(0.75,1),(0.75,0)
      ],
15.        'I': [(0,0),(0.25,0),(0.125,0),(0.125,1),(0,1),(0.25,1
      )],
16.        'J': [(0,0.125),(0.125,0),(0.375,0),(0.5,0.125),(0.5,1
      )],
17.        'K': [(0,0),(0,1),(0,0.5),(0.75,1),(0,0.5),(0.75,0)],
18.        'L': [(0,0),(0,1),(0,0),(0.75,0)],
19.        'M': [(0,0),(0,1),(0.5,0),(1,1),(1,0)],
20.        'N': [(0,0),(0,1),(0.75,0),(0.75,1)],
21.        'O': [(0.75,0.125),(0.625,0),(0.125,0),(0,0.125),(0,0.
      875),(0.125,1),(0.625,1),(0.75,0.875),(0.75,0.125)],
22.        'P': [(0,0),(0,1),(0.625,1),(0.75,0.875),(0.75,0.625),
      (0.625,0.5),(0,0.5)],
23.        'Q': [(0.75,0.125),(0.625,0),(0.125,0),(0,0.125),(0,0.
      875),(0.125,1),(0.625,1),(0.75,0.875),(0.75,0.125),(0.875,
      0)],
24.        'R': [(0,0),(0,1),(0.625,1),(0.75,0.875),(0.75,0.625),
      (0.625,0.5),(0,0.5),(0.625,0.5),(0.875,0)],
25.        'S': [(0,0.125),(0.125,0),(0.625,0),(0.75,0.125),(0.75
      ,0.375),(0.675,0.5),(0.125,0.5),(0,0.625),(0,0.875),(0.125
      ,1),(0.625,1),(0.75,0.875)],
26.        'T': [(0,1),(0.5,1),(0.5,0),(0.5,1),(1,1)],
27.        'U': [(0,1),(0,0.125),(0.125,0),(0.625,0),(0.75,0.125)
      ,(0.75,1)],
28.        'V': [(0,1),(0.375,0),(0.75,1)],
29.        'W': [(0,1),(0.25,0),(0.5,1),(0.75,0),(1,1)],
30.        'X': [(0,0),(0.375,0.5),(0,1),(0.375,0.5),(0.75,1),(0.
      375,0.5),(0.75,0)],
```

```
31.        'Y': [(0,1),(0.375,0.5),(0.375,0),(0.375,0.5),(0.75,1)
    ],
32.        'Z': [(0,1),(0.75,1),(0,0),(0.75,0)],
33.        '0': [(0,1),(0,0),(1,0),(1,1),(0,1)],
34.        '1': [(1,0),(1,1)],
35.        '2': [(0,1),(1,1),(1,.5),(0,.5),(0,0),(1,0)],
36.        '3': [(0,1),(1,1),(1,.5),(0,.5),(1,.5),(1,0),(0,0)],
37.        '4': [(0,1),(0,.5),(1,.5),(1,1),(1,0)],
38.        '5': [(0,1),(1,1),(0,1),(0,.5),(1,.5),(1,0),(0,0)],
39.        '6': [(0,1),(1,1),(0,1),(0,0),(1,0),(1,.5),(0,.5)],
40.        '7': [(0,1),(1,1),(1,0)],
41.        '8': [(0,1),(0,0),(1,0),(1,1),(0,1),(0,.5),(1,.5)],
42.        '9': [(0,1),(1,1),(1,.5),(0,.5),(0,1),(1,1),(1,0),(0,0
    )]}
43.
44. myPen = turtle.Turtle()
45. myPen.hideturtle()
46. myPen.tracer(0)
47. myPen.speed(0)
48. window = turtle.Screen()
49. window.bgcolor("#000000")
50. myPen.pensize(4)
51.
52. def morphing(letter1,letter2,t,fontSize,color,x,y):
53.     myPen.color(color)
54.     letter1=letter1.upper()
55.     letter2=letter2.upper()
56.     myPen.penup()
57.     myPen.goto(x,y)
58.     myPen.pendown()
59.
60.     #Check that the characters belong to the Alphabet
61.     if letter1 in alphabet and letter2 in alphabet:
62.         letter1Coordinates=alphabet[letter1]
63.         letter2Coordinates=alphabet[letter2]
64.
65.         dots=[]
66.
67.         #Some letters have more nodes than others. We need
    to ensure they have the same number of nodes
68.         if len(letter1Coordinates)>len(letter2Coordinates):

69.             lastDot = letter2Coordinates[len(letter2Coordinate
    s)-1]
70.             for i in range(0,len(letter1Coordinates)-
    len(letter2Coordinates)):
71.                 letter2Coordinates.append(lastDot)
72.         elif len(letter1Coordinates)<len(letter2Coordinates)
    :
```

223

```
73.            lastDot = letter1Coordinates[len(letter1Coordinate
        s)-1]
74.            for i in range(0,len(letter2Coordinates)-
        len(letter1Coordinates)):
75.                letter1Coordinates.append(lastDot)
76.
77.        numberOfDots = len(letter1Coordinates)
78.
79.        #Morphing Calculations
80.        #Calculate the new interim coordinates of each node

81.        for i in range(0,numberOfDots):
82.            dotx=letter1Coordinates[i][0] + (letter2Coordinate
        s[i][0]-letter1Coordinates[i][0])*t/10
83.            doty=letter1Coordinates[i][1] + (letter2Coordinate
        s[i][1]-letter1Coordinates[i][1])*t/10
84.            dots.append([dotx,doty])
85.
86.        #Draw the resulting morphed charcater
87.        myPen.penup()
88.        for dot in dots:
89.            myPen.goto(x + dot[0]*fontSize, y + dot[1]*fontSiz
        e)
90.            myPen.pendown()
91.
92.
93.    #Main Program Starts Here
94.    fontSize = 200
95.    fontColor = "#FF00FF"
96.
97.    name=input("Enter your name:")
98.    while True:
99.      #For each letter of the name
100.     for i in range(0, len(name)-1):
101.       for t in range(0,11):
102.         myPen.clear()
103.         morphing(name[i], name[i+1], t, fontSize, fontColor,
        -100, -100)
104.         sleep(0.05)
105.         myPen.getscreen().update()
106.
107.     sleep(1)
108.     #And back to the first letter of the name
109.     for t in range(0,11):
110.       myPen.clear()
111.       morphing(name[len(name)-1], name[0], t, fontSize,
        fontColor, -100, -100)
112.       sleep(0.05)
113.       myPen.getscreen().update()
```

91. Off-Side Detection Algorithm

In a game of football, one of the most complex rules is the offside rule. One of the roles of the assistant referees is to detect when a player is offside.

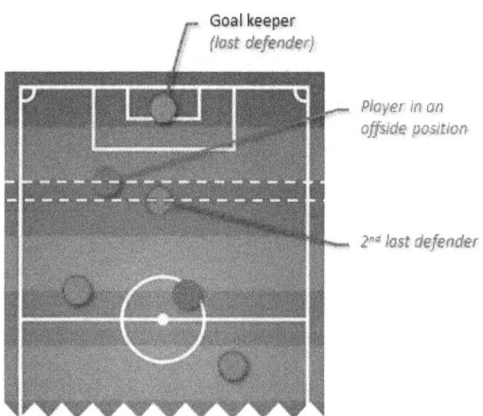

Goal keeper
(last defender)

Player in an
offside position

2ⁿᵈ last defender

A player is in an offside position if, when the ball is played by a team-mate, they are nearer to the opposition's goal line than both the ball and the second last defender (the last defender being in most cases the goal keeper).

Note that players cannot be offside in their own half of the field.

In this challenge, we are using Python Turtle to draw a football pitch and randomly position all 22 players on the pitch. We then apply an off-side detection algorithm to output on screen whether a team has one or more players who could potentially be in an off-side position.

Web Address

https://www.101computing.net/offside-detection-algorithm/

Python Code – Main.py

```
1.  #Offside Detection Algorithm
2.  import pitch
3.  import turtle
4.  from random import randint
5.
6.  pitch.drawPitch()
7.
8.  #Add Home team players (blue team) on the pitch
```

```
9.  homeTeam=[]
10. #Start by with the goal keeper
11. homeTeam.append([0,-194,1])
12. pitch.drawPlayer("blue",0,-194,"Goal Keeper")
13. #Add an extra 10 players
14. for i in range(1,11):
15.   x=randint(-130,130)
16.   y=randint(-180,160)
17.   homeTeam.append([x,y,i+1])
18.   pitch.drawPlayer("blue",x,y,i+1)
19.
20. #Add away team players (red team) on the pitch
21. awayTeam=[]
22. #Start with the goal keeper
23. awayTeam.append([0,170,1])
24. pitch.drawPlayer("red",0,170,"Goal Keeper")
25. #Add an extra 10 players
26. for i in range(1,11):
27.   x=randint(-130,130)
28.   y=randint(-180,160)
29.   awayTeam.append([x,y,i+1])
30.   pitch.drawPlayer("red",x,y,i+1)
31.
32. #Off-Side Detection Algorithm - HomeTeam
33. offSide=True
34. for player in homeTeam:
35.   if player[1]>0:
36.     offSide=True
37.     for opponent in awayTeam[1:]:
38.       if player[1]<opponent[1]:
39.         offSide=False
40.     if offSide:
41.       break
42. #Output:
43. if offSide:
44.   pitch.drawText(-140,2,"Off side position - Blue player")
45.
46. #Off-Side Detection Algorithm - HomeTeam
47. offSide=True
48. for player in awayTeam:
49.   if player[1]<0:
50.     offSide=True
51.     for opponent in homeTeam[1:]:
52.       if player[1]>opponent[1]:
53.         offSide=False
54.     if offSide:
55.       break
56. #Output:
57. if offSide:
```

```
58.    pitch.drawText(-140,-30,"Off side position -
       Red player")
```

```
1.  import turtle
2.  GREEN="#149118"
3.  screen = turtle.Screen()
4.  screen.tracer(0)
5.  screen.bgcolor(GREEN)
6.
7.  myBrush = turtle.Turtle()
8.  myBrush.width(1)
9.  myBrush.hideturtle()
10.
11. myBrush.speed(0)
12.
13. def drawText(x,y,label):
14.     myBrush.penup()
15.     myBrush.goto(x,y)
16.     myBrush.color("#FFFFFF")
17.     myBrush.write(label,font=("Arial", 16, "normal"))
18.
19. #A Procedure to draw a player at the given position
20. def drawPlayer(color,x,y,label):
21.     myBrush.penup()
22.     myBrush.goto(x,y)
23.     myBrush.fillcolor(color)
24.     myBrush.begin_fill()
25.     myBrush.circle(10)
26.     myBrush.end_fill()
27.     screen.tracer(1)
28.     myBrush.penup()
29.     myBrush.goto(x+10,y)
30.     myBrush.color(color)
31.     myBrush.write(label)
32.
33. #A Procedure to draw the pitch
34. def drawPitch():
35.     global GREEN
36.     myBrush.color("#FFFFFF")
37.
38.     #Outer lines
39.     myBrush.penup()
40.     myBrush.goto(-140,195)
41.     myBrush.pendown()
42.     myBrush.goto(140,195)
```

227

```
43.    myBrush.goto(140,-195)
44.    myBrush.goto(-140,-195)
45.    myBrush.goto(-140,195)
46.
47.    #Penalty Box - Top
48.    myBrush.penup()
49.    myBrush.goto(0,115)
50.    myBrush.pendown()
51.    myBrush.circle(40)
52.    myBrush.penup()
53.    myBrush.goto(-80,195)
54.    myBrush.pendown()
55.    myBrush.fillcolor(GREEN)
56.    myBrush.begin_fill()
57.    myBrush.goto(80,195)
58.    myBrush.goto(80,140)
59.    myBrush.goto(-80,140)
60.    myBrush.goto(-80,195)
61.    myBrush.end_fill()
62.
63.    #Penalty Box - Bottom
64.    myBrush.penup()
65.    myBrush.goto(0,-195)
66.    myBrush.pendown()
67.    myBrush.circle(40)
68.    myBrush.penup()
69.    myBrush.goto(-80,-195)
70.    myBrush.pendown()
71.    myBrush.fillcolor(GREEN)
72.    myBrush.begin_fill()
73.    myBrush.goto(80,-195)
74.    myBrush.goto(80,-140)
75.    myBrush.goto(-80,-140)
76.    myBrush.goto(-80,-195)
77.    myBrush.end_fill()
78.
79.    # Goal Box - Bottom
80.    myBrush.penup()
81.    myBrush.goto(40,-195)
82.    myBrush.pendown()
83.    myBrush.goto(40,-170)
84.    myBrush.goto(-40,-170)
85.    myBrush.goto(-40,-195)
86.
87.    # Goal Box - Top
88.    myBrush.penup()
89.    myBrush.goto(40,195)
90.    myBrush.pendown()
91.    myBrush.goto(40,170)
```

```
92.    myBrush.goto(-40,170)
93.    myBrush.goto(-40,195)
94.
95.    #Halfway Line
96.    myBrush.penup()
97.    myBrush.goto(-140,0)
98.    myBrush.pendown()
99.    myBrush.goto(140,0)
100.
101.        #Central Circle
102.        myBrush.penup()
103.        myBrush.goto(0,-40)
104.        myBrush.pendown()
105.        myBrush.circle(40)
106.
107.        screen.tracer(1)
```

92. Estimating Pi using the Monte Carlo Method

One method to estimate the value of π (3.141592…) is by using a Monte Carlo method. This method consists of drawing on a canvas a square with an inner circle. We then generate a large number of random points within the square and count how many fall in the enclosed circle.

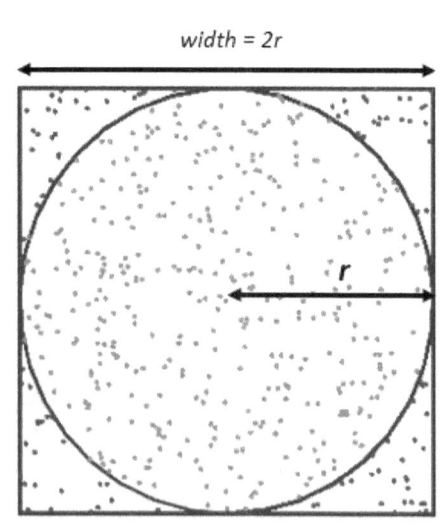

width = 2r

r

The area of the circle is πr^2,

The area of the square is $width^2 = (2r)^2 = 4r^2$.

If we divide the area of the circle, by the area of the square we get π/4.

The same ratio can be used between the number of points within the square and the number of points within the circle.

Hence we can use the following formula to estimate Pi:

π ≈ 4 x (number of points in the circle / total number of points)

In this challenge are applying this method using Python Turtle to provide a visual representation.

Web Address

https://www.101computing.net/estimating-pi-using-the-monte-carlo-method/

Python Code

```
1.  #Estimating Pi using the Monte Carlo Method
2.  import turtle
3.  import random
4.
5.  #Initialise Python Turtle
6.  myPen = turtle.Turtle()
7.  myPen.hideturtle()
8.  myPen.tracer(0)
9.  myPen.speed(0)
10. window = turtle.Screen()
11. window.bgcolor("#FFFFFF")
12.
13. #A function to draw the Canvas
14. def drawSquare(x,y,width):
15.     myPen.penup()
16.     myPen.goto(x,y)
17.     myPen.pensize(3)
18.     myPen.color("#333333")
19.     myPen.pendown()
20.     for side in range(0,4):
21.       myPen.forward(width)
22.       myPen.right(90)
23.     myPen.pensize(1)
24.
25. #A function to draw the Circle
26. def drawCircle(x,y,radius):
27.     myPen.penup()
28.     myPen.goto(x,y-radius)
29.     myPen.pensize(2)
```

```
30.    myPen.color("#333333")
31.    myPen.pendown()
32.    myPen.circle(radius)
33.    myPen.pensize(1)
34.
35. #A function to draw a dot
36. def drawDot(x,y,color):
37.    myPen.penup()
38.    myPen.goto(x,y-1)
39.    myPen.pendown()
40.    myPen.fillcolor(color)
41.    myPen.color(color)
42.    myPen.begin_fill()
43.    myPen.circle(1)
44.    myPen.end_fill()
45.
46. #Main Program Starts Here
47. radius=180
48. color = "#000000"
49. total = 2500
50. totalIn = 0
51.
52. drawSquare(-radius,radius,2*radius)
53. drawCircle(0,0,radius)
54.
55. for dots in range(0,total):
56.    x = random.randint(-radius,radius)
57.    y = random.randint(-radius,radius)
58.
59.    #Apply Pythagoras Formula to find out the distance to the
       centre of the screen
60.    distance = (x**2 + y**2)**0.5
61.
62.    #Check if dot is in the circle
63.    if distance<radius:
64.        color = "#FF0000"
65.        totalIn += 1
66.    else:
67.        color = "#0000FF"
68.
69.    #Draw Dot
70.    drawDot(x,y,color)
71.
72. myPen.getscreen().update()
73.
74. #Applying Monte Carlo's Method to estimate Pi
75. pi = 4*(totalIn/total)
76. print("Pi Estimation:" + str(pi))
```

A few hundred years ago people enjoyed betting on coins tossed on to a wooden floor and check whether they would cross a line or not.

A French mathematician called Georges-Louis Leclerc, Comte de Buffon (1707-1788) started thinking about this and worked out the probability.

This probability is called "Buffon's Needle" in his honour.

Buffon then used the results from his experiment with a needle to estimate the value of π (Pi). He worked out this formula:

$$\pi \approx 2LN / CW$$

In this formula:

- L is the length of the needle
- N is the total number of needles
- C is the total number of needles crossing a line
- W is the line spacing (Width of the wooden boards on the floor)

For this challenge, we have decided to simulate this experiment using a Python Turtle.

Web Address

https://www.101computing.net/estimating-pi-using-buffons-needle/

Python Code

```
1.  #Estimating Pi using Buffon's Needle
2.  import turtle
3.  import random
4.  import math
5.  boardWidth = 40
6.  needleLength = 30
7.  numberOfNeedles = 200
8.
```

```
9.  myPen = turtle.Turtle()
10. myPen.hideturtle()
11. myPen.speed(0)
12.
13. y=180
14.
15. #Draw the floor boards
16. for i in range(0,10):
17.    myPen.penup()
18.    myPen.goto(-200,y)
19.    myPen.pendown()
20.    myPen.goto(200,y)
21.    y-=boardWidth
22.
23. #Draw the needles
24. myPen.color("#f442d1")
25. c=0
26. for needle in range(0,numberOfNeedles):
27.    #Generate random position and direction of a needle
28.    x=random.randint(-180,180)
29.    y=random.randint(-180,180)
30.    angle=random.randint(0,360)
31.    height=(math.sin(math.radians(angle))*needleLength)
32.
33.    #Check if this needle is crossing a floor line
34.    if ((height+((y-20)%boardWidth))>(boardWidth)):
35.       c+=1
36.    if ((height+((y-20)%boardWidth))<0):
37.       c+=1
38.
39.    #Draw the needle
40.    myPen.penup()
41.    myPen.goto(x,y)
42.    myPen.setheading(angle)
43.    myPen.pendown()
44.    myPen.forward(needleLength)
45.
46. #Apply Buffon's formula to estimate the value of Pi
47. pi=2*(needleLength*numberOfNeedles)/(c*boardWidth)
48.
49. #Output key information
50. print("L = " + str(needleLength))
51. print("N = " + str(numberOfNeedles))
52. print("W = " + str(boardWidth))
53. print("C = " + str(c))
54. print("Pi = "+ str(pi))
```

94. Lissajous Curve Tracing Algorithm

Lissajous curves are a family of curves described by the following parametric equations:

$$x(t) = A \sin(at + \delta)$$
$$y(t) = B \sin(bt)$$

Lissajous curves have applications in physics, astronomy, and other sciences. Below are a few examples of Lissajous curves that you will be able to reproduce by changing the values of constant A and B in the Python code provided below.

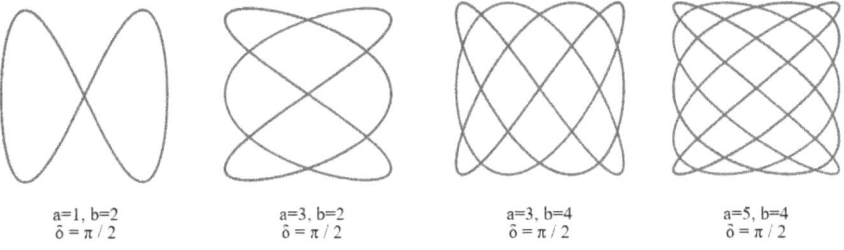

a=1, b=2
δ = π / 2

a=3, b=2
δ = π / 2

a=3, b=4
δ = π / 2

a=5, b=4
δ = π / 2

Using a very similar approach we can also trace rose curves which are a family of curves based on the following parametric equations:

$$x(t) = A \cos(kt) \cos(t)$$
$$y(t) = A \cos(kt) \sin(t)$$

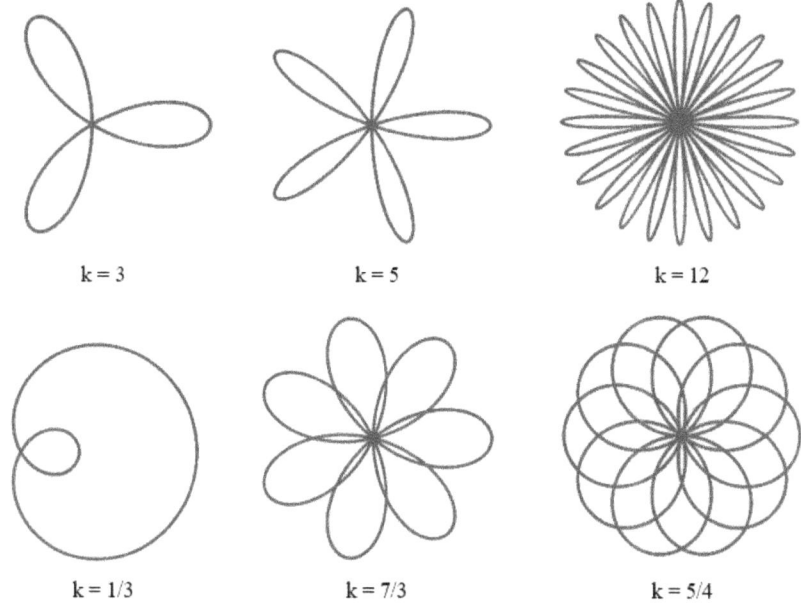

| k = 3 | k = 5 | k = 12 |

| k = 1/3 | k = 7/3 | k = 5/4 |

Web Address

https://www.101computing.net/python-turtle-lissajous-curve/

Python Code: Lissajous Curve Tracing Algorithm

```
1.  #Python Turtle - Lissajous Curve
2.  import turtle
3.  from math import cos,sin
4.  from time import sleep
5.
6.  window = turtle.Screen()
7.  window.bgcolor("#FFFFFF")
8.
9.  myPen = turtle.Turtle()
10. myPen.hideturtle()
11. myPen.tracer(0)
12. myPen.speed(0)
13. myPen.pensize(3)
14. myPen.color("#AA00AA")
15. myPen.penup()
16.
17. A = 100
18. B = 100
19. a = 3
```

```
20. b = 4
21. delta = 3.14/2
22. t=0
23.
24. for i in range(0,1000):
25.     t+=0.01
26.     #Apply Lissajous Parametric Equations
27.     x = A * sin(a*t + delta)
28.     y = B * sin(b*t)
29.
30.     myPen.goto(x,y)
31.     myPen.pendown()
32.     myPen.getscreen().update()
```

Python Code: Rose Curve Tracing Algorithm

```
1.  #Python Turtle - Rose Curve
2.  import turtle
3.  from math import cos,sin
4.  from time import sleep
5.
6.  window = turtle.Screen()
7.  window.bgcolor("#FFFFFF")
8.
9.  myPen = turtle.Turtle()
10. myPen.hideturtle()
11. myPen.tracer(0)
12. myPen.speed(0)
13. myPen.pensize(3)
14. myPen.color("#AA00AA")
15. myPen.penup()
16.
17. A = 160
18. k = 5
19. t=0
20.
21. for i in range(0,1000):
22.     t+=0.01
23.     #Apply Parametric Equations for a Rose curve
24.     x = A * cos(k*t) * cos(t)
25.     y = A * cos(k*t) * sin(t)
26.
27.     myPen.goto(x,y)
28.     myPen.pendown()
29.
30. myPen.getscreen().update()
```

The Moon's surface is covered with thousands of craters. These are caused by asteroids and meteorites colliding with the lunar surface. In this challenge, we will use Python Turtle to create a drawing of the Moon with a random selection of craters.

This challenge consists of randomly positioning craters of various sizes (radius) on the surface of the Moon. Generating random (x,y) coordinates is fairly straight forward, however the challenge is to ensure that the craters fit within the disc representing the Moon:

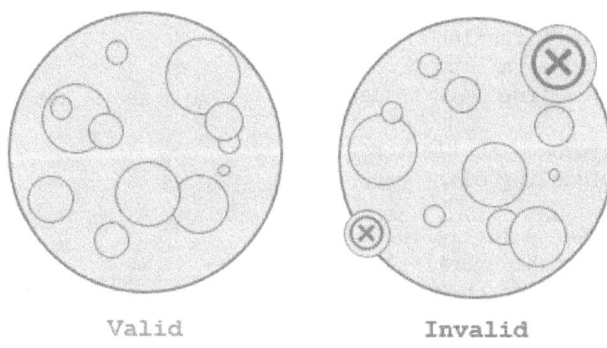

Valid   Invalid

To solve this problem, we start by generating a set of random Cartesian coordinates (x,y). Before using these coordinates to draw a crater we calculate the distance between the centre of the disc representing the Moon and the randomly generated (x,y) coordinates. To do so we use Pythagoras' Theorem. If the distance is lower than (Radius of the Moon − Radius of Crater) then we keep these coordinates to draw our crater, otherwise we generate a new set of coordinates.

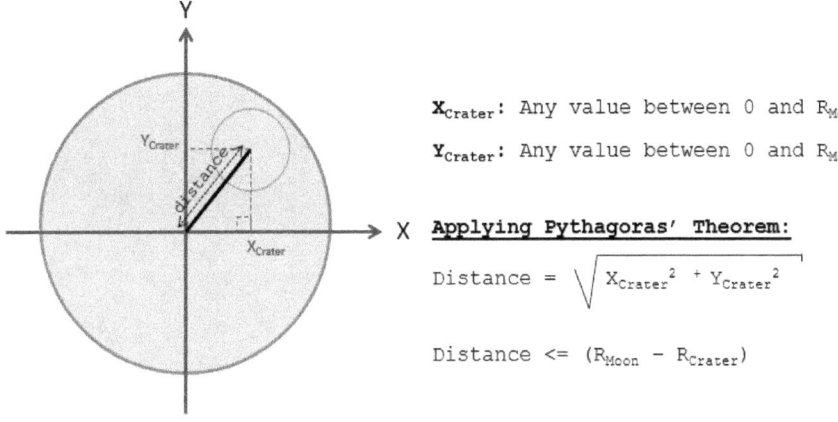

X_{Crater}: Any value between 0 and R_{Moon}

Y_{Crater}: Any value between 0 and R_{Moon}

X **Applying Pythagoras' Theorem:**

$$Distance = \sqrt{X_{Crater}^2 + Y_{Crater}^2}$$

$$Distance <= (R_{Moon} - R_{Crater})$$

Web Address

https://www.101computing.net/lunar-craters-challenge/

Python Code

```
1.  #Lunar Craters Challenge
2.  import turtle
3.  import math
4.  from random import randint
5.
6.  myPen = turtle.Turtle()
7.  myPen.tracer(0)
8.  myPen.speed(0)
9.  screen = turtle.Screen()
10. screen.bgcolor("#111155")
11. myPen.color("#888888")
12. myPen.pensize(3)
13. myPen.penup()
14. myPen.goto(0,0)
15.
16. def drawMoon(x,y,radius):
17.     myPen.penup()
18.     myPen.goto(x,y-radius)
19.     myPen.pendown()
20.     myPen.fillcolor("#AAAAAA")
21.     myPen.begin_fill()
22.     myPen.circle(radius)
23.     myPen.end_fill()
24.
25. def drawCrater(x,y,radius):
26.     myPen.pensize(1)
```

```
27.   mypen.penup()
28.   mypen.goto(x,y-radius)
29.   mypen.pendown()
30.   mypen.fillcolor("#AAAAAA")
31.   mypen.begin_fill()
32.   mypen.circle(radius)
33.   mypen.end_fill()
34.
35. #Draw the Moon
36. MOON_RADIUS = 160
37. drawMoon(0,0,MOON_RADIUS)
38. #Add 20 craters on the Moon's surface
39. for i in range(20):
40.   radius = randint(3,50)
41.   distance = MOON_RADIUS
42.   while (distance+radius > MOON_RADIUS):
43.     x = randint(-MOON_RADIUS,MOON_RADIUS)
44.     y = randint(-MOON_RADIUS,MOON_RADIUS)
45.     #Apply Pythagoras Theorem to calulate the distance from
    the centre
46.     distance = (x**2 + y**2)**0.5
47.   drawCrater(x,y,radius)
48.
49. mypen.hideturtle()
50. mypen.getscreen().update()
```

96. Curling Challenge

Curling is a sport in which players slide stones on a sheet of ice towards a target area which is segmented into four concentric circles. Two teams, each with four players, take turns sliding heavy, polished granite stones, also called rocks, across the ice curling sheet towards the house, a circular target marked on the ice. Each team has eight stones. The purpose is to accumulate the highest score for a game; points are scored for the stones resting closest to the centre of the house at the conclusion of each end, which is completed when both teams have thrown all of their stones. A game usually consists of eight or ten ends.

We have created a Python script using Python Turtle to represent the target as well as the eight stones, randomly positioned above the target. Our algorithm randomly generates x and y coordinates. Our algorithm also ensures that the stones are not overlapping as this would be impossible in a real game of curling.

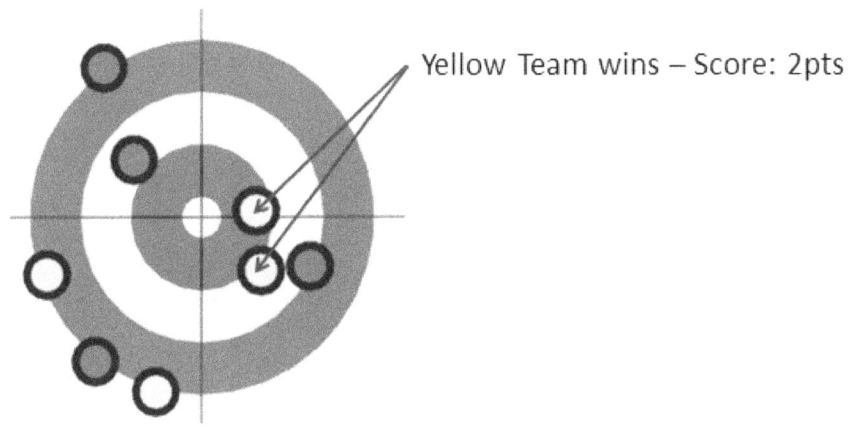

Yellow Team wins – Score: 2pts

Our code then finds out who is the winning team and calculate the score of the winning team based on the number of stones resting closer to the target than any of the stones of the opposite team.

Web Address

https://www.101computing.net/curling-challenge/

Python Code

```
1.  #Curling Challenge
2.  import turtle
3.  import random
4.
5.  def drawCircle(colorFill, size, x, y):
6.      myPen.penup()
7.      myPen.color(colorFill)
8.      myPen.fillcolor(colorFill)
9.      myPen.goto(x,y)
10.     myPen.begin_fill()
11.     myPen.circle(size)
12.     myPen.end_fill()
13.     myPen.pendown()
```

```
14.
15. def drawTarget():
16.    drawCircle("#1188FF", 170, 0,-170)
17.    drawCircle("#FFFFFF", 120, 0,-120)
18.    drawCircle("#FF0000", 70, 0,-70)
19.    drawCircle("#FFFFFF", 20, 0,-20)
20.    myPen.color("#00358c")
21.    myPen.penup()
22.    myPen.goto(-200,0)
23.    myPen.pendown()
24.    myPen.goto(200,0)
25.    myPen.penup()
26.    myPen.goto(0,-200)
27.    myPen.pendown()
28.    myPen.goto(0,200)
29.
30. def slideStone(colour):
31.    global redStones
32.    global yellowStones
33.    radius = 24
34.    overlap=True
35.    while overlap:
36.       x=random.randint(-170,170)
37.       y=random.randint(-170,170)
38.       #Check that a stone will fit at this position without ov
    erlapping with existing stones
39.       #If not generate new random coordinates until you find a
    n empty space.
40.       overlap=False
41.       for i in range(0,len(redStones)):
42.          distance = ((x-redStones[i][0])**2 + (y-
    redStones[i][1])**2)**0.5
43.          if distance<2*radius:
44.             overlap=True
45.       for i in range(0,len(yellowStones)):
46.          distance = ((x-yellowStones[i][0])**2 + (y-
    yellowStones[i][1])**2)**0.5
47.          if distance<2*radius:
48.             overlap=True
49.
50.    drawCircle("#2b2b2b",24,x,y-24)
51.    drawCircle(colour,16,x,y-16)
52.    distanceFromCenter = (x**2 + y**2)**0.5
53.    if colour=="#FF0000":
54.       return [x,y,distanceFromCenter,"Red"]
55.    else:
56.       return [x,y,distanceFromCenter,"Yellow"]
57.
58. def writeText(text):
```

```
59.    myPen.penup()
60.    myPen.goto(-130, 176)
61.    myPen.color("#000000")
62.    myPen.write(text, None, None, "16pt bold")
63.
64.  ######################################################
65.  #            Main Program Starts Here            #
66.  ######################################################
67.  myPen = turtle.Turtle()
68.  myPen.tracer(0)
69.  myPen.speed(0)
70.  myPen.shape("arrow")
71.
72.  drawTarget()
73.
74.  #Placing the stones
75.  redStones=[]
76.  yellowStones=[]
77.  redStones.append(slideStone("#FF0000"))
78.  yellowStones.append(slideStone("#FFFF00"))
79.  redStones.append(slideStone("#FF0000"))
80.  yellowStones.append(slideStone("#FFFF00"))
81.  redStones.append(slideStone("#FF0000"))
82.  yellowStones.append(slideStone("#FFFF00"))
83.  redStones.append(slideStone("#FF0000"))
84.  yellowStones.append(slideStone("#FFFF00"))
85.
86.  allStones = yellowStones + redStones
87.  allStonesSorted = sorted(allStones,key=lambda sort: sort[2])

88.
89.  winningColour = allStonesSorted[0][3]
90.  count = 0
91.  while allStonesSorted[count][3]==winningColour:
92.    count+=1
93.
94.  writeText("Winning Team: " + winningColour + " -
       Score: " +str(count))
95.
96.  #Hide the pen
97.  myPen.hideturtle()
98.
99.  myPen.getscreen().update()
```

97. Oblique Projection Formulas

The aim of this challenge is to demonstrate how the oblique projection formulas are used to convert 3D coordinates (x,y,z) into 2D coordinates (x,y).

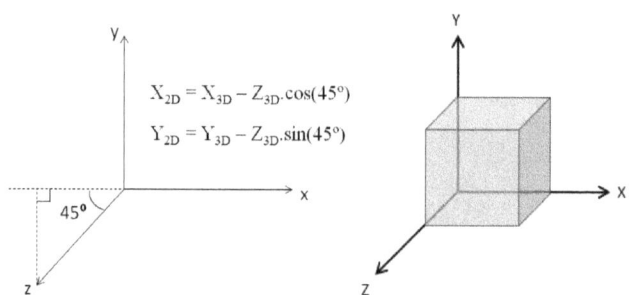

$$X_{2D} = X_{3D} - Z_{3D} \cdot \cos(45°)$$

$$Y_{2D} = Y_{3D} - Z_{3D} \cdot \sin(45°)$$

The oblique projection formulas are essential to understand how 3D models are displayed on a 2D screen. They are heavily used in 3D video games, computer animations and virtual reality.

In the Python code provided below we are applying these formulas to represent a simple 3D house on a 2D canvas using Python Turtle.

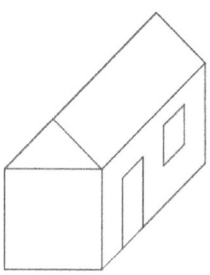

Web Address

https://www.101computing.net/oblique-projection-formulas/

Python Code

```
1.   #Oblique Projection
2.   import turtle
3.   from math import cos, sin, radians
4.
5.   myPen = turtle.Turtle()
6.   myPen.tracer(0)
7.   myPen.speed(0)
8.   myPen.shape("arrow")
9.   myPen.color("purple")
10.  myPen.pensize(2)
11.
```

```
12.  def addLabel(myPen,label,x,y):
13.    myPen.penup()
14.    myPen.goto(x,y)
15.    myPen.write(label, None, None, "14pt")
16.
17.  vertices={}
18.  vertices["A"]=[0,0,0]
19.  vertices["B"]=[100,0,0]
20.  vertices["C"]=[100,100,0]
21.  vertices["D"]=[0,100,0]
22.  vertices["E"]=[0,0,150]
23.  vertices["F"]=[100,0,150]
24.  vertices["G"]=[100,100,150]
25.  vertices["H"]=[0,100,150]
26.  # Roof
27.  vertices["I"]=[50,150,0]
28.  vertices["J"]=[50,150,150]
29.
30.  #Door
31.  vertices["K"]=[100,0,120]
32.  vertices["L"]=[100,70,120]
33.  vertices["M"]=[100,70,90]
34.  vertices["N"]=[100,0,90]
35.
36.  #Window
37.  vertices["O"]=[100,40,30]
38.  vertices["P"]=[100,80,30]
39.  vertices["Q"]=[100,80,60]
40.  vertices["R"]=[100,40,60]
41.
42.  edges=[]
43.  #edges.append(["A","B"])
44.  edges.append(["B","C"])
45.  #edges.append(["C","D"])
46.  #edges.append(["D","A"])
47.  edges.append(["E","F"])
48.  edges.append(["F","G"])
49.  edges.append(["G","H"])
50.  edges.append(["H","E"])
51.  #edges.append(["A","E"])
52.  edges.append(["B","F"])
53.  edges.append(["C","G"])
54.  edges.append(["D","H"])
55.
56.  # Roof
57.  edges.append(["D","I"])
58.  edges.append(["I","C"])
59.  edges.append(["H","J"])
60.  edges.append(["J","G"])
```

```
61.    edges.append(["I","J"])
62.
63.    # Door
64.    edges.append(["K","L"])
65.    edges.append(["L","M"])
66.    edges.append(["M","N"])
67.
68.    # Window
69.    edges.append(["O","P"])
70.    edges.append(["P","Q"])
71.    edges.append(["Q","R"])
72.    edges.append(["R","O"])
73.
74.
75.    for edge in edges:
76.        #Position pen at the starting vertice of the edge
77.        myPen.penup()
78.        x = vertices[edge[0]][0]
79.        y = vertices[edge[0]][1]
80.        z = vertices[edge[0]][2]
81.
82.        #Apply Oblique Projection Formula
83.        x2D = x - z*cos(radians(45))
84.        y2D = y - z*sin(radians(45))
85.
86.        #addLabel(myPen,edge[0],x2D-10,y2D+5)
87.        myPen.goto(x2D,y2D)
88.
89.
90.        #Move pen to the ending vertice of the edge
91.        myPen.pendown()
92.
93.        x = vertices[edge[1]][0]
94.        y = vertices[edge[1]][1]
95.        z = vertices[edge[1]][2]
96.
97.        #Apply Oblique Projection Formula
98.        x2D = x - z*cos(radians(45))
99.        y2D = y - z*sin(radians(45))
100.
101.       myPen.goto(x2D,y2D)
102.       #addLabel(myPen,edge[1],x2D-10,y2D+5)
103.
104.   myPen.hideturtle()
105.   myPen.getscreen().update()
```

98. Cell Phone Trilateration

Mobile phone tracking is a process for identifying the location of a mobile phone, whether stationary or moving. Localisation may occur either via multilateration of radio signals between several cell towers and the phone, or simply via GPS.

Mobile positioning is used by telecommunications companies to approximate the location of a mobile phone and enables to offer location-based services and/or information to the mobile user.

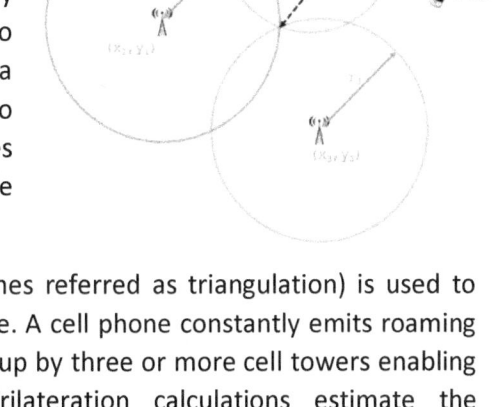

Cell tower trilateration (sometimes referred as triangulation) is used to identify the location of the phone. A cell phone constantly emits roaming radio signals that may be picked up by three or more cell towers enabling the triangulation to work. Trilateration calculations estimate the coordinates of a mobile device using the coordinates (longitude, latitude) of nearby cell towers as well as the estimated distance of the device from the cell towers (e.g. either based on signal strength or by measuring the time delay that a signal takes to return back to the towers from the phone).

In this challenge we will investigate the Maths equations used in trilateration calculations. We will simplify the process by using a 2D model of the problem based on (x,y) coordinates (as an alternative to longitude/latitude coordinates). The math equations are given at the web address provided below. Our Python program will use Python Turtle to randomly position three cell towers and one cell phone and will apply the trilateration formulas to calculate the exact location (coordinates) of the cell phone.

https://www.101computing.net/cell-phone-trilateration-algorithm/

Python Code

```
1.  #Cell Phone Trilateration Algorithm
2.  import turtle
3.  from random import randint
4.
5.  def drawCellTowers():
6.    myPen = turtle.Turtle()
7.    myPen.hideturtle()
8.    myPen.tracer(0)
9.    myPen.speed(0)
10.   window = turtle.Screen()
11.   window.bgcolor("#F0F0F0")
12.
13.   x1 = randint(-150,-80)
14.   y1 = randint(-150,150)
15.   x2 = randint(80,150)
16.   y2 = randint(20,150)
17.   x3 = randint(80,150)
18.   y3 = randint(-150,-20)
19.   x = randint(-60,60)
20.   y = randint(-60,60)
21.   r1 = ((x-x1)**2 + (y-y1)**2)**0.5
22.   r2 = ((x-x2)**2 + (y-y2)**2)**0.5
23.   r3 = ((x-x3)**2 + (y-y3)**2)**0.5
24.
25.   myPen.color("#ff5744")
26.   myPen.penup()
27.   myPen.goto(x1-5,y1)
28.   myPen.pendown()
29.   myPen.goto(x1+5,y1)
30.   myPen.penup()
31.   myPen.goto(x1,y1-5)
32.   myPen.pendown()
33.   myPen.goto(x1,y1+5)
34.   myPen.penup()
35.
36.   myPen.goto(x1,y1-r1)
37.   myPen.pendown()
38.   myPen.circle(r1)
39.
40.   myPen.color("#41befc")
41.   myPen.penup()
42.   myPen.goto(x2-5,y2)
```

```
43.    myPen.pendown()
44.    myPen.goto(x2+5,y2)
45.    myPen.penup()
46.    myPen.goto(x2,y2-5)
47.    myPen.pendown()
48.    myPen.goto(x2,y2+5)
49.    myPen.penup()
50.
51.    myPen.goto(x2,y2-r2)
52.    myPen.pendown()
53.    myPen.circle(r2)
54.    myPen.penup()
55.
56.    myPen.color("#52bf54")
57.    myPen.goto(x3-5,y3)
58.    myPen.pendown()
59.    myPen.goto(x3+5,y3)
60.    myPen.penup()
61.    myPen.goto(x3,y3-5)
62.    myPen.pendown()
63.    myPen.goto(x3,y3+5)
64.
65.    myPen.penup()
66.    myPen.goto(x3,y3-r3)
67.    myPen.pendown()
68.    myPen.circle(r3)
69.
70.    myPen.getscreen().update()
71.    return x1,y1,r1,x2,y2,r2,x3,y3,r3
72.
73. #A function to apply trilateration formulas to return the (x
    ,y) intersection point of three circles
74. def trackPhone(x1,y1,r1,x2,y2,r2,x3,y3,r3):
75.    A = 2*x2 - 2*x1
76.    B = 2*y2 - 2*y1
77.    C = r1**2 - r2**2 - x1**2 + x2**2 - y1**2 + y2**2
78.    D = 2*x3 - 2*x2
79.    E = 2*y3 - 2*y2
80.    F = r2**2 - r3**2 - x2**2 + x3**2 - y2**2 + y3**2
81.    x = (C*E - F*B) / (E*A - B*D)
82.    y = (C*D - A*F) / (B*D - A*E)
83.    return x,y
84.
85. #Generate and represent data to be used by the trilateration
    algorithm
86. x1,y1,r1,x2,y2,r2,x3,y3,r3 = drawCellTowers()
87.
88. #Apply trilateration algorithm to locate phone
89. x,y = trackPhone(x1,y1,r1,x2,y2,r2,x3,y3,r3)
```

```
90.
91. #Output phone location / coordinates
92. print("Cell Phone Location:")
93. print(x,y)
```

99. Lighthouse Animation Challenge

The purpose of this challenge is to use a Python program to demonstrate how frame-based animations can be implemented.

For this challenge we are using the *Processing.py* library.

The code below will run the *setup()* procedure once, when the program starts. Then the *animateLighthouse()* procedure will be called 20 times per second (based on the frame rate), indefinitely.

This code makes use of two transformations:

- A translation: 2D translations are often used to re-position or animate objects on screen (gliding effect)
- A rotation: in this case, a rotation is applied to animate the light beam. The angle of rotation increments by 0.5 degrees between each frame.

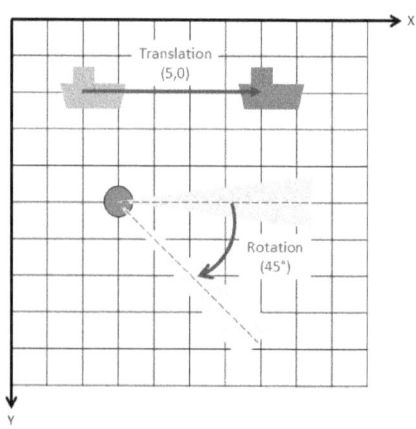

Web Address

https://www.101computing.net/lighthouse-animation-challenge/

```
1.  #Lighthouse Animation Challenge
2.  from processing import *
3.
4.  angle = 0
5.  lighthouseX = 150
6.  lighthouseY = 150
7.  translateX = -100
8.
9.  def setup():
10.     frameRate(20)
11.     size(400,400)
12.     strokeWeight(1)
13.
14. def animateLighthouse():
15.     global angle, translateX, lighhouseX,lighhouseY
16.
17.     background(50,140,180)
18.     fill(255,0,0)
19.
20.     #Draw the lighthouse
21.     stroke(0,0,0)
22.     ellipse(lighthouseX,lighthouseY,30,30)
23.
24.     #Draw the boat
25.     translateX = translateX + 2
26.     if translateX>400:
27.       translateX = -100
28.     translate(translateX,40)
29.     fill(255,0,0)
30.     beginShape()
31.     vertex(0, 15)
32.     vertex(70, 15)
33.     vertex(60, 30)
34.     vertex(10, 30)
35.     vertex(0, 15)
36.     vertex(10, 15)
37.     vertex(10, 0)
38.     vertex(30, 0)
39.     vertex(30, 15)
40.     endShape()
41.
42.     translate(-translateX,-
    40) #Cancel translation so that it does not apply to the lig
    htbeam
43.
44.     #Draw the light beam
```

```
45.    stroke(255,255,0)
46.    fill(255,255,0)
47.
48.    angle+=0.5
49.    if angle>=360:
50.      angle=0
51.    #Center of rotation is (0,0)
52.    #By using a translation we create a rotation effect from
     (lighthouseX,lighhouseY)
53.    translate(lighthouseX,lighthouseY)
54.    rotate(radians(angle))
55.    triangle(0,0,400,0,400,90)
56.
57. draw = animateLighthouse
58. run()
```

100. Target Detection Algorithm

In Star Wars movies, most spaceships are fitted with laser cannons to shoot enemy spaceships. To assist the pilot, these spaceships have built-in targeting computers that enable them to aim the cannon and inform them when their target is within reach. When this is the case, the algorithm informs the pilot with the following message:

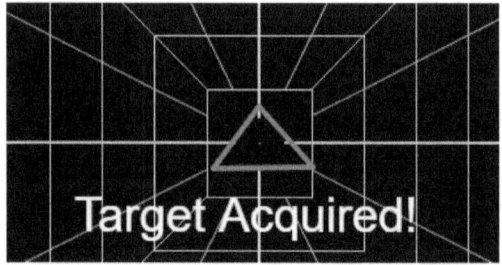

We have retrieved the code used in a Star Wars Tie Fighter spaceship. The code is used to aim the laser cannon. However this spaceship is not fitted with a target acquisition algorithm to inform the pilot when to shoot.

Your aim is to upgrade this code to detect when the enemy spaceship is within reach of the laser cannon.

To do so you will need to check if the X, Y coordinates of the cannon aim (mouse pointer) is within the A B C triangle representing the enemy spaceship.

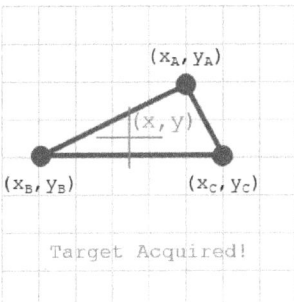

You will need to complete the code provided at the web address given below.

Web Address

https://www.101computing.net/target-detection-algorithm/

Python Code

```
1.  # Target Detecion Algorithm
2.
3.  from processing import *
4.  from math import cos, sin, radians
5.  from random import randint
6.
7.  delay = 10
8.
9.  def setup():
10.     strokeWeight(1)
11.     frameRate(20)
12.     size(400,400)
13.
14.
15. def drawLine(x1,y1,x2,y2):
16.     global X,Y
17.     #Draw a line on screen
18.     line(x1+X,y1+Y,x2+X,y2+Y)
19.
20. def drawSpaceship(xA,yA,xB,yB,xC,yC,color):
21.     stroke(color[0],color[1],color[2])
22.     strokeWeight(4)
23.     line(xA,yA,xB,yB)
24.     line(xB,yB,xC,yC)
25.     line(xC,yC,xA,yA)
26.
```

```
27. def drawGrid():
28.     background(10,10,10)
29.
30.     #Draw grid lines
31.     stroke(255,185,0)
32.     strokeWeight(1)
33.     for i in range(-2000,2000,1000):
34.         drawLine(-2000,i,-40,i/50)
35.         drawLine(2000,i,40,i/50)
36.         drawLine(i,-2000,i/50,-40)
37.         drawLine(i,2000,i/50,40)
38.     for i in range(-2000,2000,40):
39.         drawLine(i,i,i,-i)
40.         drawLine(i,-i,-i,-i)
41.
42.     strokeWeight(2)
43.     drawLine(-2000,0,-20,0)
44.     drawLine(20,0,2000,0)
45.     drawLine(0,-2000,0,-20)
46.     drawLine(0,20,0,2000)
47.
48.
49. def startGame():
50.     global X,Y
51.
52.     X = (mouse.x);
53.     Y = (mouse.y);
54.     print(X,Y)
55.
56.     drawGrid()
57.     targetAcquired=False
58.
59.     #Above line AB?
60.     aboveAB=False
61.     if Y>=(mAB*X + pAB):
62.         aboveAB=True
63.     #Above line AC?
64.     aboveAC=False
65.     if Y>=(mAC*X + pAC):
66.         aboveAC=True
67.     #below line BC?
68.     belowBC=False
69.     if Y<=(mBC*X + pBC):
70.         belowBC=True
71.
72.     if belowBC and aboveAB and aboveAC:
73.         targetAcquired=True
74.
75.     if targetAcquired:
```

253

```
76.     #Turn spaceship to red
77.     drawSpaceship(xA,yA,xB,yB,xC,yC,(255,0,0))
78.     f = createFont("Arial",36,True)
79.     textFont(f,36)
80.     fill(255)
81.     text("Target Acquired!",70,360)
82.   else:
83.     drawSpaceship(xA,yA,xB,yB,xC,yC,(255,255,255))
84.
85.   fc = environment.frameCount
86.
87. #Randomly position spaceship on grid by generatring coodinat
    es of vertices A, B and C.
88. xA=randint(60,340)
89. yA=randint(60,340)
90. xB=xA-randint(30,50)
91. yB=yA+randint(30,50)
92. xC=xA+randint(30,50)
93. yC=yA+randint(30,50)
94.
95. #Calculate the linear equations (slopes and slope intercepts
    ):
96. # Line (AB) y = mAB.x + pAB
97. # Line (AC) y = mAC.x + pAC
98. # Line (BC) y = mBC.x + pBC
99.
100.        mAB = (yA -yB)/(xA-xB)
101.        pAB = yA-mAB*xA
102.        mAC = (yA -yC)/(xA-xC)
103.        pAC = yA-mAC*xA
104.        mBC = (yB -yC)/(xB-xC)
105.        pBC = yB-mBC*xB
106.
107.        draw = startGame
108.        run()
```

Chapter #10: Object Oriented Programming

All previous 100 challenges are based on procedural programming. It is essential that you are fully confident with all the techniques we covered so far before moving on to the next stage of programming known as **OOP: Object Oriented Programming**.

The aim of this last challenge is not to teach all of the concepts of OOP programming. This challenge will however provide a basic introduction to what Object Oriented Programming is. It will also invite you to use the **PyGame library**, an OOP library specifically designed to add a Graphical User Interface (GUI) to your programs. This library will allow you to start creating your own video games.

This last challenge will focus on:

- Classes and Objects,
- Methods and Properties,
- PyGame Library,
- Creating our first game based on a Graphical User Interface (GUI).

101. Pong

Pong is one of the earliest arcade video games, first released in 1972 by Atari. It is a two-player game based on table tennis. The game features simple 2D graphics. It consists of two paddles used to return a bouncing ball back and forth across the screen. The score is kept by the numbers at the top of the screen.

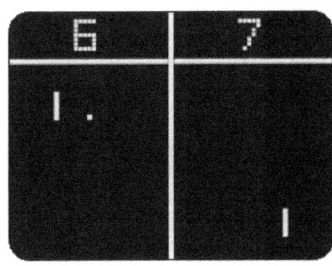

In this challenge you will recreate a game of Pong using Python and the Pygame library. The Pygame library is the perfect library to build basic 2D arcade games and to start developing your OOP skills. (Object-Oriented Programming). You can find more about the Pygame library and about OOP concepts using the web addresses provided below.

Web Address

https://www.101computing.net/pong-tutorial-using-pygame-getting-started/

Download the Pygame Library

http://www.pygame.org/

Pygame Trinket

https://trinket.io/features/pygame

Find out more about Object-Oriented Programming concepts

https://www.101computing.net/object-oriented-programming-concepts/

```
1.   # Import the pygame library and initialise the game engine

2.   import pygame
3.   from paddle import Paddle
4.   from ball import Ball
5.
6.   pygame.init()
7.
8.   # Define some colors
9.   BLACK = (0,0,0)
10.  WHITE = (255,255,255)
11.
12.  # Open a new window
13.  size = (700, 500)
14.  screen = pygame.display.set_mode(size)
15.  pygame.display.set_caption("Pong")
16.
17.  paddleA = Paddle(WHITE, 10, 100)
18.  paddleA.rect.x = 20
19.  paddleA.rect.y = 200
20.
21.  paddleB = Paddle(WHITE, 10, 100)
22.  paddleB.rect.x = 670
23.  paddleB.rect.y = 200
24.
25.  ball = Ball(WHITE,10,10)
26.  ball.rect.x = 345
27.  ball.rect.y = 195
28.
29.  #This will be a list that will contain all the sprites we
     intend to use in our game.
30.  all_sprites_list = pygame.sprite.Group()
31.
32.  # Add the car to the list of objects
33.  all_sprites_list.add(paddleA)
34.  all_sprites_list.add(paddleB)
35.  all_sprites_list.add(ball)
36.
37.  # The loop will carry on until the user exit the game (e.g
     . clicks the close button).
38.  carryOn = True
39.
40.  # The clock will be used to control how fast the screen up
     dates
41.  clock = pygame.time.Clock()
42.
```

```
43.   #Initialise player scores
44.   scoreA = 0
45.   scoreB = 0
46.
47.   # -------- Main Program Loop -----------
48.   while carryOn:
49.       # --- Main event loop
50.       for event in pygame.event.get(): # User did something

51.           if event.type == pygame.QUIT: # If user clicked cl
      ose
52.               carryOn = False # Flag that we are done so w
      e exit this loop
53.           elif event.type==pygame.KEYDOWN:
54.               if event.key==pygame.K_x: #Pressing the x
      Key will quit the game
55.                   carryOn=False
56.
57.       #Moving the paddles when the use uses the arrow keys (
      player A) or "W/S" keys (player B)
58.       keys = pygame.key.get_pressed()
59.       if keys[pygame.K_w]:
60.           paddleA.moveUp(5)
61.       if keys[pygame.K_s]:
62.           paddleA.moveDown(5)
63.       if keys[pygame.K_UP]:
64.           paddleB.moveUp(5)
65.       if keys[pygame.K_DOWN]:
66.           paddleB.moveDown(5)
67.
68.       # --- Game logic should go here
69.       all_sprites_list.update()
70.
71.       #Check if the ball is bouncing against any of the 4 wa
      lls:
72.       if ball.rect.x>=690:
73.           scoreA+=1
74.           ball.velocity[0] = -ball.velocity[0]
75.       if ball.rect.x<=0:
76.           scoreB+=1
77.           ball.velocity[0] = -ball.velocity[0]
78.       if ball.rect.y>490:
79.           ball.velocity[1] = -ball.velocity[1]
80.       if ball.rect.y<0:
81.           ball.velocity[1] = -ball.velocity[1]
82.
83.       #Detect collisions between the ball and the paddles
84.       if pygame.sprite.collide_mask(ball, paddleA) or pygame
      .sprite.collide_mask(ball, paddleB):
```

```
85.        ball.bounce()
86.
87.    # --- Drawing code should go here
88.    # First, clear the screen to black.
89.    screen.fill(BLACK)
90.    #Draw the net
91.    pygame.draw.line(screen, WHITE, [349, 0], [349, 500],
   5)
92.
93.    #Now let's draw all the sprites in one go. (For now we
   only have 2 sprites!)
94.    all_sprites_list.draw(screen)
95.
96.    #Display scores:
97.    font = pygame.font.Font(None, 74)
98.    text = font.render(str(scoreA), 1, WHITE)
99.    screen.blit(text, (250,10))
100.   text = font.render(str(scoreB), 1, WHITE)
101.   screen.blit(text, (420,10))
102.
103.   # ---
   Go ahead and update the screen with what we've drawn.
104.   pygame.display.flip()
105.
106.   # --- Limit to 60 frames per second
107.   clock.tick(60)
108.
109. #Once we have exited the main program loop we can stop the
   game engine:
110. pygame.quit()
```

```
1.  import pygame
2.  BLACK = (0,0,0)
3.
4.  class Paddle(pygame.sprite.Sprite):
5.      #This class represents a car. It derives from the "Sprit
    e" class in Pygame.
6.
7.      def __init__(self, color, width, height):
8.          # Call the parent class (Sprite) constructor
9.          super().__init__()
10.
11.         # Pass in the color of the car, and its x and y posi
    tion, width and height.
12.         # Set the background color and set it to be transpar
    ent
13.         self.image = pygame.Surface([width, height])
14.         self.image.fill(BLACK)
15.         self.image.set_colorkey(BLACK)
16.
17.         # Draw the paddle (a rectangle!)
18.         pygame.draw.rect(self.image, color, [0, 0, width, he
    ight])
19.
20.         # Fetch the rectangle object that has the dimensions
     of the image.
21.         self.rect = self.image.get_rect()
22.
23.     def moveUp(self, pixels):
24.         self.rect.y -= pixels
25.         #Check that you are not going too far (off the scree
    n)
26.         if self.rect.y < 0:
27.           self.rect.y = 0
28.
29.     def moveDown(self, pixels):
30.         self.rect.y += pixels
31.         #Check that you are not going too far (off the scree
    n)
32.         if self.rect.y > 400:
33.           self.rect.y = 400
```

```
1.  import pygame
2.  from random import randint
3.  BLACK = (0, 0, 0)
4.
5.  class Ball(pygame.sprite.Sprite):
6.      #This class represents a car. It derives from the "Sprit
    e" class in Pygame.
7.
8.      def __init__(self, color, width, height):
9.          # Call the parent class (Sprite) constructor
10.         super().__init__()
11.
12.         # Pass in the color of the car, and its x and y posi
    tion, width and height.
13.         # Set the background color and set it to be transpar
    ent
14.         self.image = pygame.Surface([width, height])
15.         self.image.fill(BLACK)
16.         self.image.set_colorkey(BLACK)
17.
18.         # Draw the ball (a rectangle!)
19.         pygame.draw.rect(self.image, color, [0, 0, width, he
    ight])
20.
21.         self.velocity = [randint(4,8),randint(-8,8)]
22.
23.         # Fetch the rectangle object that has the dimensions
     of the image.
24.         self.rect = self.image.get_rect()
25.
26.     def update(self):
27.         self.rect.x += self.velocity[0]
28.         self.rect.y += self.velocity[1]
29.
30.     def bounce(self):
31.         self.velocity[0] = -self.velocity[0]
32.         self.velocity[1] = randint(-8,8)
```